82053

GENTLEMEN VOLUNTEERS

The Story of American Ambulance Drivers
in the Great War
August 1914–September 1918

ARLEN J. HANSEN

Foreword by George Plimpton

ARCADE PUBLISHING · NEW YORK

This book is dedicated to the volunteer ambulance drivers in the Great War, for their heroics amid horrors, their manners amid madness.

FIRST EDITION

"my sweet old etcetera" is reprinted from *Complete Poems: 1904–1962* by E. E. Cummings, Edited by George J. Firmage, by permission of Liveright Publishing Corporation. Copyright © 1926, 1954, 1991 by the Trustees for the E. E. Cummings Trust. Copyright © 1985 by George James Firmage.

Library of Congress Cataloging-in-Publication Data

Hansen, Arlen J., 1936–1994
    Gentlemen volunteers : the story of American ambulance drivers in the Great War,
  August 1914–September 1918 / Arlen J. Hansen. —1st ed.
       p.   cm.
    Includes bibliographical references and index.
    ISBN 1-55970-313-X
    1. World War, 1914–1918 — Medical care — United States. 2. American Field Service —
  History. 3. Ambulance drivers — United States — History. I. Title
  D807.U6H36 1996
  940.54'7573 — dc20   95-18638

Published in the United States of America by Arcade Publishing, Inc., New York
Distributed by Little, Brown and Company

10 9 8 7 6 5 4 3 2 1

Designed by API

BP

PRINTED IN THE UNITED STATES OF AMERICA

Contents

Foreword

A certain lord, neat, and trimly dress'd,
Fresh as a bridegroom; and his chin, new-reap'd,
Showed like a stubble-land at harvest home:
He was perfumed like a milliner,
And twixt his finger and his thumb he held
A pouncet-box, which ever and anon
He gave his nose and took 't away again.

And as the soldiers bore dead bodies by,
He called them untaught knaves, unmannerly,
To bring a slovenly, unhandsome corpse
Betwixt the wind and his nobility.

The above verses (from Hotspur's report to the king after the Battle of Holmedon in *Henry IV, Part I*) would hardly qualify to describe the noncombatants who drove ambulances in Europe during the Great War, though, in fact, a large number were recruited from New England prep schools and Ivy League universities. These were upper-class gentry — perhaps typical of them Richard Norton (the 42-year-old son of Harvard's distinguished professor of art history, Charles Eliot Norton), who among other affectations carried not a snuffbox but wore a monocle. He was described by a fellow member of his ambulance section, the writer John Dos Passos, as follows: "Dick Norton, aesthete, indomitable archeologist, the man who smuggled half the Ludovici throne out of Italy, a Harvard man of the old nineteenth-century school, snob if you like, but solid granite underneath." Once Norton became actively involved with his ambulance corps he was able to persuade Henry

James (who else!) to write laudatory copy about it for the newspapers.

Among Norton's compatriots in the earliest days of the Service were H. Herman Harjes, a 39-year-old partner of the Morgan-Harjes Bank in Paris; A. Piatt Andrew, a 41-year-old Princeton graduate; and Edward Dale Toland, a 28-year-old Main Line Philadelphian, who had boarded a steamer in August, 1914, and gone to Europe "simply to see the excitement and the French people in wartime" (his idea of a vacation!) and, caught up in the real events, stayed on to help form the first American volunteer ambulance unit.

Back home the main recruiter and fund-raiser for Andrews's Field Service was a banker, Henry Sleeper, of the Lee Higginson & Co. in Boston — the campuses of the eastern prep schools and colleges his favorite hunting grounds. One might well assume that the best source for manning an ambulance corps would be the garages and repair shops of New England, there to find men schooled in how to make the temperamental machines of that era function. Instead, one would have thought Sleeper was searching out candidates for an extremely exclusive men's club — the criteria for membership not the ability to take apart a manifold but good bloodlines and impeccable manners. In his recruiting letter, Richard Norton's brother Eliot insisted that ". . . a volunteer must be a man of good disposition possessed of self-control — in short, a gentleman."

One is instantly reminded of the recruiting after the Second World War of so-called "white shoes undergraduates" for service in the Central Intelligence Agency — focusing in particular on prep-school graduates who had gone on to Harvard and Yale. It should be noted that the romantic zeal of those picked ultimately led to such disasters as the Bay of Pigs. Better to have amateurs driving ambulances than foreign policy!

There appear to have been three types who joined the ambulance corps: (1) humanitarians (men like Toland and Harjes), (2) pacifists (John Dos Passos, E. E. Cummings), and (3) those itching to get actively involved in the war (Ernest Hemingway, Archibald MacLeish, et al.). By the time the United States entered the war in April, 1917, and the ambulance corps were absorbed by the Red Cross and the U.S. Army, over 3,500 Americans had served in their ranks.

A lot of it had to do, of course, with the romantic idea of warfare in those early days of the conflict — so vividly described in such books as Barbara Tuchman's *The Guns of August* . . . the troops off to the front to the cheers of the crowd, the waving of banners, envied by those either too young or too old to fight. For some, of course, ambulance driving was too tame; they wanted to become more actively involved. Such was the case of James H. McConnell, for whom driving an ambulance wasn't enough. He resigned from the American Field Service and joined the Lafayette Flying Escadrille; soon afterwards he was shot down by the Germans and killed. At the time, he was writing about his service overseas, a posthumously published work titled *Flying for France.*

The number of those who drove ambulances in Europe and subsequently became famous literary figures is astonishing — among them William Slater Brown, Louis Bromfield, Malcolm Cowley, Harry Crosby, E. E. Cummings, John Dos Passos, Julien Green, Ramon Guthrie, Robert Hillyer, Ernest Hemingway, Sidney Howard, John Howard Lawson, Archibald MacLeish, Charles B. Nordhoff (whose reminiscence about the Field Service was called *The Fledgling,* and who after the war collaborated with James Hall to write the famous sea trilogy about the mutiny aboard the *Bounty*), William Seabrook, and Edward Weeks, who wrote about his service in the book *My Green Age* and was subsequently for many years the editor of the *Atlantic Monthly.* Many of the other writers mentioned incorporated their impressions of the war in their work, most notably John Dos Passos in *One Man's Initiations* and *Three Soldiers*, Ernest Hemingway in *A Farewell to Arms*, and E. E. Cummings in *The Enormous Room.*

In addition, a number of nonliterary former volunteers wrote books about their experiences — indeed so many that some must have worried if they had picked a title already chosen by another. Here are some of them: Leslie Buswell's *Ambulance No. 10*, William Yorke Stevenson's *At the Front in a Flivver*, Philip D. Orcutt's *The White Road of Mystery*, Julien Bryan's *Ambulance 464*, Robert Imbrie's *Behind the Wheel of a War Ambulance*, Amy O. Bradley's *Back of the Front in France*, Martin W. Sampson's *Camion Letters*, and Arthur H. Gleason's *Our Part in the Great War.*

Perhaps the most famous book associated with the volunteer experience is E. E. Cummings' *The Enormous Room.* Cummings found himself in trouble with the Field Service for fraternizing overly with the French and then with the French for admitting he didn't hate the Germans — the latter indiscretion landing him in an internment camp near Paris, the Dépôt de Tirage. Here, by his account, over a three-month period he had the time of his life; he was, of course, eventually to use his experience in the camp as background for *The Enormous Room*, in which, modeling the book on the structure of *The Pilgrim's Progress*, he looked into the personalities of his fellow prisoners and their psychological reactions to the squalid and harsh circumstances of their internment.

As for Ernest Hemingway, his interest in the volunteer ambulance corps was sparked by a friend of his on the *Kansas City Star*, Theodore Brumback, who had spent the summer of that year (1917) driving ambulances in France. Brumback, a twenty-year-old whose most distinguishing feature was a glass eye, not only persuaded Hemingway and a fellow journalist, Winslow Hicks, to enlist but rejoined himself. The three men left for Europe in the spring of 1918. They felt they would be infinitely more involved in witnessing what was going on at the front than the so-called war correspondents, who were in effect restricted to London and Paris and filed stories given them by the officials and bureaucrats running the war.

In fact, stationed in Italy, Hemingway saw very little action. One day in June 1918, he told his friend Brumback (according to a letter Brumback wrote Hemingway's parents): "I'm fed up. There's nothing here but scenery and too damn much of that. I'm going to get out of the ambulance section and see if I can find out where the war is."

This he did, volunteering for what was called canteen service — delivering cigarettes, chocolates, postcards, toilet kits, and so on to troops at the front, which he did by bicycle. On the eighth of July he was badly wounded at Fossalta by a mortar burst. In a letter to Malcolm Cowley in 1948 he described the moment: "Then there was a flash, as when a blast-furnace door is swung open, and a roar that started white and went red." Despite his wounds he carried a soldier who had been hit by the same mortar blast back toward the command post; on the way he was wounded again, this time by machine-gun fire. Eventually rescued, he lay for two hours in a dressing station repeating the prayer, "Now I lay me down to sleep . . ."

Arlen Hansen is somewhat deprecating about Hemingway's

service — pointing out that he only drove an ambulance one or two times before he took off for Fossalta, a move that is made to seem almost a desertion. Perhaps Hansen felt that Hemingway's actions (in a sense, leaving his post) were not in keeping with the values laid down by Eliot Norton in his recruiting letter — "self-control" being one of them.

But then one should remember that "volunteer" is derived, loosely, from the Latin word *voluntarius* — namely one who undertakes an action without external constraint and who thus performs of one's own free will . . . a property that one often associates with heroism, especially if the cause is an honorable one. This account is full of such volunteers.

George Plimpton

Acknowledgments

Before Arlen J. Hansen died of cancer on August 12, 1993 he worked diligently to finish this book, although often in a great deal of pain. His family and friends supported him throughout, and after his death continued to see that the work was published.

The following organizations and people are to be specifically recognized as extremely helpful in the creation of this book: The Hoover Institution Archives, The American Field Service Archives and Museum, The Houghton Library of Harvard University, The National Archives Washington, D.C., The University of the Pacific Library, and The Bancroft Library at the University of California, Berkeley. I am also very grateful for their insight and expertise, to Alan Albright and to William L. Foley, who has also generously contributed photographs and documents from his matchless collection.

A special thanks to Charles, Jeff, Jim, John, Katie, Kip, Laura, and Tess for their counsel, readings, and rewritings of the manuscript. I am greatly indebted to Dick Seaver, Arcade's publisher, who was most helpful to Arlen and now to me, and also to senior editor Tim Bent, who was always encouraging.

Lynn Hansen

Introduction

Nothing is so simple as words can make it seem.
Le temps a dégradé tous les monuments.

During the first years, Americans re-
ferred to the hostilities of 1914–1918 as the "European War." Once the
Yanks joined the fighting in April of 1917, however, it became the
"World War." The Europeans, on the other hand, always considered
this indescribably ghastly conflict the "Great War." Americans are
sometimes surprised to see that the casualties listed on World War I
monuments *(monuments aux morts)* in French villages invariably out-
number similar monuments for World War II. Actually, the Great War
was the lesser war for the United States (about 320,000 casualties,
including wounded, compared with over 1 million, including
wounded, during World War II). In France, however, the first war
constituted 51 months of uninterrupted fighting (2.8 million casualties,
including wounded), whereas the German occupation during World
War II effectively suspended the fighting in France from the summer of
1940 to the spring of 1944. The weaponry developed for this war was at
once more accurate, efficient, mobile, and destructive than anything
the world had previously seen. New technologies produced such inno-
vative horrors as long-range artillery that could lob a 750-pound shell
over six miles, machine guns that could fire six hundred rounds a minute, U-boats, warplanes, tanks, flamethrowers, mine-launchers, and
phosgene and other suffocant gases. In little more than four years, the
international slaughter now referred to as the First World War involved sixteen nations and 61 million troops. The fighting produced
34.5 million casualties of the following types and proportions:

TYPE OF CASUALTY	PERCENTAGE
Battlefield deaths	20
Unable to be transported (died)	8
Transported recumbent *(couchés)*	12
Transported sitting *(assis)*	20
Ambulatory (still requiring care)	40[1]

France suffered in particular, with 895,000 battlefield deaths. Another 420,000 men died from wounds or sickness, a fact that reflects the state of the medical service of the day.[2] These figures would have been even worse, no doubt, were it not for the ambulance service.

When the German army invaded Belgium on August 4, 1914, the ambulance corps of the French army consisted of horse-drawn wagons designed for the Franco-Prussian War of 1870–1871.[3] At the time, the French had only two sections of motorized ambulances, with twenty cars in each section, although the superiority of motorized ambulances was self-evident. From the very beginning, the French army faced two problems regarding their ambulance service: getting their hands on cars (automobile production was, understandably, a low priority in Europe) and finding qualified drivers (able-bodied men were needed in the trenches).

A potential resolution of this dilemma lay in the United States. American manufacturers, who were already turning out Packards, Cadillacs, and Fords at an impressive rate, were always on the lookout for new markets. Moreover, hundreds, if not thousands, of American boys had been caught up in the automobile craze and loved to get behind a steering wheel and drive — anything, anywhere. With the Allies' blessing, young Americans eagerly began volunteering for ambulance duty in Europe almost immediately after war broke out. They even offered to bring their own cars.

Initially, the majority of the volunteers came from Ivy League universities and Eastern prep schools. According to the American Field Service *Bulletin* of 8 December 1917, 348 volunteers had joined the American Field Service from Harvard; 202 from Yale; 187 from Princeton; 122 from Cornell; 70 from California; and 58 from Stanford. Columbia, MIT, and Penn provided the American Field Service over 40 volunteers; Chicago, Amherst, Michigan, Williams, Syr-

acuse, Wisconsin, Washington (St. Louis), and Illinois sent more than 30. In addition, four of the very first drivers came from St. Paul's School in Concord, New Hampshire; and Phillips Academy, Andover, sent an entire section. There were also several hundred young men with similar backgrounds who drove for the Norton-Harjes sections (such as John Dos Passos and E. E. Cummings) or for the American Red Cross in Italy in 1918 (Julien Green and Ernest Hemingway). In addition to succumbing to the romantic dream of driving a motorized ambulance in glorious battle, many of these young men had been to Europe on personal grand tours, some had friends or relatives living there, and nearly all feared that the very Anglo-Franco culture they venerated was in jeopardy. For many of them, the act of volunteering tended to be a conservative gesture, a manifestation of their desire to serve and protect the established sociopolitical systems of Republican France and Imperial England. As the war progressed and the press and the public turned against Germany, the volunteer fervor spread from Tory, Ivy League classrooms to white-collar offices and middle-class living rooms throughout the United States.

Ambulance work evolved into two general categories. One was a sort of jitney duty that took place well behind the front lines, and concerned the transfer of wounded soldiers *(blessés)* from one hospital to another, from sanitary trains to urban hospitals, or, in the coastal sectors, to and from hospital ships.[4] Jitney duty normally involved a daily routine with regular hours, seldom taking the drivers closer to the front than the outlying hospitals in small or mid-size cities like Montdidier or Amiens. The various civilian and military hospitals in Paris, and other major medical centers such as Bordeaux or London, had their own ambulances pick up and distribute the *blessés* who arrived on daily sanitary trains. For the first six months of the war, rear-line jitney duty was the only type of work American volunteers were allowed.

The second type of ambulance duty took the drivers as close to the trenches as the roads allowed. Ambulances working the front lines brought wounded men from the advanced dressing stations *(postes de secours)* back to evacuation hospitals, which could usually be reached by car in about forty-five minutes. Typically, a wounded soldier was taken by his comrades directly to a first-aid station set up in the trenches. From there he would be carried by stretcher-bearers (*brancardiers*) through a communication trench leading back to the nearest *poste de secours*. Ideally, the *postes* would be located less than a mile from the first-line trenches in some type of bombproof structure, such as a specially timbered cave or a reinforced farmhouse cellar.

At the *postes de secours*, on-duty physicians cleaned and dressed the wounds, immobilized fractures, or, in the most severe cases, performed emergency amputations. At the beginning of the war, *blessés* were kept at the *postes* until an ambulance could get there, but the American ambulanciers introduced a different practice, one greatly appreciated by the wounded soldiers. "Before the coming of the American cars, ambulances came up to the *postes de secours* only when called," one driver noted, pointing to the change the Americans made. "The American Section established a service on the spot," he said, "so that the waiting was done by the driver of the ambulance and not by the wounded."[5] From the *postes de secours*, the driver took his *blessés* back to a triage hospital (triage is the act of dividing the wounded into three types: those requiring immediate treatment, those that could be sent straight to a rear-line hospital, and those destined for the moribund ward), if there was one, and then on to an evacuation hospital safely beyond the range of enemy guns. There, the injured men were carefully examined, and treated if necessary, before being sent further back by train to a fully equipped urban hospital. As much as historians or military administrators would like to classify, standardize, or otherwise sort out the various types of hospitals into evacuation — as opposed to, say, triage — hospitals, the fact is that each medical unit pretty much defined its own function, depending on staff, proximity to the battlefield, and available equipment. For example, the evacuation hospitals particularly close to the front often performed triage, whereas others seldom did.

The great majority of American drivers served in one of three major volunteer groups.[6] The first corps in the field was the Harjes Formation, a small contingent consisting of five Packards. Established by H. Herman Harjes, the senior partner of the Morgan-Harjes Bank in Paris, this ambulance unit was sometimes called the Morgan-Harjes Section. Richard Norton's Anglo-American Volunteer Motor-Ambulance Corps was initially sponsored by the British Red Cross and supported by the London-based St. John Ambulance Association. In 1916, Norton and Harjes combined their efforts under the auspices of the American Red Cross, after which the units became known as the Norton-Harjes, or Red Cross, Sections. The third volunteer group evolved from a field service sent out by the American Military Hospital in Paris (Neuilly). A. Piatt Andrew organized this scattered assortment of ambulances originally intended to relieve the overworked hospitals north and west of Paris, into an autonomous corps called the American Ambulance Field Service. The AAFS (later abbreviated to simply AFS) eventually became the most complete volunteer operation in France. In addition to overseeing several ambulance and camion (truck) sections, Andrew's organization ran its own repair park, training camp, and stateside recruiting and fund-raising network.

As the war progressed, the American volunteer units grew steadily. Richard Norton's Anglo-American Volunteer Motor-Ambulance Corps consisted of twenty-five ambulances in operation in June of 1915. By November, a month before he and Harjes merged their sections, Norton had sixty cars in the field. By Christmas of 1915, Harjes had expanded his formation to forty ambulances; in addition, he had established a ski team of fifty Norwegian and American volunteers to serve in the Vosges. When the United States declared war on Germany on April 6, 1917, the combined Norton-Harjes operations numbered thirteen sections, with well over one hundred ambulances and two hundred men. Andrew's American Field Service had increased even more dramatically, with thirty complete sections in the field in April.

By the time the U.S. Army took over these organizations in October of 1917, over 3,500 Americans had served as drivers. The story of these gentlemen volunteers — a chronicle of heroics and horrors, manners amid madness — has never been fully told.

Arlen J. Hansen

Part I
The Three Beginnings

The most important thing that a nation can safe-guard is its *amour propre*, and these young men have helped our country to save its soul. There is not an American worthy of the name who has not incurred a deep debt of gratitude towards these young men for what they have done.   THEODORE ROOSEVELT

The gentleman who signed the boys up was a New York Lawyer and he talked about their being gentleman volunteers and behaving like gentlemen and being a credit to the cause of the Allies and the American flag and civilization that the brave French soldiers had been fighting for so many years in the trenches.

JOHN DOS PASSOS

These drivers are men of high education. They are the very pick and flower of American life, some of them professional men, but the greater number of them young men on the threshold of life, lads just down from college or in their last student years. All life lies before them in their own country, but they have put that aside for an idea, and have come to help France in her hour of need. . . . To this company of splendid and gentle and chivalrous Americans be all thanks and greetings from the friends and allies of sacred France.

JOHN MASEFIELD

In addition he must realize that sometimes an am-bulance corps has, for quite a period of time, very little to do; the result is that the time hangs heavy on the men's hands and there is a great chance for a troublemaker to make trouble, and accordingly . . . a volunteer must be a man of good disposition, possessed of self-control — in short a gentleman.

ELIOT NORTON, RECRUITING LETTER

1

The Harjes Formation

In March of 1910, a group of Americans living in Paris opened a small, semiphilanthropic hospital just off the Boulevard Victor Hugo in the suburb of Neuilly. When the war broke out in August of 1914, the American Hospital became a natural focal point for the concerned American colony. They donated money, equipment, and automobiles, and even offered their personal services, to help the war effort. Learning that the American Hospital intended to treat wounded soldiers by setting up tents in the hospital's gardens if necessary, French officials were directed by a Dr. Févier, surgeon general of the French Army, to offer the Americans the unfinished Lycée Pasteur to use as its "ambulance," or military hospital. (*Ambulance* can be a misleading term. The Americans, like the English, use the word to denote a motorized vehicle designed to carry patients to hospitals. For the French, *ambulance* designates a military hospital. In this text, *ambulance* in lowercase refers to vehicles, and *Military Hospital* replaces *Ambulance*, though I am aware there are those who prefer American Ambulance of Paris to American Military Hospital because the latter suggests that the American military was involved, and this was most emphatically not the case.) The Lycée Pasteur, which had been requisitioned by the French government, was an elaborate arrangement of red-brick school buildings just beyond the Maillot gate in Neuilly, six blocks from the American Hospital.[1] After the war, the Lycée Pasteur reclaimed its buildings on the Boulevard d'Inkerman, and the Americans were reimbursed for some of their construction expenses. The ante-bellum American Hospital, which got a new building in 1926, still carries on its work today at its old location, just off the Boulevard Victor Hugo.

The French offer of Lycée Pasteur carried with it two conditions. First, the American Hospital Board had to agree to underwrite the completion of the buildings and grounds, at a cost of $400,000. Second, the Board had only twenty-four hours to accept. Neither of these stipulations daunted the Hospital Board's two principal powers: former Ambassador Robert Bacon, its president, and Anne Harriman Vanderbilt, the second wife of William K. Vanderbilt. Once introduced, the deal was done.[2] On August 14, 1914, the day after accepting the offer, Bacon appointed a Board of Governors for the American Ambulance of Paris. The roster of the Ambulance Board alone is sufficient to demonstrate that this board had the wherewithal, clout, and connections to get things done: Mrs. Henry P. Davison (her husband later directed the American Red Cross), Mrs. E. H. Harriman, Mrs. Myron T. Herrick (wife of the popular ambassador to France), Mrs. Whitelaw Reid, Mrs. Montgomery Sears, Mrs. Bayard Van Rensselaer, and Mrs. Harry Payne Whitney, among other names of equal luster.[3]

To help recruit the medical staff and oversee the completion of the lycée buildings (which needed mostly interior work: lighting, heating, and cabinetry), the Ambulance Board named an administrative Ambulance Committee.[4] Working together, these two groups soon had the American Military Hospital up and running — in the nick of time. According to a report later filed with the American Hospital Board, the first four wounded soldiers were received on September 6. As the French and British continued to drive the Germans back from the Marne in mid-September, the number of blessés rose steadily. Ninety-one were admitted to the Military Hospital on the 15th of September; 146 on the 16th; 209 the following day; and during the second half of September and the first half of October, the average number of patients per day reached 238.[5]

Yet all this medical service would not have been helpful without a means of getting the blessés to the hospital. Mrs. Vanderbilt and Harold White, manager of the Ford Motor Company's French assembly plant, had already addressed the matter of transporting the wounded.[6] With financial assistance from Mrs. Vanderbilt, White donated ten Ford chassis, which were outfitted as ambulances by a local carriage builder. A crude plank floor was extended from the gas tank out over the rear axle, an overarching canopy of canvas covered the rear compartment, and a single board was strapped across the top of the gas tank for the driver to sit on. That was all — no side doors, no roof over the cab, no windshield.

The first drivers signed on in no less improvised a manner. J. Paulding Brown, whose pleasure tour of Europe had been interrupted by the outbreak of the war, showed up at the Military Hospital one day in early September of 1914, and "15 minutes later was an ambulance driver."[7] Brown's "first of a series of interesting trips into the environs of Paris" was made on September 7, and thereafter "for several weeks we were busy along the Marne gathering in wounded and bringing them back to Paris."[8]

Once the Germans had been pushed above the Aisne in late September, the French holding stations were necessarily beyond the reach of the Military Hospital's Fords, and the usefulness of the ambulances temporarily waned. Sanitary trains now constituted the principal means of transporting the wounded from the front to La Chapelle, the renovated rail station at the northernmost edge of Paris. This former railway depot had been transformed into an official receiving station to which all Paris-bound hospital trains brought their wounded. Once a warehouse-like barn with a huge unloading platform, this cold and stark station was made over into a warm, pleasant, and efficient distribution center. On the platform facing the railroad tracks were four newly constructed barracks, each painted a different color. The wounded were taken from the railroad cars directly into one of these structures, where nurses gave them hot soup and bread, and dressed them in fresh bandages if necessary. Using cards coded according to the color of the barracks, clerks wrote down the names of the wounded, four per card, grouped according to type of injury. Then the cards were distributed to the drivers, whose ambulances were lined up in stalls. After selecting his or her stretcher-bearers from a common pool, the driver sent them to the barracks corresponding to the card's color, where they picked up the four *blessés* named on the card. Once the *blessés* were loaded into the ambulance, the driver took off for the appropriate hospital — say, the American Military Hospital if the four *blessés* required facial surgery — or to the Val du Grâce for special types of amputation. The only hitch was that no station, not even the wondrously efficient La Chapelle, could keep pace with the daily slaughter and the resultant backlog of trains. One night, Harold Howland noted, "There were two trains standing alongside the La Chapelle station and one inside, and eight more waiting in the yards outside the city to come in."[9]

The most expedient means of distributing *blessés* from La Chapelle to the numerous hospitals was by automobile, but ambulance work was regarded by many as incidental, not integral, to a hospital's true and proper functions. In that trips into the field were no longer practical and, for Americans, were actually prohibited by military policy, the Ambulance Committee of the American Military Hospital hesitated before deciding officially to add a transportation department to its operations.[10] Some on the Committee felt that whatever ambulance service the American Military Hospital required could be handled by other motor corps operating in the city, including units from Spain, Canada (whose drivers were all women), and Scandinavia. In addition, they knew that eventually an ambulance service would probably be co-opted by the military, which would, understandably, take over the control and deployment of the vehicles. The Hospital seemed to have little to gain by setting up its own ambulance service. Most of the medical administrators felt that a hospital's job was to treat the wounded, not to fetch them.

Other factors worked against the inclusion of a transportation department in the American Military Hospital's operations. Given the magnitude of the Hospital's undertaking and its policy of treating the most challenging cases, particularly men in need of facial reconstruction,[11] an ambulance service would be a drain on the Hospital's finances and personnel. The American Military Hospital had become a highly respected and successful institution by concentrating its efforts on the medical aspects of its service. By the end of 1915, it had an impressive number of beds in operation — 575, with another 50 ready for emergencies.[12] Although the hospital staff was serving largely without pay, the Board spared no expense on medical technology, which gave rise to the criticism that the Hospital was extravagant.[13] Still, despite the Hospital's emphasis on treatment rather than transportation, its ambulances had already proved their worth at the holding stations in Meaux, Lizy-sur-Ourcq, and Coulommiers during the Battle of the Marne. The cars were also of considerable use in distributing the wounded who continued to arrive at La Chapelle. So, by late February of 1915, the Military Hospital Board finally con-

sented to form a Transportation Committee, which would oversee the
formation and operation of an ambulance service. Not surprisingly,
transportation matters were relegated to the bottom of the Hospital's
budgetary and organizational priorities. New ambulances were occasionally purchased with money raised in the United States by William
Hereford, a New York banker who was the chief fund-raiser for the
entire American Hospital organization. Some contributors specified
that their donations go toward buying ambulances, giving Hereford
no choice but to spend the money on cars. Nevertheless, by December of 1916, when the hospital was spending over $1,000 per day to
handle nearly 1,600 wounded, the number of ambulances working
directly out of the Neuilly hospital had increased from the original ten
to just thirty-five.[14]

The American Military Hospital was not unique in its attitude
toward ambulance units. Until the early spring of 1915, few hospitals
recognized the importance of independent ambulance services, particularly when it came to trench warfare. When armies marched,
the armies' mobile hospitals could follow the troops and pick up the
wounded at assembly points. In this war, however, not only was the
French Army stationary, but its medical facilities were often based in
converted civilian hospitals and other civic buildings, which were
invariably a moderate distance from the front, far enough to be out of
artillery range. The wounded had to be hauled back to these urban
hospitals, but neither trains nor horse-drawn wagons provided an
entirely satisfactory means of transporting them. The blasted, sea-
sonally boggy terrain over which the *blessés* had to be carried would
not sustain railroad beds, and the wagons moved so slowly that the
wounded were exposed far too long to enemy fire. Cars, in short, were
the answer. However, as was the case with the American Military
Hospital in Paris, most civilian hospital boards and their administrative surgeons were not accustomed to supporting or managing an
extensive ambulance service.

A typical case was Mrs. C. Mitchell Depew, who converted half
of her Château d'Annel at Longueil, some nine miles north of Compiègne, into a splendid forty-bed hospital. The American Mrs. Depew
was a long-time resident in France and a close friend of General
Joffre, who helped her obtain the necessary medical licenses. Mrs.
Depew and her staff opened the hospital on August 27, but when

German troops poured across the region three days later, everyone, including members of her own family, had to leave. Returning a month later, they reopened their hospital and, according to Dr. Harvey Cushing, who visited the Château d'Annel the following March, "have been continuously busy [ever since]." Cushing, a Harvard surgeon who was inspecting various regional clinics on behalf of the American Hospital Board, counted "seven nurses for the 40 patients [and] an ambulance corps of four Ford cars."[15]

But Dr. Cushing was wrong in one matter. Mrs. Depew's hospital may have been in full operation when he visited it in March of 1915, but between the preceding September and the end of January it had been virtually without patients. Earlier, in November of 1914, two French generals (Berthier and Dziewonski) directed the *médecin en chef* at Montdidier to deliver his overflow of wounded to her hospital. However, because the Montdidier doctor had no ambulances to spare and because Mrs. Depew had not obtained the requisite *laissez-passers* (permits) or sufficient gasoline to run her own ambulance service, Mrs. Depew's hospital was without the means of bringing in any patients, Montdidier's overflow included.[16] Not until the end of January, by which time Mrs. Depew had obtained three ambulances, the appropriate passes, and a ration of gasoline, did the Longueil hospital have a legitimate ambulance service. Accordingly, when Cushing arrived in March, the hospital had ambulances (Cushing counted an additional one, making four in all) and a full component of forty *blessés*.

Largely owing to the French ban on foreign nationals in the field, the American volunteer ambulance services were slow to be accepted by French officials, but once the usefulness of the American cars and drivers was recognized, the demand grew instantly. The experience of Edward Dale Toland captures the pace and nature of the change in attitude toward American ambulance drivers. Toland, a 28-year-old Philadelphia gentleman, boarded the *S.S. Laconia* out of New York in late August of 1914, intending "simply to see the excitement and the French people in wartime."[17] Having spent the previous six years in the engineering and banking businesses, the Princeton alum (1908) was intrigued by "the prospect of an indeterminate holiday." Instead, the unassuming and modest Toland got caught up in the rush of events and before he knew it was helping to form the very first American volunteer ambulance unit.

Having been in Paris the previous year, Toland was stunned by what he saw upon arrival on September 14. The entire length of Avenue de l'Opéra revealed "not a soul on the sidewalks," and that evening the usually hectic Place de la Concorde was "as dark and still as a country churchyard," Toland wrote in his diary.[18] In early September, United Press reporter William Shepherd had stood on Avenue de l'Opéra and looked in its shops and down its side streets. "No human being is in sight," Shepherd observed in *Confessions of a War Correspondent.* "The prairies of Texas were never more silent." In contrast, Will Irwin's first chapter in *The Latin at War* depicts Paris as unfazed during this period, with its populace as contented and outgoing as ever. Irwin admitted that his sample was skewed, however: "Naturally, I know the American colony in Paris better than the French . . . , [and] they are for the most part wealthy or well-to-do, and before the war they were an idle set." The city was still reeling from the terrors of the first weeks of the war. During August, three million German troops had raced across the western front, carried by 550 trains a day rolling through Belgium, to bear down upon the French capital. The German advance was finally halted and turned back a few miles outside Paris in early September, just before Toland's arrival. By late September, the German western flank had been driven north of the Aisne, where both sides eventually dug in. Nevertheless, many Parisians remained convinced that the German threat was not over, and that made them wary and sometimes capable of ugly conduct that winter.

Toland spent his first day at the Cooper-Hewitt Hospital, a small operation near the Bois de Boulogne. Although splendidly equipped, the fifty-bed Cooper-Hewitt was completely empty — not a single patient, despite the savage fighting that had taken place recently along the Marne, literally within earshot of Paris. "The French officials in Paris do not seem to want wounded men brought in here," Toland was told by a Mrs. F, who managed the hospital (Toland does not give her full name). Throughout the city, she said, "There are some six hundred beds now prepared with first-class equipment and staff all ready and waiting for them." The officials, she figured, "are afraid the possibility of a siege is not over, or else they are afraid that the moral effect on the French public will be bad."[19]

Mrs. F told Toland that the only way to get patients into these small private hospitals was to ignore the officials and operate one's own ambulance service, as she had done for her other hospital, the converted Majestic Hotel. The night before Toland's arrival, Mrs. F and her aides had driven a huge omnibus out to the army's holding station at Montereau, some sixty miles outside Paris, and brought back twelve *blessés*, who had been virtually abandoned there. What she had seen at the Montereau station was almost more than she could bear: hundreds of wounded men piled on filthy straw, all wounds septic "beyond description," no bandages or gauze or anesthetics, no surgeons, and maybe one nurse for every fifty men. Sadly, her "horrible old rattle-trap of an omnibus"[20] had room for only a small fraction of the men requiring emergency attention. Mrs. F's passionate account of this experience so impressed Toland that the former banker instantly blurted out an offer to help the Majestic's operations in any way he could. So much for the indeterminate holiday he had envisioned.

One day, while working at the Majestic as a volunteer orderly, Toland heard that a trainload of British wounded, slowly making its way to the coast, would stop briefly at Villeneuve St. Georges, six miles outside Paris, the following morning. "The thing that is most needed," he wrote in his diary that night, echoing Mrs. F's sentiments, "is to get the men off the field and to a place where they can have some sort of attention."[21] Despite the proscription against civilian travel beyond the gates of Paris, Toland, along with one of the Majestic's surgeons and a French nurse, decided to intercept the train when it stopped at Villeneuve St. Georges and bring the most seriously wounded back for immediate care.

Thanks to the nurse's personal charm and her quick tongue, the group got past the various sentries and reached the Villeneuve St. Georges station well ahead of the British hospital train. However, no amount of time could have prepared them for the train's gruesome cargo. Some twenty small boxcars were crammed with maimed and bleeding men lying on wisps of straw loosely scattered over the floor boards. Far too many needed immediate attention for the Majestic's omnibus-ambulance to carry, so the irrepressible nurse went to work again, this time on the Villeneuve St. Georges station master, and enchanted him completely. He found them an empty railroad car with enough space for twenty-two *couchés*, and ordered it attached to a train about to depart for Paris. Despite the impeding efforts of the civilian and military authorities, Toland and the others were able to bring dozens of severely wounded men to the Majestic that night.

There are several explanations for the abundance of horrific scenes of brutalized men at the holding stations. The new warfare technology accounted for a large percentage of the numerous conspicuous casualties. Fragmentation shells such as the so-called Daisy Cutter exploded on impact and were designed to maim and cripple rather than kill outright. Thus, in this war, siege artillery became antipersonnel weaponry. Shrapnel produced three times as many casualties as bullets. The newly designed pineapple ridges on hand grenades maximized the number of jagged bits of hot metal that burst randomly about, maximizing the ability of grenades to rip up human flesh. The machine gun, especially the Germans' Maxim, gave the solitary soldier a disproportionately large capacity for carnage with a single sweep of his gun.[22] Perhaps nothing was more efficient as a disabling weapon than gas: at first the suffocants, greenish-yellow chlorine and colorless phosgene; later, mustard gas, which produced progressive conjunctivitis or painfully crippling blisters.[23] Men died slowly from all of this new weaponry — or, perhaps worse, didn't die at all, surviving with permanent disability or mutilation, a living reminder of the Great War's horrors.

There were nontechnological reasons as well for the boxcars overflowing with wounded, and the huge numbers of *mutilés de guerre*. During the first months of the war, the French military authorities tended to accept a notion attributed to Lieutenant Colonel Louzeau de Grandmaison, chief of training on the General Staff: ardor wins wars. Never mind weapon power or troop numbers, this view argued, an army that displays an unconquerable spirit will be victorious and, thus, French military strategy called for *l'attaque à outrance*, all-out attack.[24] As one historian put it: "The 1913 [French] manuals contained no prescription for retreat."[25] Consequently, the number of casualties rose as French ardor rose, and the ardor soared the closer the Germans got to Paris.

Ironically, advances in treatment and medical knowledge may also have contributed to the suffering during the First World War. In 1901, the Austrian-born pathologist Karl Landsteiner, working in the

United States, discovered the secret of blood types (A, O, B, AB), which made transfusions more practical. Many wounded who would previously have been regarded as untreatable were now being shipped back to urban hospitals for transfusions in the hope that their limbs, or lives, could be saved. Moreover, the recently developed practice of debridement, which prevented gangrene by immediately removing damaged tissue from wounds, kept still others alive long enough to endure the boxcar rides. In earlier wars, many of the raving, suffering men that Toland and Mrs. F encountered would have been silently abandoned or buried at the battlefront, out of public view.

To get these wounded men to urban hospitals, some type of transportation service was necessary, but ambulances were difficult to come by, at least for Mrs. F. It was a simple matter of greed, she concluded. "There are a good many motors which could be put at the disposal of hospitals," she stated bitterly, "but it is quite hard to get hold of them." People who owned motorcars, she said, were acting in the "most cowardly and selfish way." Although Mrs. F had extracted promises from several owners, she invariably discovered, when she went to pick up the cars, that neither the machines nor their owners were in town. The cars had been taken to the country and safely ensconced, presumably, on the grounds of family estates.[26]

Toland was shocked by the hypocrisy of car owners who reneged on their promises, but he was even more disturbed by the behavior of some hotel owners. Certain hotels made an ostentatious show of having been converted into hospitals, although these same hotel-cum-hospitals showed little real concern about actually treating patients. For instance, the glamorous Ritz Hotel generously reserved sixty-four beds for hospital use. It purchased some state-of-the-art medical equipment and hired two dozen nurses. Yet, the Ritz's management accepted no patients, protesting that it could not admit any *blessés* without authority from the officials of the *Bureau de Santé* (Department of Health). Literally speaking, that was true. However, Toland countered, "we told them they would never get any patients if they waited for authority from [the Health Department]."[27]

The advantages of such tactics were immediately apparent, assuming the hotel's management did not foolishly set aside so many beds that it undercut business. The idea was to hire a few nurses (but no expensive surgeons), giving the operation a veneer of sincerity, and perhaps even to invest in some medical equipment. It was imperative to announce the conversion by flying Red Cross flags conspicuously. A hotel could continue its normal routine without actually bothering about hospital work — until, of course, the licenses were issued by the bureaucracy. There was little need to worry — the labyrinthine Parisian bureaucracy worked at a snail's pace in the best of times. The point of such deviousness was to make sure German artillery spotters or troops, in the event that Paris was taken, might believe the hotel was a hospital. Best of all, the hotel's management did not have to put up with any bleeding *blessés* or imperious surgeons making things unpleasant for the hotel's clientele.

Toland sensed a change in the Majestic's attitude right after the Germans had settled in along the Aisne and the threat of a further assault on Paris had virtually disappeared. "Our relations with the management of this hotel," Toland said, "are decidedly unpleasant." The cause was obvious: "I am quite sure that the only reason the hotel was given as a hospital was as a sort of insurance proposition." In other words, Toland writes, "Now that there is no chance of the Germans getting in here [Paris], I think they [the Majestic's management] would jolly well like to kick us all out."[28]

When the French and German armies took up defensive positions during the relatively peaceful winter of 1914–1915, the small private hospitals in Paris became undersubscribed, if not superfluous. Civilian-managed mobile field hospitals were rumored to be in the offing. These field hospitals, it was held, would include both medical and automobile units, and would be set up just behind the trenches, within driving distance of the army's holding stations. Having heard about these field units, Toland noted that "It has been my wish to do this sort of work, and I feel I could be of far more use out there than in a [Paris] hospital."[29] He arranged a meeting with Robert Bacon, the President of the American Hospital Board, to talk it over. A man of considerable influence, Bacon had been President Theodore Roosevelt's third (1909) Secretary of State and President Taft's Ambassador to France. Toland's session with Bacon on September 25 turned out to be most frustrating. "There isn't any chance of getting to the front," Bacon had explained to him. "The English and French armies won't have any outsiders messing about their work."[30] Bacon was alluding to the French policy banning all nonmilitary personnel, including those from neutral or nonaligned countries, from traveling into battle zones.[31]

On October 1, Bacon introduced Toland to Dr. Edmund Gros, one of the chief medical officers at the American Military Hospital in Neuilly, who proposed that Toland come to work for them. As President of the American Hospital Board, Bacon added that the American Military Hospital "would offer me [Toland] more opportunities than the Majestic Hotel Hospital." The hospital in Neuilly was a much larger operation, Bacon pointed out, with a capacity of six hundred patients. Moreover, it was about to establish a small ambulance unit for transporting *blessés* to and from the hospital. Driving an ambulance for the Military Hospital, Toland felt, was "more like the work I have been wishing to do."[32]

Bacon mentioned a second, even more appealing, possibility to Toland. H. Herman Harjes, the 39-year-old Senior Partner of the Morgan-Harjes Bank in Paris, was planning to organize a mobile field unit under the sponsorship of the French military hospital, the Val de Grâce. Harjes, Bacon said, intended his field service to work in cooperation with both French medical and military officials (thus avoiding the ban against allowing neutrals in a war zone) in the Compiègne-Montdidier sector, where the battle lines had not yet completely stabilized. If Toland so wished, Bacon would try to get him into Harjes' unit. "It is exactly what I want," Toland wrote in his diary that evening.[33]

The next morning (October 2, 1914), Mrs. Herman Harjes, an active member of the Ambulance Board, as well as the prime force behind her husband's field service, made Toland an offer: Would he be willing to go to the front with the Morgan-Harjes *Ambulance Mobile de Premiers Secours* to set up a field hospital, complete with its own ambulances? Toland replied without hesitation that he would, and so for the next week he helped set up the Morgan-Harjes field hospital and ambulance service.

At 6:00 A.M. on Saturday, October 9, two chauffeur-driven Packards left Paris in search of a location for Harjes' field hospital. They wanted to choose a spot as close to the front as possible, enabling them to have prompt access to the wounded.[34] In this initial scouting party were Mr. and Mrs. Harjes, their chief surgeon (an

American), a head nurse, a French corporal ("who is to represent the army and keep military records, etc."), and Edward Toland. Other personnel and equipment were soon added to this nucleus, including two operating surgeons, a few paramedics, and at least three more Packards.[35] Four Ford ambulances, donated by J. P. Morgan, were said to be on the way from New York.

In the village of Ricquebourg, halfway between Compiègne and Montdidier, the scouting party found a beautiful and spacious châ-teau, which seemed suitable, though it needed some repair and mod-ernization (for example, running water) before it could function as a hospital. The château was also within three hundred yards of a French battery that invited the attention of enemy fire. Nevertheless, the Harjes group was assured, should the German infantry break through, that they would have plenty of time to evacuate. The group settled in and work began the next day.[36] For the first time, an American volunteer unit was setting up a hospital and ambulance service in the field, relatively close to the battle lines.

Two of Toland's favorite surgeons from the Majestic Hotel Hos-pital, Drs. Joll and DeQuelen, came out on October 11 to help the Harjes crew get started. Their operational model, naturally, was the Majestic, where the ambulance service (that is, the omnibus that Toland and Mrs. F occasionally drove) was secondary to the medical service. Drivers were members of the general hospital staff rather than an independent ambulance corps. Accordingly, when Clarence Mitchell joined the Harjes unit, he and the others who drove its ambulances regarded themselves as employees of a hospital, and therefore undertook whatever hospital chores needed to be done. "I have been working in the wards a good deal," Mitchell wrote his parents in December of 1914, "and this morning I put in chopping wood."[37] Ambulance driving was simply one of the tasks he was assigned as an employee of the field hospital.

Given the extensive renovation required, and the proximity of the French battery, the setup at the Ricquebourg château didn't work out, so on October 26 the Harjes unit relocated to Compiègne. Less than a week later, Harjes drove out from Paris with instruc-tions for his group to move again, this time to a château outside Montdidier belonging to French Minister of Finance Monsieur Klotz. Significantly, the instructions to move had originated at the

4th Corps of the French Second Army, which was expecting a large battle and a concomitant number of wounded.[38] In other words, the Harjes group was complying with, or at least responding to, a French Army request.

The following day, November 2, the *médecin en chef* of the Montdidier district and the chief surgeon of the largest hospital at Montdidier arrived, apparently uninvited and unannounced, to inspect Harjes' medical facilities. After giving their approval, the officials suggested that some of the Montdidier patients might be transferred to Harjes' hospital. On the morning the transfer was to begin, a fierce battle broke out near the small town of Roye, and all available vehicles were pressed into emergency duty. By order of the Montdidier *médecin en chef*, every ambulance, including the five Harjes Packards, was sent to one of the rear-line holding stations in the region around Roye. Each of the Packards, which were big cars — the one Toland was driving was a six-cylinder Packard 30 — had room for six stretchers, and ended up transporting 250 *couchés* (stretcher cases; those *blessés*, or wounded men, able to sit up were called *assis*), most of whom were taken to Montdidier hospitals. Rolling all day and through most of the night, the Harjes ambulances played a far more prominent role than had the hospital to which they were assigned. Indeed, it was the biggest day the Harjes *Ambulance Mobile de Premiers Secours* had had so far.[39]

A few days later, French officials ordered the Harjes Packards back into the field, again without consulting the Harjes hospital. "About three in the afternoon," Toland wrote in his diary, "the Médecin Chef sent for all of our cars again. . . . I was detailed to car No. 9. When we got to the [holding] station they had fifty men to take to Breteuil, twenty-two kilometers west of us."[40] French military and medical officials had found Harjes' ambulances efficient and convenient — an eminently valuable autonomous service on which they could call regardless of the hospital to which it was formally attached. Gradually, Harjes' ambulance corps began to split off from the hospital unit and function independently. The Morgan-Harjes operation was evolving into two discrete groups: the medical staff, whose job it was to maintain a functional hospital, and the ambulance drivers, whose services were increasingly being called upon by second-line French officials.

As the separation between the medical and ambulance personnel formalized, the differences between the type of volunteer each attracted became more distinct. Signing up for hospital duty was quite unlike offering to drive an ambulance. Hospitals were hectic and crowded, yet guided by strict rules, and staffed with other overworked angels of mercy; ambulance driving was usually carried out alone. In an ambulance, you were alone, heading blindly down a bomb-cratered, unmarked dirt road to god-knows-where in a rattletrap of a car. Each job appealed to individuals with fundamentally different motives, attitudes toward the war, skills, expectations, and degrees of recklessness. The two sorts of work reinforced personality traits. If the volunteer ambulance driver and the volunteer hospital worker weren't that different when they arrived, the demands and pressures of their disparate jobs soon made them so.

The Morgan-Harjes unit was growing increasingly interested in and attractive to men who were more familiar with automobiles than with hospital work. When Clarence Mitchell decided to sail for France after the war broke out, he thought the type of assistance he could offer would be medical, not mechanical. He hadn't calculated exactly what he would do when he got to Paris, but he figured he would probably help out at the American Military Hospital in Neuilly. Upon his arrival in Paris on October 17, Mitchell presented a letter of introduction to an official at the Morgan-Harjes Bank. The official, who knew relatively little about the Neuilly hospital, said that Harjes had a unit "just behind the firing line and needs another man who understands automobiles, and I [Mitchell] can probably have the job."[41]

Two weeks later, after hurriedly practicing his driving and passing the requisite test, Mitchell was assigned to the Harjes unit. Despite anxious projections by the 4th Corps of the French Second Army (which had instructed Harjes to move his unit to Monsieur Klotz's château outside Montdidier), the sector was still rather quiet when Mitchell arrived, so he spent his first days making trips to and from the local train station. The action picked up (Mitchell called it a "rush") on November 5, and the drivers of the Harjes Packards, including Mitchell and Toland, were instructed to proceed beyond the train station and pick up wounded men from the Warsy and Dancourt assembly points a few miles behind the trenches.

SPRING CREEK CAMPUS

Mitchell soon felt as if the Harjes ambulances had become part of the French Army. "This job beats working in the American [Military] Hospital four ways at once," he wrote his parents on November 11, 1914. "The field work is exciting and very good exercise. . . ."[42] Mitchell and the other Harjes drivers were now largely spared the drudgery of hospital duty and made available for emergency calls from French officials. Although not yet allowed to travel to the *postes de secours* at the very front, neither were Harjes' drivers confined to doing tiresome jitney work, shuttling back and forth between city hospitals and train stations.

In the winter of 1914–1915, the demand for ambulance drivers and their cars spread throughout France, even in Paris, where only a few months earlier the American Ambulance Board had displayed only a minimal commitment to its transportation service. The attitude of the Board had changed. "I had a note from the American [Military] Hospital," Mitchell observed in December, "offering me a driving job, and one from F[rancis] C[olby] asking me to join his ambulance corps."[43] By February of 1915, the British Army started allowing British Red Cross groups, such as the Friends' Ambulance unit, to work the British Expeditionary Force's advanced dressing stations, a change in policy that incurred Mitchell's envy and admiration. "The English Red Cross men are nervy beyond belief," he wrote, "and the casualties among them are very high, even among the ambulance drivers who run up in daylight to the second line of trenches."[44]

The conversion of local hospitals and civic institutions near the battle zones into military hospitals was virtually completed by the early spring of 1915. Anyone setting up a hospital or clinic finally realized that they needed their own ambulance corps to bring *blessés* into them. Mrs. Harry Payne Whitney, who completely refurbished a sixteenth-century seminary in the small village of Juilly (population 400) into a second American Military Hospital provides an example. Hospital B, as Mrs. Whitney's clinic was called, opened February 1, 1915, but it had no operational ambulance service.[45] Consequently, when Mitchell visited Hospital B a week later, he found "electric lights, steam heat, scientific sewerage, bath tubs, [and] two hundred and fifty beds — but no patients."[46] This problem was rectified when Mrs. Whitney and the American Hospital Board in Paris arranged for a corps of ambulances to serve her hospital.

Given the disproportionate abundance of medical facilities in the Montdidier sector, as compared with the paucity of ambulance service, Harjes dropped the hospital branch from his operations in mid-February. "Our hospital is closed," Mitchell wrote on February 19, 1915, "but our ambulance service is to be kept going."[47] Indeed, Harjes' unit now included volunteers whose full-time job it was to drive its ambulance fleet, which consisted of two six-cylinder Packards, a 35-horsepower Renault, and, when operational, three worn-out 1907 Panhards (as well as a 1907 Renault light truck).[48] Although later augmented by other vehicles and some new drivers, this group was all that remained of the original Morgan-Harjes *Ambulance Mobile de Premiers Secours* that Harjes and his wife had organized in late September of 1914. With the medical component dropped, the operation became strictly an ambulance service, known officially as the Harjes Formation.

From February to June, the Harjes Formation was attached to a regional evacuation hospital and assigned vital, if routine, duty. The hours between 8:00 A.M. and 9:00 P.M. were divided into three shifts, during which at least one ambulance was on duty. The Formation's on-duty drivers transported *blessés* who came in on the regularly scheduled sanitary trains, helped distribute the sick and wounded brought in from the front by French Army convoys, and delivered urgent cases that arrived randomly and unannounced from the front throughout the day. The off-duty Harjes ambulances were kept on alert. It was strictly jitney work.

Like the Harjes Formation, the ambulance corps headed by Richard Norton and A. Piatt Andrew were also attached to rear-line bases during late 1914 and early 1915. In these first months, Norton's unit was attached to the British Red Cross headquarters in Boulogne, and Andrew initially was overseeing the cars and drivers dispatched by the American Military Hospital in Neuilly. Both units were deployed in regions controlled by the British Expeditionary Force, north of the Harjes Formation, and they were all also pretty much limited to jitney duty, although their collective hearts ached for work more demanding and consequential.

The tedium of the American volunteers' life ended in the summer of 1915. The Harjes, Norton, and Andrew volunteer units grew dramatically, and their services became essential to the French Army.

As their respective affiliations with regional base hospitals were dropped, the American units all became first-line ambulance services attached to specific divisions of the French Armies. Soon, Americans seemed to be everywhere up and down the French front, as Andrew observed. "In 1915," he said, "the little American ambulances could be seen scurrying over the flat plains of Flanders, on the wooded hills of northern Lorraine, and in the mountains and valleys of reconquered Alsace."[49]

2

Richard Norton and the American Volunteer Motor-Ambulance Corps

"He seems to be a very decent sort," a volunteer for a rival unit said of Richard Norton, "excepting that he wears a monocle."[1] Norton's eyepiece gave him the air of a cocksure English aristocrat or, rather less flattering, considering the times, a Prussian. Certainly there were reasons for his self-assured bearing. Richard's father was Charles Eliot Norton, Harvard's internationally celebrated professor of art history, and his mother, Susan Sedgwick, had Boston Brahmin blood. Himself a Harvard graduate (A.B., 1892; Ph.D.), Norton had served as director of the American School of Classical Studies in Rome from 1899 to 1907, after which he supervised the archeological excavations at Cyrene (1910–1911). John Dos Passos, who served in one of Norton's ambulance sections, characterized him this way: "Dick Norton, aesthete, indomitable archeologist, the man who smuggled half the Ludovici throne out of Italy, a Harvard man of the old nineteenth-century school, snob if you like, but solid granite underneath."[2] The preponderance of evidence indicates that for all his affects, Richard Norton was a gifted leader and organizer. He got things done, even if he had to do them himself — and frequently he did.

During the first few weeks of the war, Norton spent his time in London and Paris pretty much as any 42-year-old gentleman of leisure might. He attended luncheons and receptions, cocktail parties and dinners. However, his diary entries of those days reveal that it was not the usual social gossip that caught his ear.[3] Rather, he filled his daily log with stories of the war, some quaint and ironic, others graphic and disconcerting.

His richest days were spent with acquaintances who had just returned from the front — until September 20, 1914, that is. His diary entry for this date marks Norton's decision to devote his considerable energies and talents to active war-relief work. The day began like most other days. "Lunched with Eric Wood, who had seen some of the fighting but tells fairy tales," he noted in his diary that night. He didn't dismiss his dinner conversation as lightly.

> Dined with Magnin, Stewart & Lachaise [of the American Military Hospital]. They say that they were notified the other day that at Soissons there were some 600 wounded in various houses & shelters & only a few old women to give them water etc. Many of the wounded reach the American hospital a week after being wounded & all that time having been without any care beyond the first bandaging . . .

These descriptions obviously show a touched Norton, and in the second paragraph of his diary entry that night he noted his feeble and, no doubt, far-fetched response.

> Suggested to Lachaise that small portable houses . . . be put about at junctions of railways or other suitable places near [the] fighting line where the wounded could be looked after until they can be brought back to the hospitals.

Norton felt something should be done. But the last sentence of his diary entry seems to change the subject entirely: "The rules regarding motorists who want to see the fighting are stiffer than ever & the military authorities say the Americans give them more trouble than anyone."

The sequence of his thoughts suggests a growing revelation. They proceed from (1) hearing about the grotesque treatment of the wounded, to (2) suggesting portable shelters near the battle lines, to (3) motoring to the front. From there it's only a small leap to a hypothetical number 4: motorcars could be used in the fields, rather than portable shelters, to expedite the treatment of wounded soldiers. Indeed, Norton was soon at work on a project to expand and extend the ambulance service of the American Military Hospital in Neuilly.

He wasn't able to get to his project the next day, for he had some personal business to attend to at the Prefecture of Police. On the following day, September 22, however, he twice drove out to the American hospital, the second time "to arrange with Colby about more motor ambulances." Francis T. Colby was a driver for the American Military Hospital at the time, so he was familiar with the condition, number, and function of its ambulances. Norton returned the next morning to make still "further arrangements with Colby about ambulances," after which he knew what he had to do: "Plan to go to England tomorrow to raise money & men. Idea to get Ford cars at $1,000 apiece fitted as ambulances."[4]

In Richard Norton — a man with influential social connections, sorely needed organizational skills, and an appreciation of practical action — the volunteer ambulance service found new impetus. He was not to be stopped — not, at least, until three years later, when Norton ran up against the devious and obstinate U.S. Army, incurring the personal enmity of General John J. Pershing (see Chapter Nine).

Norton left for London right away, and hit the ground running.

> Saw Agnew about the ambulance company. He thinks well of it & gave me a letter to Sir Luke Fildes who [has] given me one to Sir Fred Trevis. Also spoke to Mrs. McEwen who is working along similar lines. Jordan says he is too poor to help.

He now had two pledges of support, one turndown, and two letters introducing him to other potential supporters — all on the day he arrived in London. As it turned out, raising money and enlisting volunteers were relatively easy jobs for Norton. His socially prominent connections proved generous, and his friends eager. Upon learning of the project, Norton's friend Arthur Kemp signed on and brought a car and driver along with him. So did Alan Loney, William P. Clyde, D. P. Starr, and W. G. Oakman, among others.

Then came the first setback. While in London, building his base of support, Norton received some bad news from Colby in Paris.[5] The American Military Hospital in Neuilly was about to organize a motor-ambulance corps of its own, presumably to be sent into the field, which meant that Norton's original plan was no longer viable. Apparently the hospital had sufficient cars and men to expand without Norton. They didn't need his ambulance corps.

Denied the sponsorship of the American Military Hospital, Norton decided to inquire about operating under the aegis of the British Red Cross (BRC) Society. Having already gotten commitments of cars, drivers, and some basic start-up funds, Norton was well received by the BRC, except for one matter. The head of the Motor Department, a man by the name of Rogers, refused to accept any Ford cars. For some inexplicable reason (Norton attributed it to "hanky-panky"), Rogers insisted that instead of Fords the unit use English-made Wolseleys. Until Norton got rid of his Fords, the BRC would not agree to sponsor his corps of volunteers.

Almost perversely, the British War Office also thwarted Norton's early efforts, using a ploy similar to the one they had tried on one Baker and his Quaker unit in August. General McPherson told Norton that the War Office was sending 120 of its own ambulances to the British Army and didn't need any more. Norton testily replied that 120 cars didn't seem very many for a front 220 miles long. Unfazed, McPherson added that because they were speaking of a corps of *American* volunteers, the Hague Conference guidelines dictated that the offer must come from the United States Government and that all of the belligerents would have to be notified. Exasperated, Norton put the matter to McPherson directly: did he or did he not want the cars? "If you put it that way," McPherson replied feebly, "we should not like to refuse." A feeble response was all Norton needed. He would proceed.[6]

There's no reasonable accounting for the obstructive disposition of the Red Cross or War Office, although several possible explanations come to mind: turf protection, reluctance to change, Norton's nationality, fear that an ambulance corps would create more work, and the pressure to make an instantaneous decision. None of these by itself explains the wooden, inflexible, and ambiguous responses Norton invariably elicited whenever he had to deal with the BRC or War Office. Perhaps the best way to understand their conduct is as a 1914 form of stonewalling, the response of choice among many bureaucracies past and present.

Elsewhere, the developments were more encouraging. When he called on Lord Norrys and Sir Claude MacDonald of the St. John Ambulance Association, Norton found them "very keen for our cars and [posed] no difficulties."[7] They would try to help Norton any way they could. Another stroke of good fortune occurred when William Clyde, one of his volunteers, introduced Norton to Lieutenant Colonel A. J. Barry, a military officer assigned to the British Red Cross.[8] Barry immediately won Norton's respect by candidly noting that "McPherson is no good & puts all sorts of trouble in people's way." Moreover, Barry had just come from the front, and he knew how great the need for ambulances truly was.[9]

A few days after Colonel Barry had returned to his post behind the French lines in Amiens, Norton got a surprising letter from him. Barry wrote Norton that his ambulances would be "very welcome" in the Amiens sector. Furthermore, Barry offered to return to London and help straighten out the difficulties Norton was having with the British Red Cross and the War Office.[10] Given Colonel Barry's unique position with the military *and* the British Red Cross, the prospect of his being able to work out a solution was promising.

However, even Barry couldn't budge the Red Cross. Rogers' Motor Department simply refused to accept Fords, and that was that. An appeal to the head of the British Red Cross Society, the Honorable Arthur Stanley, got Barry no further. Stanley argued that if Barry were to take Norton and his Americans to Amiens, other British volunteers who currently held less appealing duty would make trouble.[11] Frustrated by the Red Cross, Barry turned to the army and called upon the War Office, where General McPherson was effectively a lame duck, about to be replaced (if he hadn't been already). This time, with McPherson's influence muted, the War Office was genuinely pleased to accept Norton's offer.[12]

Possessing the endorsement of Lord Norrys' St. John Ambulance Association, and now holding the approval of the War Office, Norton and Barry were finally able to persuade the Red Cross to withdraw its objections. The British Red Cross decided it would sponsor Norton's group, Fords and all. Braced by the good news, Norton immediately called on the American ambassador in London and got the proper letters, which he carried directly to the French

Embassy. There he was issued the necessary visas and passes for his fleet of cars and drivers.[13]

Norton knew no pause, for the very next day, October 18, 1914, three of Norton's men — Loney, Starr, and Gideon — left for the Channel. On the 19th, "Kemp in his Rolls-Royce, Oakman & Robinson in the Cadillac, Berry in a Ford ambulance & I [Norton] in a Ford touring [car] left London," bound for Folkestone. After spending most of the 20th crossing the Channel on a steamer, they arrived in Boulogne that evening, and so on October 21, one month to the day after committing himself to his war-relief project, Richard Norton had his American Volunteer Motor-Ambulance Corps, some fifteen cars in all, at work in the fields of the war.

The first seven months, roughly from late October to mid-May, tested Norton's skills as a leader and organizer. In that Barry had invited Norton's corps to join him in the Amiens area, Norton's ambulances were actually operating within the purview of the French Second Army. In other words, American volunteers sponsored by the British Red Cross were effectively working for the French Army.

Such a situation guaranteed organizational chaos. Norton's most immediate superior within the British Red Cross chain of command — in theory at least — was Colonel Barry. Barry (wisely) seems never to have considered himself Norton's organizational superior. Ranked above Barry was a succession of inept British Red Cross officials stationed at the BRC continental headquarters in Boulogne. These officials periodically issued perfunctory commands that usually proved either unworkable or just plain silly. On occasion, the main office of the British Red Cross Society in London issued new regulations or new interpretations of old ones. These Norton had to attend to — sometimes by dashing back to London to point out their impracticality. Still higher, ruling over all national Red Cross societies, stood the august International Red Cross in Geneva; Norton had to take care that he and his men complied with its stipulations.

Norton had another line of command to contend with as well: that of the French military. Reluctant to let American volunteers work the front lines, the French Armies used their own ambulances to carry wounded from the battlefield. The medical divisions behind the lines, however, needed ambulances for jitney work. This amounted to little more than transporting patients from one hospital to another, carrying incoming wounded to an appropriate hospital, or evacuating the patients to trains bound for larger hospitals in Paris or cities along the coast. So Norton's ambulances, which had been expected to perform jitney work around Amiens, were headquartered in Doullens, where seven hospitals were overseen by *Médecin en Chef* Dr. Coutourier. He was thus Norton's immediate French superior. Stationed in the regional offices at Amiens was General Dziewonski, who outranked Coutourier and frequently rescinded or peremptorily changed the doctor's directives. Norton therefore had to reckon with Dziewonski as well, not to mention the entire string of French generals all the way up to Joffre and Pétain, any one of whom felt free to pop in on the American volunteers and issue spur-of-the-moment commands.

It was bad enough having a dozen or so bosses, but when they issued contradictory, vague, and impractical orders by means of an inchoate bureaucracy, it could be downright paralyzing. Unless you're Richard Norton, that is. He seemed to know when to listen to his superiors' orders, when to ignore them, and when to challenge them.

Consider the difficulties Norton and Barry had getting supplies during the first three months. On October 24, the day after Norton's Corps arrived at Doullens, Arthur Kemp drove to Boulogne to pick up some things Colonel Barry had ordered from the British Red Cross headquarters there. Kemp found the BRC office "in a worse muddle than ever & unable to give him the supplies." He returned empty-handed. A few days later, Colonel Barry decided to go to Boulogne himself to find out what was going on. He too returned frustrated and empty-handed. "Things at Boulogne are more in a mess than ever," he reported to Norton. "The Red Cross refuse to give us anything & say we must get all supplies from the French."[14] Norton was dumbfounded. Such a policy ran counter to his hard-won agreement with Stanley and Rogers in London. The British Red Cross had consented to be Norton's sponsor; it was to provide for the general upkeep and operation of his Corps.

Fortunately for Norton, he had an ace in the hole — a couple of them, actually — to make sure his operation was not completely at the mercy of the British Red Cross. He had arranged with his brother Eliot in New York to serve as a recruiter and fund-raiser for the

Corps. By diligently writing letters and submitting reports to their prospective donors, the Norton brothers began cultivating a sizable number of stateside supporters. In addition, over lunch one day, Norton and Henry James discussed the work of the American Volunteer Motor-Ambulance Corps. James was "most kind and interested" and offered "to write something about it."[15] Five days later, James sent an open letter (under the title "The American Volunteer Motor-Ambulance Corps in France")[16] to a variety of journals in the United States. After describing the Corps' work in laudatory terms, James concluded with an appeal for funds to be sent to "Mr. Eliot Norton, of 2 Rector Street, New York." In prose typical of the later James, he writes,

> What I therefore invite all those whom this notice may reach to understand, as for that matter they easily will, is that the expenses of our enlightened enterprise [James, according to the *New York Times* (March 21, 1915), was Chairman of Norton's organization] have to be continuously met, and that if it has confidence in such support it may go on in all the alert pride and pity that need be desired. . . . The members of the Corps . . . wish more of their friends would come and support it either personally or financially — or, best of all, both.

A month later, at a New Year's Eve luncheon, James told Norton he was eager to write still more on behalf of Norton's Corps.

Compared with this steady independent support, the British Red Cross was a model of inconsistency. In December, for example, while he was still unable to get basic supplies, Norton met with Sir Saville Crossley in Boulogne. Sir Saville spontaneously gave him "another car, an Argyle, with chauffeur, for our Corps." Sir Saville's generosity did not change Norton's opinion of the BRC's operations, however. "The mismanagement of the Red Cross," he noted, "[is] incredible."[17]

On his way back to Doullens that evening, Norton stopped in Montreuil, where a new 200-bed hospital for Indian troops was near completion. The Montreuil officials, Norton noted, were "very pleasant & most grateful for the work we [had] done for them in these last days." Norton saw, however, that to be successful the new hospital would need at least one ambulance, so he turned over the Argyle and its driver to them on the spot. They "were delighted," he wrote, "when I told them I would leave the Argyle car." Assuming the authority to deploy the ambulances and drivers from his Corps as he saw fit, Norton knew it would be a long time, if ever, before the BRC would get around to sending an ambulance to this hospital. "When I told them that I knew there [were] many cars at Boulogne doing nothing," the Montreuil medical officers were shocked. They "could not understand why none had been provided for them."[18] (Two days later, French Field Marshal (General) Joseph Joffre ordered several of the BRC automobiles and drivers in Boulogne and the near vicinity back to England, "as they are doing no good and only joyriding.") The Montreuil officials must have been new at dealing with the Boulogne office of the British Red Cross.

Nearly three months after Kemp had returned empty-handed from Boulogne, the BRC still refused to issue goods and materials to Norton's men, even to the point of withholding brassards and other means of identification. So Norton headed to London himself, arriving on January 14. Before the Red Cross offices closed that afternoon, he had an answer. Some "minor officials" in the office told him that his unit was "not officially recognized by the Red Cross and so they [could] do nothing about it [the supply problem]." Norton also learned that "the Hon. Arthur Stanley admits that he forgot last Oct. when he accepted our corps to make any official note of it to the Red Cross authorities."[19] This was the sort of mismanagement that enraged Norton. Over the weekend, however, the matter was miraculously cleared up. A trace of cynicism colors Norton's words of Monday evening: "It seems as though at last the Red Cross would recognize us officially and see to the upkeep of our cars as the Hon. Arthur Stanley promised us last Oct."[20]

The British Red Cross wasn't the only one mucking things up. The French authorities had a knack for it too. For instance, one briskly cold winter day, Norton and Colonel Barry were asked to transfer sixteen *assis* and two seriously wounded *couchés* from a hospital in Doullens to a *train de ravitaillement* (resupply train). When their ambulance carrying the *couchés* got to the station, they were told that it was forbidden for army supply trains to carry stretcher cases. Norton and Barry had to hoist the *couchés* back into the ambulances and haul them back to the hospital. Ambulance trips, as they well knew, were always a painful experience for stretcher-bound men, so this transfer and retransfer in freezing weather seemed almost unforgivable. "Dr. Coutourier had been given this order [not to transfer *couchés*] but apparently forgot it," Norton angrily observed. "I told him what I thought of his management & the *Médecin Inspecteur en Chef* said my remarks were *tres juste*."[21]

Norton was not one to withhold an opinion. In the early months, he tended to vent his frustrations with French authorities in relatively quiet tones, such as he did the morning he needed a pass to go to Montdidier. Calling upon the head of the French Red Cross in Doullens, Norton was told to go to the station commander at the city hall. There he was sent from office to office, until finally someone told him he would have to go to Cagny (south of Amiens, some twenty-five miles away) and see the commander there. From Cagny, he was sent to Dury (fifteen miles west), where he finally got his pass. When he finally arrived in Montdidier , he found no work to do. One can read the fatigue and exasperation in his laconic diary entry: "This being sent from pillar to post happens frequently."[22]

Norton's sharpest comments were invariably directed at his paid Red Cross drivers.[23] Norton would have preferred American drivers, or so he said: "The [British] chauffeurs were mainly wasters & slackers," he wrote on January 18, 1916. "These Frenchmen are of a type who won't do more than they have to. If I could get good energetic Americans they would be the best." During one long convoy, some of the cars took the wrong road, "owing to the stupidity of the drivers," as Norton put it.[24] On the return trip a few days later, Norton took special precautions: "Clyde and I led to show the [drivers] the road but they managed to take a wrong turn though we were not 100 yds ahead and they had been over the road several times already. . . . Lord they are stupid."[25]

Norton even had some complaints about Colonel Barry, who, he said, "has about as much sense to run a convoy as a child."[26] In particular, Norton was most frequently perturbed by Barry's inclination to take off on pleasure drives. "Barry left for Beauvais, Boulogne and I do not know where else on a joy ride," Norton jotted in his diary. "It was damn nonsense his going but on the whole it is easier if he is not fussing about here."[27] As long as his affiliation with the British Red Cross teamed him up with Barry, Norton's criticism of the

Colonel didn't slacken. "Everyone agrees," Norton once carped, "that A. J. [Barry] is the worst organiser possible and as he can neither talk nor understand French he gets things badly mixed."[28] And yet, when Norton dropped his affiliation with the British Red Cross at the end of 1915 and Barry went off to run his own unit, Norton was sorry to see him go: "Cold gray day and I feel cold and gray. I hate this breaking up as not withstanding Barry's peculiarities he has been a pleasant companion."[29]

Norton could be critical, it seems, of everyone. Of reporters: "Saw Graves and Barrow of the Daily Mail. Both as useless as ever" (5/10/15). Of the ambulances sent out by Harjes and the American Military Hospital: "The rules are to be stiffened . . . due to the lax methods of the American Ambulance [Hospital] at Neuilly and to the Harjes section" (11/11/15). Of Sir Arthur Lawley, the head of the British Red Cross, whom Norton told to get his facts straight: "Called Lawley down when he said it was of my volition we left the BRCS [British Red Cross Society]" (12/21/15). Of a French medical officer at Verdun, whom he called "an excitable ass" (12/15/16). In words that reveal an ugly side to his anger, Norton wrote of the Germans: "Glad to see the London Times advises the use of gas bombs. There is no use of thinking of game laws when you have to kill vermin and the Boche have put themselves in that class" (5/7/15) and "[the French infantry] are taking no prisoners but killing everyone — a good thing" (3/31/17).

As sharp as his words could be, Norton's actions could be equally swift and severe. On one occasion a driver named Baker, whom Norton had berated for failing to wash a car, openly rebuked Norton for treating "the hired chauffeurs" differently from "the private owners [volunteers] who happened to have more money." Norton fired Baker on the spot: "I discharged him before he knew what had hit him. I can not make out whether it is socialism, general idiocy, or the fact that most Red Cross chauffeurs are slackers or medically useless that is getting in to these men."[30]

Norton himself was no shirker. He worked in the machine shops (usually barns), overhauling engines and redesigning ambulance chassis. He "waded through knee-deep mud" with a lantern, pointing out shell holes for George Tate, his chauffeur, who was driving slowly behind him on a four-mile evacuation trip that took two-and-a-half hours.[31] On the night of June 6, 1915, he drove until 1:30 A.M. and then was up early leading three convoys through heavy bombardment two hours later, continuing until 8:00 that evening. Norton also made personal sacrifices for his men: "At the hospitals the doctors feed us well if we can get there and I have seen that all the men got down to them. I have not been able to get there except at lunch today. . . ."[32] Richard Norton was as demanding of himself as he was of others. Prompt and decisive, he expected his men to be equally dependable and resolute.

Swift, unambiguous actions were frequently required, in that someone had to make decisions; someone decisive, and the British authorities weren't — not, at least, from Norton's perspective. On February 22, 1915, the British Red Cross first brought up the matter of shifting Norton's Corps from the area controlled by the French into an area where they could serve the British Army. The prospect was appealing for a number of reasons, and Norton responded positively. Less than a month later (March 16, 1915), he was told to be prepared to make the shift within six weeks. Four months after that, Norton still had heard nothing further about transferring to a post where his men could serve the British troops. In late June, Colonel Barry went to London to get the matter straightened out, but he learned little. "All that is suggested is that [Norton's Corps] should go to Etaples and wait there 'till something turns up,' " Barry reported.[33]

Not only did the vagueness of this response fail to satisfy Norton, but by this time he had established a new relationship with the French Second Army, which had begun to depend on him to work their front lines. Abandoning the French merely to go to Etaples and wait for something to turn up seemed foolish — and immoral. So, Norton was off to London again, leaving on July 7. Somehow, perhaps by the sheer force of his personality, he got the answer Barry was unable to get.

> There is little or no chance of work with the British Army. All their units that leave here are well supplied with ambulances. . . . The idea of our going to Etaples was simply due to some of the Army officials saying it would be nice to have a corps of cars in reserve there but they had no idea of giving us any work.[34]

Amid the muddle and confusion of the first seven months, Norton ran his Corps pretty much as he pleased. He had assumed the authority to give the Indian hospital in Montreuil a new car on the spot. He assigned a volunteer and chauffeur to take a woman searching for her son around to nearby military hospitals and headquarters.[35] One night in January, when two nervous officers showed up in search of an ambulance to take an injured woman to Paris, Norton kindly obliged them.[36] The woman had been run over by an army car, the officers said, and had suffered a broken leg. Moreover, Norton gave his volunteers the freedom to probe the regions around Doullens and Amiens at their will, performing whatever relief work they might find. Norton's Corps may have appeared to be a three-ring circus, with men going off every which way, but each man knew that he was working for a formidable ringmaster.

Let November 20, 1914, serve as a representative day. Arthur Kemp went to Boulogne on personal business, taking Gideon — who was getting bored and irritable from inaction — with him. Two other volunteers, Starr and Berry, went to Montdidier in the Daimler to help out there, as they saw fit. Egerton also drove down to Montdidier, separately. Cave went to Senlis to see if Norton's cars might happen to be needed there (they weren't). The rest of the unit spent the morning evacuating patients from the Doullens hospitals, and in the afternoon Colonel Barry and Norton went to Amiens, the regional medical headquarters, to catch up on the action there. In other words, much time during these early months was spent out in the field *looking for work*, the individual volunteers trying on their own to find a job that needed doing.

Two of Norton's men returned one day from Mrs. Depew's hospital in Longueil and reported that it "is well organized but lacks ambulances & seems to be unable to get passes, etc." Norton was quick to respond: "Think I will go down [to Longueil] tomorrow & see if we can't help them," he wrote in his diary that evening.[37] When he saw her predicament, Norton reported to General Dziewonski that he intended to get some cars for Mrs. Depew's hospital. Sure enough, three weeks later, when Norton spoke to Lord Norrys in Boulogne, Norton was promised "two of the St. John's ambulance cars for Mrs. Depew's hospital."[38]

In the meantime, Norton had already sent Alan Loney with a car to help out at the Longueil hospital. But it wasn't long before Loney asked — read "begged" — to return to Doullens, although Mrs. Depew protested that were Loney to leave she would need another car with two men. When Loney was finally relieved, he reported to Norton that Mrs. Depew's hospital "is run like a children's school with all sorts of petty rules." One day, for example, she had Loney post a notice saying that "anyone using anyone else's overcoat would be fined 2 Francs."[39] By mid-January of 1915, Mrs. Depew had persuaded a number of friends to drive for her. When Norton dispatched two new men to her on the 20th, she sent them right back — with a letter saying that because she had just received three ambulances, she no longer needed Norton's cars or drivers. "She did not even say thank you!" Norton wrote in his diary that night, choosing to punctuate his note with an exclamation point, which he seldom did.

When they weren't doing their usual jitney work, searching for jobs on their own, or helping out at other hospitals, Norton and his men undertook new ways of serving the troops. During the winter of 1914, Norton got the idea of a soup truck, which he drove around to encampments in places such as Hébuterne and Sailly and ladled out hot soup to the soldiers.[40] On idle days, Norton and his men drove to various French operational headquarters and turned over for distribution an assortment of shirts, mufflers, socks, cigarettes, and other items that had been provided by the British, French, and American Red Cross societies.

All of this free-lancing activity changed, however, in May of 1915. At the end of April, while he was still waiting to see if his Corps were to be shifted to the British Army, Norton was told that should his unit be assigned to the British, his cars would have to be refitted to meet new specifications. Sir Arthur Lawley stipulated that any ambulance corps serving the British Army must have at least fifty cars, each capable of carrying four stretcher cases and designed with an aisle down the middle for an attending physician.[41] A week later, Norton spoke with Lawley's aide, Major Campbell, and learned that the War Office would probably modify their requirements. They might like each ambulance to have a middle aisle, but they probably wouldn't *insist* on it.[42] Three days later, this regulation was indeed relaxed, as Norton noted: "Major Campbell told me [Norton] that the British authorities have again changed their minds and decided that it is not essential for ambulances to have the central gangway but that 4-stretcher convertible ambulances will do."[43] The proposal to require an attending doctor did not come up.

The first bit of relief from British indecision came on May 16. At 9:30 in the morning, *le Directeur du Service Automobile de la 2nd Armée* (an officer named Ballut) told Norton that his volunteers would be "attached to one of the Army corps and work just like a French military section at the front." The next day, matters were clarified even further when Norton and Barry met with Ballut at Cagny. "All details," Norton noted, were "arranged very easily. He says we will be attached to [a French] army corps tomorrow or the next day." Promptly at 6:00 the next morning, the French officials arrived to number Norton's cars (in accord with the French system) and to issue him registration cards *(livrets matricules)*. Three days, and the job was done.

The reassignment meant that Norton's headquarters had to be moved out of Doullens, which was too far behind the lines. When they did get settled down, first at Varennes and then at Baizieux,[44] the volunteers discovered that their freewheeling days were over. Now there were specific assignments made by the military, most notably the exacting *service de garde* — outpost duty. Norton's ambulances were assigned to serve the three principal outposts of the 11th Corps of the French Second Army: those at Albert, Martinsart, and Courcelles (which was dropped a few days later and replaced by Bray).[45] At least one ambulance was to be sent to each outpost every night, and sometimes the work could be unrelenting. On May 25, for example, one of Norton's volunteers, a man named Mulville, was on outpost duty at Albert when a mine exploded during the night. The destruction was prodigious, the casualties numerous. Throughout the night Mulville made three trips carrying wounded to Bertrancourt and Senlis. Each trip involved seventy-five miles of "pitch black driving" with a car full of wounded soldiers — some stunned into quiescence, others writhing and moaning in pain.

Although having the French military issue specific, if demanding, orders was no doubt preferable to waiting for the British to make up their minds, Norton soon found that all bureaucracies shared certain inescapable features. The events of June 10, 1915, illustrate the point. Norton, it will be seen, did not spare himself the hazardous outpost duty.

Took one of the cars with Sibley to [the outpost at] Hébuterne. The others with me were Barrington and Bucknell. Were kept busy all night & early this morning while I was at [a dressing station near the trenches] came in for a fairly heavy shelling. One shrapnel bullet went through the car just missing a wounded man we had just put in. Others fell all round & about us. Reached home about 10:30. After lunch helped with evacuations of hospitals in P.M. Rouberti [the French liaison officer] sent word this P.M. there was to be an attack tonight & to send out 6 cars instead of 3 to Mailly. With some difficulty arranged this as the cars were late in returning from evacuation. Just as they were starting came another message to say that after all 3 would do. Another message from the Médecin en Chef at Auchaux asking why we were not there. He has made some mistake as we were not asked to go. Barry tells me Sawyer feels injured by my sarcasm when he complained at Hébuterne the other night about going into the fire zone.

Whether working for the British Red Cross officials in Boulogne or the French in Doullens and Amiens, Norton and his men always seemed to meet up with the same thing: confusion, hard work, mixups, hurt feelings, last-minute changes of orders, and fatigue. Only, here at the front, the experience was more intense — and downright dangerous.

But clearly there had been one major change. Prior to May of 1915, neither the British nor French would allow American ambulances to approach their front lines. Harjes' unit was initially kept back near Montdidier, miles from the trenches, and only in emergencies was allowed to evacuate front-line holding stations, such as those at Warsy and Dancourt. The reason for prohibiting Americans was to prevent "meddling," as Robert Bacon had earlier implied in his conversation with Edward Toland, in October. In mid-May, however, virtually out of the blue, Norton was assigned to the front by the French Second Army. Something had changed the French attitude and, concomitantly, its policies regarding the American volunteer ambulance units.

Norton's diary betrays no curiosity about the change in policy. Perhaps he knew what caused the change, perhaps he didn't; it is even possible he didn't want to know. The fact of the matter is, the policy change was effected by a man Norton disliked and distrusted: A. Piatt Andrew. In April of 1915, Andrew pulled off a remarkable coup that immediately persuaded the French authorities to allow American ambulances — Andrew's, Harjes', and Norton's — to work as close to the front lines as the roads and shelling permitted, and the army's need dictated.

3

A. Piatt Andrew and the American Ambulance Field Service

In the winter of 1914, Robert Bacon, the President of the American Hospital Board, received an appeal from Abram Piatt Andrew of Gloucester, Massachusetts. It was not one that Bacon could regard lightly, for he knew the 41-year-old bachelor personally, and A. Piatt Andrew (Princeton, 1893) had an impressive background. He had served as an assistant professor of economics at Harvard (1900–1909), as director of the United States Mint (1909–1910), and as assistant secretary of the Treasury (1910–1912). Bacon also knew that in September Andrew had lost a primary run-off for the Essex County congressional seat to the incumbent, a fellow Republican named Augustus Peabody Gardner. Finally, Bacon owed Andrew one: while at Treasury, Andrew had hired Bacon's son as his personal secretary.[1]

In his letter, Andrew asked Bacon for a position with the American Military Hospital in Neuilly, but the only work Bacon had to offer at the time was driving ambulances. That was good enough for Andrew. He accepted immediately. After outfitting himself with "a whole equipment of sheep-lined coats and vests, even Jaeger underwear," Andrew sailed out of New York on the *Touraine* on December 19, 1914.[2]

Writing to his parents even before he had received Bacon's reply, Andrew offered his reasons for deciding to go to France.

> [T]he possibility of having even an infinitesimal part in one of the greatest events in all history — the possibility of being of

> some service in the midst of so much distress — the interest of
> witnessing some of the scenes in this greatest and gravest of
> spectacles — and above all the chance of doing the little all
> that one can for France.[3]

Perhaps he also needed a change in scenery after the disappoint-
ing election. Nonetheless, the "little all" he sought to do proved to be
very much indeed. Once Andrew got to France and established himself, he proved relentless in expanding the function and securing the
status of the American volunteer ambulance service. The man's accom-
plishments in organizing, deploying, and eventually taking over the
American Military Hospital's ambulance corps were simply amazing.

Arriving in Paris on the morning of December 30, 1914,[4] Andrew spent his first week gathering the necessary papers, obtaining
his identity card, and registering with the police. Getting a driver's
license was no easy matter for Andrew, who was unaccustomed to
driving a Model T, with its three floor pedals. After nearly hitting a
trolley, a flock of sheep, and an assortment of pedestrians (his licens-
ing officer used the word *assassin* during the test drive), Andrew was
grudgingly given his license.[5] Andrew also had to paint his newly
built Model T slate blue, like all the others, road test it, and outfit it
with new tires. (The original tires were usually replaced with larger
765 x 105s — nonskids, often, on the rear.) "All of this has been done
out of doors in the mud at Neuilly, often in a drizzling rain," Andrew
said. During his first days in Paris he also shopped for a uniform,
sleeping bags, blankets, shoes, shirts, towels, and other personal
supplies.

The American Military Hospital had already begun to experi-
ment with sending some of its cars out into the field to serve regional
hospitals.[6] According to one account, on November 7, 1914, a squad
of ten cars commanded by Robert McClay was sent to the British
front and attached to the Indian Army Corps.[7] In December, the
hospital sent six vehicles, five Fords and one lorry, to help the hospitals in Amiens.[8] This squad was probably the one that later moved
to the Dunkirk sector to serve the British Army there, in that a squad
of five ambulances from the Neuilly hospital was said to be in the
Dunkirk area in early January.[9] Andrew had gotten his papers together too late to leave with the third squad, a contingent of ten cars

that left for Beauvais on January 6.[10] Ready and eager to go, Andrew was promised a spot with the next outbound group, but its departure orders did not come through for two weeks.

These two weeks gave Andrew a chance to renew some old, and valuable, acquaintances. Whereas Richard Norton tended to associate with people of influence in cultural, artistic, and academic circles, A. Piatt Andrew was more politically inclined. His years working in Washington, as well as his attempt to run for Congress, had given him a taste of politics and interested him in people with a political cast of mind. While teaching at Harvard, for example, Andrew made friends with a visiting French professor of political economics, André Tardieu, who was now serving on General Joffre's staff at the *Grande Quartiers Général* (General Headquarters) in Chantilly.[11] It was a good connection, but it was not the only access Andrew had to the GQG. While studying German in Jena in 1898, Andrew had become friends with Gabriel ("Gaby") Puaux. After serving as an infantry captain and having seen action at the Marne, Gaby was transferred in January to Chantilly, where he also joined Joffre's General Staff.[12] While waiting in Paris, Andrew had lunch with Gaby's wife and parents, and they spent the early evening together enjoying a patriotic program at the Théâtre Française.[13] His friendship with the Puauxes and Tardieu was no doubt sincere, for these were genial, attractive people, but he was doubtless aware that they were also valuable contacts.

After the two-week delay, Andrew finally left Paris for Dunkirk on January 20 in a section of twenty men and twelve ambulances.[14] He was given the night shift (6:00 P.M. to 8:00 A.M.), "driving wounded from the trains to one or another of the score of hospitals in Dunkirk and the neighboring towns, or to the hospital steamers that carry them to Boulogne or Brest."[15] Jitney work, in other words, but he made the most of it. At the time, Dunkirk was being shelled almost daily by a new long-range cannon the British could not locate. When the bombardment was particularly destructive, Andrew went out into the city looking for wounded civilians. One evening he found

> the body of a customs officer and two badly maimed fellow officials lying in pools of blood on the sidewalk. They had been innocently walking in the quiet night. I picked up the

> dead body, still warm and pliant, and with difficulty got it into
> the machine. The arms insisted on falling down every time
> that I crossed them over the poor fellow's breast. Then, for the
> first time in my life, I drove a hearse, as we [Andrew had
> another driver with him] carried the lifeless body to one of the
> hospitals. Later, we went down on the dock and found three
> other fellows badly torn and wounded and took them to one of
> the hospitals.[16]

Because there were no trains for him to meet that night, Andrew was
able to work until 2:00 in the morning, when "we got our last
wounded man to a hospital."

Although he appreciated the necessity and importance of ambulance work, Andrew was not entirely satisfied with jitney driving.
Bacon too must have sensed that Andrew's talents were not being put
to full use driving cars, for — apparently without the knowledge of
the Transportation Committee — he stepped in and created a new
position for Andrew: Inspector General of the American Ambulance
Field Service.[17]

One explanation for Bacon's unilateral action may be that some
of his hospital squads were having discipline problems. Richard Norton, though not a sympathetic source, noted that an Amiens doctor
told him the leader of one squad of American hospital ambulances in
that sector "is very disobliging and also drinks."[18] Rumors about
slack discipline among the American Military Hospital's volunteers
appeared again in Norton's log of April 2, 1915, when one of Norton's
drivers returned from Abbéville and reported that the American
hospital's drivers were violating curfew. "They give as their reason,"
Norton's man reported, "that they are Americans and that the English
[who were in control of the Abbéville sector] can not make rules to
govern them." Given rumors like these, Bacon may have decided that
someone was needed to ride herd on the various squads his hospital
had sent out, especially as the men who were scattered around Belgium and Northern France were beyond the direct supervision of the
hospital and its Transportation Committee.

Andrew himself was excited about the new assignment. "The
ambulance committee," he wrote his parents on March 2, 1915,

> have promoted me and I am now a staff officer. . . . An auto-
> mobile has been put at my disposal, and I am hereafter to visit

> and inspect the work of our various [ambulance] sec-
> tions. . . . It is the most interesting job I can imagine . . . , and I
> am to make of it what I can.[19]

No one, not even Bacon, could have guessed what Andrew, holding
an apparent carte blanche, would eventually "make of" the new
position. The members of the Transportation Committee, however,
were vaguely leery of the resolute Andrew, as well they should have
been, given their own lackadaisical and self-aggrandizing tendencies.

One week after taking over his new position, Andrew left on an
inspection tour, a five-day trip visiting ambulance drivers at Beauvais,
St. Pol, Abbéville, Dunkirk, Paris-Plage, Hesdin, and St. Riquier.
What he learned, he had already suspected, for it was a problem he
himself had experienced: the volunteers were bored with jitney work.
Upon his return to Paris on March 14,[20] Andrew began some serious
politicking. He went to the French GQG in Chantilly, where his old
friends, André Tardieu and Gaby Puaux, introduced him to Captain
Aimé Doumenc, General Joffre's chief adviser on transportation. The
volunteers were mostly eager, energetic college men, Andrew told
Doumenc, and were tired of driving from train stations to hospitals
and back. These spirited young men, Andrew argued, needed to be
near the action — that's what they'd come over for.

Doumenc was dubious.[21] The French policy was to not allow
American volunteers at the front because it would be imprudent to
allow neutrals, who may very well have pro-German sympathies, to
circulate freely among the trenches or artillery batteries. Moreover, if
they were allowed at the front, the American volunteers would naturally have to conform to the regulations, restrictions, and discipline of
the French military authorities. These requirements surely would be
unenforceable, in that the French military could hardly claim jurisdic-
tion over noncombatant American citizens.[22]

The official French policy notwithstanding, Captain Doumenc
consented to let Andrew send a small section to Alsace on a trial basis,
provided Andrew could get the approval and cooperation of Captain
de Montravel, commandant of the French Army Automobile Service
of the East. Virtually without delay, Andrew headed east and south
through the Marne (valley) to Vittel (some seventy miles below
Nancy), where de Montravel was headquartered. "At first I thought

he [Andrew] had come to find out what kind of work [his] units might do in the hinterlands," de Montravel later recalled. The Captain was soon disabused of this notion.

> He [Andrew] confided to me his deepest desire, ardently shared by all of his young colleagues, to serve at the front, to pick up the wounded from the front lines . . . , to look danger squarely in the face; in a word, to mingle with the soldiers of France and to share their fate![23]

De Montravel enthusiastically agreed to an on-site trial, stating further that if the experimental section worked out, he would help Andrew persuade Doumenc and the other French authorities to reconsider their policy.

Andrew raced back to Paris, arriving in the evening of March 29. He spent the next few days putting together a carefully chosen group of drivers, including at least three men who had been at Harvard when Andrew was teaching there: Lovering Hill, Dallas McGrew, and, as section leader, Richard Lawrence. "The future of our service depends upon them, and I told them so," Andrew observed.[24] There was a thrilling sense of a change in the air. The sixteen men and twelve cars that represented Andrew's chance to revitalize his corps left Paris on Saturday, April 3, 1915, the day before Easter.

Section Z, as this unit was initially called, reported to de Montravel and other officers at Vittel before proceeding further. All accounts agree that the spirit of the volunteers, who stood for inspection beside their shiny ambulances at 6:00 A.M. every morning, was impressive. Dallas McGrew recalled that the men had their Fords neatly "lined up and polished . . . , radiators and [gas] tanks filled." When the French inspecting officer appeared, McGrew claimed years later, "he invariably found the drivers standing at attention next to their cars, one foot placed on the crank protruding from the radiator. At a signal from the section chief the drivers would stamp heavily on the cranks and ten motors would spring to life simultaneously."[25]

Regardless of McGrew's recollections, which are probably somewhat inflated, Andrew noted in a contemporaneous account (a

letter dated April 14, 1915) that Captain de Montravel and Lieuten-
ant Paquet had indeed been impressed by the men of Section Z.
Accordingly, two days after arriving in Vittel, the volunteers "were
sent a little farther east, and two days after that still farther, and now,"
Andrew wrote, "they are stationed just this side of the pass that marks
the boundary of Alsace."[26] Andrew was referring to the city of St.
Maurice-sur-Moselle, but as the French forces pushed deeper into
Alsace, Z Section kept pace by moving to Mollau and then to
Moosch.[27]

Andrew's elite group and their cars so delighted the French that
even Joffre's staff in Chantilly heard about Section Z's accomplish-
ments. Unlike the heavy ambulances of the French, the speedy and
highly maneuverable Model Ts could negotiate the virtually impassable mountain terrain of the Vosges, even the snowy steepness of
Guebwiller and Hartmannswillerkopf. The American drivers themselves, fresh out of college, displayed the same sprightly toughness
that characterized their Fords.

Section Z passed its test with flying colors. Preston Lockwood,
one of the drivers, noted that "until our light, cheap cars were risked
on these roads a wounded man faced a ten-mile journey with his
stretcher strapped to the back of a mule or put on the floor of a hard
springless wagon."[28] The volunteers changed all that. Weaving
around and through mule-train convoys, they scooted up and down
roads so narrow that two vehicles could seldom pass, so exposed to
enemy artillery that headlights and horns were prohibited, and so
steep that the drivers wore holes in their shoes from depressing the
low-gear pedal hour after hour.

The French had never seen ambulance drivers like these before.
They wanted more. "Captain de Montravel liked our first section so
well that he wanted another right away, so we got back the section
from Beauvais, and revamped it somewhat, and succeeded in getting
it off for the east . . . ," Andrew wrote proudly of his second trial
group, Section Y.[29] In his personal assessment, Andrew noted that
every day the men demonstrated "how efficiently they dispatched the
work of carrying [the wounded] to the hospitals; how ready and
willing they all were; how expert in repairing their machines . . . ;
[and] what thoroughbred gentlemen they all were."[30]

Nonetheless, the official policy restricting the movement of

American volunteers needed to be revised before Andrew could freely assign his sections to front-line French divisions. With de Montravel's enthusiasm and the splendid performance of Z Section supporting his cause, Andrew met with Captain Doumenc at GQG in Chantilly. Together they worked out an agreement that effectively changed French policy restricting the travel of the American volunteers.

The memorandum of agreement made several understandings explicit: (1) a French officer was to be the official commander of each American ambulance section; (2) volunteers were to enlist for six months (no coming and going, willy-nilly); (3) they were to wear the uniform of the American Field Service, with grenades of the French Automobile Service, but no other insignia of military rank; and (4) the cars were to be registered and attached to the Automobile Service of the French Army with which the sections were connected.[31] In addition, Andrew "assured the [French] Government . . . that no man would be accepted for [the ambulance] service who was not known to be loyal to the cause of the Allies. . . ."[32] To this end, Andrew's Field Service would require its volunteers to provide "three letters from men of standing in their communities, testifying to their character and unquestioned loyalty to the allied cause."[33]

As noted in the official *History of the American Field Service in France,* this agreement marked a new relationship between the American volunteers and the French military. In effect, on this date in April of 1915, the American Ambulance Field Service became "a distinct organization with functions, relations, and a personnel of its own."[34] In all but the official sense, the American volunteers were now virtual members of the French Army. They were to receive the same wages and provisions as the *poilus* (literally meaning "hairy ones," the term was widely used for French infantrymen during World War I) and to regard themselves as subject to the same military regulations and discipline. The salient point was that, finally, American volunteer ambulance drivers could be freely assigned to the front. The jitney days were over. The change in French policy also affected Harjes' and Norton's drivers — which explains why, shortly after the agreement was signed in Chantilly, Norton's unit could begin working with the 11th Corps of the French Second Army at the front.

The new relationship that Andrew had so fervently sought with the French, however, created tension between him and his superiors at the American Military Hospital. Satisfied with the status quo, the complacent Transportation Committee did not want Andrew's men directly involved with the French Army, preferring instead looser and less demanding affiliations with regional hospitals. Moreover, the Committee felt that Andrew had circumvented their authority by deliberately making an end-run around them and negotiating privately with Doumenc and the French GQG.

Despite the growing friction between Andrew and the Transportation Committee, he was momentarily cheered by some good news he received in mid-July. "The army administration has withdrawn the French ambulances," he wrote home, "so we Americans alone are carrying all the wounded in Alsace."[35] Such an act confirmed the French military's trust in Andrew's men and their work. Similarly, Richard Norton learned the following September that "all French ambulances were to be withdrawn from the 11th Corps and the whole service . . . [is] to be entrusted to us. This is the biggest compliment," he noted, "that could be paid to us."[36] With various divisions of the French Army relying exclusively on them, the American volunteers had become essentially irreplaceable. Andrew, for one, felt relatively secure in this position, despite his rocky relationship with the Transportation Committee, but Richard Norton remained somewhat uneasy.

Some time after Herman Harjes had gotten his ambulance unit under the sponsoring umbrella of the American Red Cross in June of 1915 (see Chapter Seven), the French General Headquarters proposed that all American volunteer units be subsumed under it.[37] The ARC would coordinate the several ambulance operations and occasionally send them miscellaneous supplies, a few cars, and even, perhaps, some limited funds. Norton, whose group had been foundering in the indecision and indifference of the British Red Cross and War Office, assented to the proposal, with the understanding that his section would stay attached to the French Second Army. Tired of dealing with the British Red Cross, who had begun complaining about his use of American drivers, Norton noted solemnly in his diary on 30 December 1915: "So after 15 months . . . I begin the New Year with a purely American corps under [the] American Red Cross."

Unlike Norton, for whom the American Red Cross represented

something like stability, Andrew had no compelling reason to come in under the ARC organizational umbrella. Indeed, Andrew had cause not to join the American Red Cross, which was a neutral organization equally dedicated to serving the Central Powers as well as the Allies.[38] As Andrew had persuaded Doumenc and the French GQG staff, he and his volunteers were not neutral and made no claim to be. They were serving the cause of France. Their motto emphasized it: *Tous et tout pour la France* ("Everyone and all for France"). Even the certificate each AFS volunteer received mentioned the "fidèle à l'ancestrale amitié de la France & des Etats-Unis" and displayed an American volunteer with his arm around a *poilu*'s shoulder.[39] "We have preferred," he said, "not to be affiliated with an organization which inevitably also has agencies in Germany, Austria, Bulgaria, and Turkey."[40]

There was another reason for Andrew's not joining up with the American Red Cross, even though his relations with the Transportation Committee in Neuilly were becoming increasingly strained. By virtue of his contacts and his own diligence, Andrew had built an effective and practically autonomous organization. His efforts in the field and at the French GQG were paying off; his sections were thriving, multiplying; he was freeing up French ambulance drivers so that they could serve the war effort in other ways. Under Andrew's management, the American Ambulance Field Service was helping France win the war, or at least helping keep the Boche at bay. He was understandably unwilling to risk compromising its operation by submitting it to Red Cross administration. Andrew wanted fewer supervisors, not more.

After the French had reversed their policy, Andrew undertook to fulfill their requests for more ambulance sections. Z Section, which had performed so magnificently in Alsace, was expanded to a full-size unit of twenty cars and a few auxiliary vehicles and designated as Section Sanitaire Américaine 3, which was abbreviated S.S.U. to distinguish it from the English unit Section Sanitaire Anglais [some drivers maintain that the "U" stood for "Unité" (Unit), others that it stood for "(Etats) Unis" (United States)]. To comply with Captain de Montravel's enthusiastic request for a second section, Andrew recalled a squad of ten cars from Beauvais, labeled it Section Y (before expanding it into S.S.U. 2),[41] and sent it to the Lorraine battlefields around Pont-à-Mousson. The various squads that had been assigned originally to the Dunkirk sector were combined and reconstituted as S.S.U. 1 — and also brought south, to work with a French division stationed along the Somme. A fourth section was created in November of 1915, and Andrew began outfitting a fifth section in April of 1916.

Alarmed by this rapid growth of the Field Service, the American Military Hospital's Transportation Committee decided to bring Andrew back in line — by cutting off his funds. In a letter to Bacon (June 29, 1916), Andrew charged that

> not one single sou from [the funds raised in] New York has been devoted to the Field Service since the first of last December, and when yesterday I made a final appeal before the Committee to Mr. Benét to sign the order for $13,000 worth of spare parts, he still refused to do so.[42]

Not about to be stopped by the Committee's action, Andrew cabled William Hereford in New York to buy the desperately needed spare parts out of Andrew's private bank account.

By the spring and summer of 1916, the funding of the Field Service was becoming a major point of contention. Through donors who wrote him directly, Andrew knew his Field Service was not getting its share of the funds that had been collected by Hereford.[43] "Contributions in New York intended for the Field Service," Andrew added in the letter to Bacon of June 29, "ought to be so marked over there and similarly ear-marked over here. . . ." Then relations worsened. When twenty-seven Ford chassis intended for Andrew's Field Service arrived in Bordeaux, the Transportation Committee, as part of its efforts to block Andrew, blithely refused to authorize men or funds to bring the automobiles up to Paris, forcing Andrew to make his own arrangements.

At the end of his rope, Andrew wired Bacon in the States on July 16, 1916, asking him to suggest to the Neuilly officials that the Field Service be granted its own treasurer and separate administration. Bacon waffled.[44] He didn't want to let Andrew or his sections down, especially considering the worldwide acclaim the Field Service was receiving for its courageous and steadfast work at Verdun.[45] Yet

Bacon insisted that "the one thing which, above all others, he wished to avoid" was the separation of the Field Service from the American Military Hospital.[46] In mid-July, in the heat of Andrew's persistence, Bacon did what any shrewd executive might do: he left the matter in Anne Vanderbilt's hands and went to Mexico. "We have no feeling of gratitude to Mr. Bacon for any of the changes that have taken place," Andrew wrote Henry Sleeper after the matter had been resolved. "He did *nothing.*"[47]

Mrs. Vanderbilt had come to France early in July. "She immediately saw our difficulties," Andrew wrote his parents, "and briskly and crisply set about to clear them away. . . ."[48] Her assistance and guarantees of financial support gave Andrew all the encouragement he needed. Andrew nominally shifted the affiliation of his Field Service to the original (civilian) American Hospital by naming a new governing committee (Andrew himself and his assistant Stephen Galatti were two of the three members) and making it respond directly to Bacon. In so doing, Andrew made the Field Service a subdivision of the original American Hospital, parallel to, and independent of, the Military Hospital, which was also a subdivision of the old American Hospital.[49] "Benét, Lopp, and Kipling will henceforth have nothing to do with the Field Service," Andrew said of the Transportation Committee,[50] which was left in control of only a handful of ambulances charged with hauling wounded from train stations such as La Chapelle to the American Military Hospital and other officially sanctioned hospitals in Paris.

Andrew felt immensely grateful to Anne Vanderbilt for standing by him during these difficult times and, good politician that he was, wanted to repay her. In a letter to Lovering Hill, who headed a Field Service section near Verdun, Andrew admitted to being "very anxious that we show her our appreciation of what she has done for us. . . ."[51] Andrew's idea was to take Mrs. Vanderbilt on a tour of the Field Service sections, all of which were in the Verdun sector. It was a risky proposition, given the state of affairs around Verdun in August of 1916, but such a tour would permit "her to know as much as possible about the conditions of life and the work of our men at the front [so] that we may have the benefit of her interest in the future," Andrew told Hill.

Accordingly, during the first week of August, Mrs. Vanderbilt, disguised in nurses' whites to identify her as a nonbelligerent (should they happen to fall into enemy hands) and also to spare her the fawning attention of French officers, accompanied Andrew on a visit to the Verdun front. All reports of this tour attested to Mrs. Vanderbilt's intelligence, vitality, and courage — as well as her growing esteem for the work the drivers were doing.[52] Her own account described a midnight artillery attack that drove her, in her robes and sleeping cap, into a dim, dank cellar, where dozens of pajama-clad men crouched anxiously.

Meanwhile, the response of the Transportation Committee to Andrew's battle for independence was petulantly to kick him out of the Lycée Pasteur buildings and order him off the property of the American Military Hospital. "They [the Committee] have asked us to leave the Hospital grounds and to provide for our men elsewhere," Andrew wrote Bacon, "and have been rather insistent upon our leaving with least possible delay."[53] Not only was Andrew prepared for such an exigency, he had the renewed assurances of financial support from Mrs. Vanderbilt. He had set his sights on a highly desirable location on the Right Bank, in the middle of the posh section of Paris known as Passy.[54] Drawing on his stock of connections, Andrew had by mid-July persuaded the owners, Baron Hottinguer and Comtesse de la Villestreux, to rent him their magnificent estate at 21 rue Raynouard.[55] "We have found a delightful old 18th century house," Andrew wrote his parents,

> which, though in the heart of Paris, is surrounded by acres of romantic and deserted gardens — a place not lived in for a decade — and it is now being fitted up with dormitories, refectory and living rooms for the boys, and offices for all our staff. Within a week we shall have everything transferred.[56]

In addition to its grandeur, the mansion and five-acre estate also had historical significance. Rousseau had taken its waters; Ben Franklin had walked its gardens; Balzac had explored its grounds while living in the house across the street; and Bartholdi, the sculptor of the Statue of Liberty, had strolled in its orangerie to relax.[57] Now it was to be the home base and headquarters of the American Field Service.[58]

While setting up his new headquarters, Andrew was also firming up his financial operations. He no longer wanted Hereford to be his stateside fund-raiser and representative. First of all, the New York banker had not seen to it in the past that Andrew got the funds he was due. More recently, Andrew learned that Hereford was less than satisfactory as a recruiter. Toward the end of July, Andrew received a note from a Harvard friend saying that "a great many fellows from Harvard have gone over to drive ambulances, but the best ones have been switched off into the Harjes outfit." The note went on to imply that Hereford was brusque and indifferent in his dealings with prospective recruits. The writer's point was reinforced when two other volunteers told Andrew that "information [about the American Field Service] in New York is very vague and all the initiative has to come from the individuals who want to come over."[59] Hereford, Andrew figured, was too busy and too passive to handle the stateside affairs of his Field Service properly.

Unlike Richard Norton, who tended to rely on his supporters' altruistic good will, Andrew was an aggressive tactician. Whereas Norton had Henry James writing laudatory copy to newspapers appealing for funds, Andrew took steps to set up over a hundred active recruiting and fund-raising committees throughout the entire United States. In the late summer of 1915, Andrew established a cooperative tie with the American Fund for French Wounded (AFFW), a large and efficient humanitarian society that Mrs. Vanderbilt had first introduced him to. Andrew's Field Service delivered the AFFW's gifts of clothing, foodstuffs, blankets, and other items of succor to the wounded at the front.[60] In return, Anne Morgan, who was treasurer of the AFFW, provided Andrew with direct access to its local committees (of which there were hundreds) in the United States.[61] This was a priceless list of contacts — names and addresses of sympathetic American citizens. He got a windfall of free publicity when the September 1915 issue of the AFFW's widely circulated bulletin was devoted entirely to the American Field Service.

Hereford was clearly not the man to take advantage of Andrew's groundwork. Andrew therefore persuaded his good friend from Gloucester, Henry Sleeper, who was associated with the Lee Higginson & Co. bank in Boston, to take over as his official representative and chief fund-raiser in the States. To assist him, Sleeper engaged two energetic and imaginative young men, John Hays Hammond, the heir of a wealthy mining engineer, and Leslie Buswell, a tireless campaigner and former actor who had served in the ambulance corps. Once local AFS committees were established, Sleeper and his staff provided them with programs and speakers for recruiting and fund-raising purposes. The most lucrative program was the illustrated lecture, a short talk (often by a former driver) accompanied by a moving picture of the drivers in action. Pro-German hooligans occasionally tried to break up these meetings, sometimes causing them to be rescheduled or even canceled.[62]

Sleeper and his staff also took advantage of the pro-Allies sentiment on American campuses.[63] Once they learned of the work of the American Field Service, several professors involved themselves directly by raising money and recruiting drivers, despite the national policy of neutrality. Some, such as Professor Martin Sampson of Cornell, actually helped organize (as well as inspire) a unit of volunteers.[64] Other professors, Charles Townsend Copeland of Harvard, for example, openly encouraged their students (Waldo Peirce and Harry Sheahan, for example) "to go over to Europe and help in any way that we could."[65] Administrators got involved as well. Prep-school headmasters such as Stearns at Phillips Academy, department heads such as Christian Gauss at Princeton, and college presidents such as George D. Olds at Amherst granted permission for their students to leave school without penalty and with readmission unimpeded. Coleman Clark noted, for instance, that "the Dean [at Yale] said that I would receive full credit for all I had done so far [this was in the middle of the spring semester]; he said that going abroad with the American Ambulance was a fine thing to do, and that he would not discourage anyone contemplating doing it."[66]

Another enterprise originated by Andrew in France and carried out by Sleeper and his staff in Boston was to produce two books describing the ambulance drivers' experiences: Buswell's *Ambulance No. 10: Personal Letters from the Front*, and *Friends of France: The Field Service of the American Ambulance Described by Its Members*. In addition to tending to make ambulance work sound gloriously exciting and grandly humanitarian, these books each contained an endpaper explaining the goals of the American Ambulance Field Service, asking for money, and inviting men to volunteer. Moreover, within the text of his book, Buswell unabashedly appealed for funds: "If all [the] people in America only knew what this Section and our work mean to the soldiers [in France], money would not be long in coming."[67]

Other drivers wrote articles for magazines and letters to home-town newspapers, which inevitably increased the American public's awareness of Andrew's Field Service. In one piece, for instance, Andrew himself wrote, "At the very start, let me say that . . . we have preferred that our Service in France should not be officially affiliated with [the American Red Cross]. . . . It is important to make clear the distinction between the two organizations [the American Field Service and the American Red Cross] because not infrequently generous Americans who have wanted to help our Service have mistakenly sent money or recruits intended for us to the Red Cross."[68] Andrew, obviously, was still fuming from the mix-ups that had occurred when Hereford was handling the funds.

Having established itself financially and administratively by the end of August of 1916, the American Ambulance Field Service could drop the word *ambulance* from its title, in that the Field Service was no longer affiliated with the American "Ambulance," that is, the Military Hospital. With Andrew now solely in charge, the American Field Service prospered as never before. When he turned his corps over to the U.S. Army a year later, in the autumn of 1917, Andrew had built the AFS up to thirty-four ambulance and fourteen camion (truck) sections. The truck sections alone accounted for eight hundred American volunteers.[69] In addition to these eight hundred truck drivers, when the U.S. Army took over the American Field Service, it acquired

> about twelve hundred [ambulance drivers] with nearly a thousand ambulances . . . [,] a spacious headquarters and reception park in the heart of Paris, its own construction and repair park and supply depot, its own training camp, its own share in the French automobile officers' school, its own home and hospital for men convalescing and on furlough . . .[70]

Andrew had indeed built a mighty operation, one that even the U.S. Army couldn't quite bring down.

Whether it was Harjes' experimentation with both hospital and ambulance units, Norton's wrestling with the slippery British Red

Cross and War Office, or Andrew's maneuvering to reverse French policy and free his corps from the American Military Hospital, the turf battles with bureaucracies had been fought and, for the most part, won by mid-1916. Thereafter, the volunteers confronted challenges of endurance, psychological stability, patience, physical strength, mechanical deftness, courage, and will — challenges that could prove at times even more frustrating than those posed by obstinate bureaucracies. After mid-1916, the volunteers as noncombatant drivers carrying wounded men had no specific antagonists, no Office of This or That to complain about or appeal to. The drivers might struggle against their own fatigue or fear one night, and an impassable road or fouled spark plug the next, but there was no institution to contend with, just as there was no human enemy to face.

As a consequence, the experiences of the volunteers working the front were profoundly complex and contradictory. In a single day they witnessed the worst that war had to offer: the wounded, maimed, and lifeless soldiers, or bits of soldier, at the front. That same day, however, they also might see the verdant countryside and elegant châteaux of La Belle France lining the unscathed roads leading back to the base hospitals beyond the reach of artillery. They heard the screams and pleas of *"doucement!"* ("slow down!") from *les blessés* being jostled around in the back of their ambulances, which they nevertheless drove full-speed through the pitch-black night with lights off, over roads pocked by shells and littered by blasted debris and the fetid carcasses of horses, in order to get to a hospital before the screaming, pleading *blessés* became *les morts*. The life of the front-line ambulance driver wasn't anchored by routine. By 1916, Harjes', Norton's, and Andrew's volunteers had come a long way from their innocent, uncertain, and trial-and-error beginnings.

Part II
Works and Days

4

Under Fire[1]

Preston Lockwood squinted through the snowy twilight as he maneuvered his ambulance up the steep roadpath deep into the Vosges of Alsace. It would be thirty minutes yet before he reached the front lines. Keeping his Model T in low gear to maintain traction, Lockwood spotted the stooped figure of a lone *poilu* slogging through the snowdrifts just ahead of him. The *poilu* stopped and turned when he heard Lockwood approach. Packing thirty-five pounds of kit, as well as a bolt-action rifle and two ammunition belts, the French soldier must have been climbing for hours — and in these conditions he would have several more to go.

Lockwood knew what would happen next. The weary *poilu* might not flag him down and plead openly for a ride, but the look of exhaustion on his face and the contortion of his twisted shoulders would make the plea all but explicit. Lockwood would have to shout, *"C'est défendu,"* and continue driving. The Hague Conventions dictated that only wounded, sick, or deceased military personnel could be carried in ambulances. Section 3, like its predecessor, Z Section, had to be absolutely circumspect. The fate of the Field Service, as "Doc" Andrew had told the drivers, depended on them. Still, it was difficult for Lockwood to refuse men a lift, especially when he knew that under other circumstances the *poilus* would do anything for him, from pushing his car out of a ditch to sharing his canteen. More depressing still, Lockwood also knew that as he drove past this hapless *poilu*, the soldier would nevertheless smile and call out, without sarcasm, *"Merci quand même!"* (Thanks all the same!).

As Lockwood's Model T neared the *poilu,* the man began waving frantically and positioned himself in the center of the narrow road.

Surrendering his traction and momentum, Lockwood stopped the car and waited as the middle-aged man, his kit jouncing on his back, ran up to him. The soldier tugged on his cap and tried to catch his breath in the wintry, high-altitude air. Then he broke into a broad smile. Lockwood's heart sank.

The *poilu* reached into the car suddenly and forced a vigorous handshake on Lockwood. Between gasps of frosty air, he told Lockwood that he had heard rumors about ambulances being driven by American volunteers, that a friend had written him about being rushed to a hospital in an American ambulance, and that this was his first chance to meet and thank in person one of the splendid *volontaires américains*. Pointing toward the front lines in the black distance, where rumbles and flashes of artillery imitated thunder and lightning, the *poilu* waved Lockwood on. "Continue, please," he said. "Perhaps you will bring *me* back tomorrow."[2]

Like a chorus in a Greek tragedy, the old men sat in the deserted wine shop, protected by stacks of sandbags and warmed by a wood-burning stove. Plenty of wood could be found in Verdun these days, after all the bombardments of the last nine months. The first snow of winter was falling. Mercifully heavy, it obscured the debris lying in the city's streets and blanketed the ash-black skeletons of burnt homes. Outside the wine shop stood a two-wheeled horse cart and an old-fashioned seesaw fire pump, covered with a patched and tattered tarpaulin.

The men were *pompiers*, volunteer firemen, the last civilian residents of Verdun. A lookout was posted on the second floor, where a telephone switchboard stood ready to send and receive messages from other *pompier* lookouts scattered throughout the battered, ruined city. No one questioned why, given the already ubiquitous devastation, anyone would bother putting out a fire. But there they waited, retired gendarmes, schoolmasters, farmers, clerks, and ex-soldiers, whose bodies were too broken for any work but this.

They looked up in unison when Henry ("Harry") Sheahan waved at them through the wine shop window. A stooped, ancient figure wearing a shiny helmet opened the door and motioned him in to get warm. Harry shook hands all around, had his back slapped numerous times, was offered bread and cheeses, and tasted three different regional, raw wines. However, he could not stay long. He was sorry. He was only out for a walk. Some wounded might have been brought into the *poste,* he explained, and he needed to get back there in case they needed to be taken to one of the hospitals down the hill.

The stooped man in the shiny helmet accompanied him out the door. "I must show you something odd, *mon vieux,*" he said. "Just around this corner and through those cellars." Leading Harry by the hand, the old *pompier* took him to a solitary house — miraculously, still intact, except for the large ground-floor window, which was cracked. He pointed inside.

The tableau inside the window absorbed Harry. On the mantel above the fireplace were photographs of families and pretty women. A stack of yellowed newspapers lay neatly on an *étagère,* below a shelf of books. Near the front window stood a dining table, its cloth spread, the place settings and silver laid out in proper order. A ceramic tureen, its lid covered with a light film of ash, occupied the center of the table. A dull green, feathery fungus carpeted the contents of a serving bowl, while suspended webs of dust drifted and floated in the wine glasses. One chair was tipped over backward.

"Officers were quartered here," the old man whispered in Sheahan's ear. "They were called very suddenly and never came back. They stepped out of the middle of their lives."[3]

The *médecin en chef* at Fort de Vaux enjoyed his work, both as a surgeon and as an army officer. But the dead bodies, which were piling up faster than his aides could bury them, got in his way. So he ordered that the drivers of Section 1 carry the dead bodies back to Verdun as part of their regular duties. When the drivers complained to their French liaison officer about this, the lieutenant agreed with them. Using ambulances to haul stacks of corpses was a waste of gas and the drivers' time. The ensuing confrontation between the lieutenant and the *médecin en chef* produced a compromise. The drivers would carry corpses for the surgeon if the bodies were fresh, but not if they were cold and stiff.[4]

Section 1 was billeted for a while in the town of Jaulzy, on the southern bank of the Aisne, halfway between Compiègne and

Soissons. The artillery fire along the Aisne front was so fierce and widespread that the Section had to serve nine *postes de secours*. To do so, they used a relay station at the small village of Vic-sur-Aisne on the north bank of the river about half a mile from the front. The drivers worked 24-hour shifts at a château there, driving up to the *postes* to get the *blessés* and transporting them back to various field or evacuation hospitals. Sometimes, if an ambulance train happened to be available, they were sent to the railhead at Pierrefonds.

Robert Imbrie arrived at Vic-sur-Aisne promptly at 8:00 on February 9, 1916, amid the usual morning din. The French batteries nearby had begun their bombardment, and the Germans began responding shortly thereafter, pounding the nearby village of Roche. No calls had come in to the town's relay station, so the drivers simply waited, knowing that sooner or later they would have more work than they could handle. Around noon, the German range contracted, and the shell fire edged closer to the château. Imbrie was returning from mess, when suddenly he saw a fellow driver drop flat to the ground. A split-second later Imbrie heard an earsplitting screech, followed by a huge crash — like a ton of lumber falling — and a rising cloud of dust half a block away. The other driver lay frozen, his arms over his head. Another shell hit. And another.

Imbrie stood motionless, watching the dirt and chunks of debris and metal explode into the air. Immobilized partly by fear, partly by panic, but mostly by curiosity, Imbrie stood fixed. He had never encountered shelling so close before. His mind was surprisingly calm, and he didn't sense any weakening of his knees until moments later, when he started to run back to the château. He knew drivers would be needed now. As he raced down the road through the wreckage and the *éclat* of the incoming fire, he was nearly run over by an ambulance speeding away. The calls had arrived. The back wall of the château had been blown away, but inside sat Imbrie's Model T, Old Number Nine, unscathed and ready to roll.

And roll it did. For the next twelve hours, Imbrie drove the roads of the Aisne as if he were a goggled driver racing around the Brickyard oval at Indianapolis. Imbrie picked up three *couchés* at Roche and delivered them, top speed, to the triage hospital at Attichy, then raced back to Vic-sur-Aisne posthaste to get his next assignment. He was promptly sent off to the dressing station at Vingre. The shelling had not let up, and a freezing rain had begun to fall, transforming the road into a canal of mud with the viscosity of axle grease. Only the high clearance of the Model T enabled Old Number Nine to proceed, slipping and sliding and spinning its wheels in the gluey gunk.

It took him nearly two hours to travel three miles, but Imbrie finally reached the *poste*, little more than a sandbag-reinforced dugout with a corrugated tin roof. The *poste* was so close to the front that while he was frantically loading his *blessés*, Imbrie could hear the popping of small-arms fire and the muffled bursts of grenades in between the battery salvos. Imbrie departed as soon as the men were loaded. The mud was starting to freeze, but still he crept along in low gear because his *blessés* were so badly wounded they couldn't abide even the slightest jostling. He didn't like being a slow-moving target for German artillery, yet it was a matter of "save first," Imbrie told himself, rather than "safety first."

As the gray daylight faded, the landscape grew depressingly bleak. The road, a half-frozen mire, passed through what was once a grove but was now a collection of tree trunks, stripped and bare. Beyond the road stretched fields of muck, undulate and pocked from shells. Above Imbrie the salvos screamed continuously, and around him lay a few random clumps of gluey earth and shards of road stone. Once in a while, a soldier's head would appear turtle-like at the narrow entrance of a dugout alongside the road and then quickly disappear. It was a colorless, barren patch of the world.

Imbrie got the *blessés* to St. Luke's Hospital at Compiègne by 7:00 that evening, and returned immediately to Vic-sur-Aisne. The cook had saved him a bit of dinner, which he gobbled down. He tried to shake the fleas out of his sleeping bag and started to roll up in it when another call came. This time it was the *poste* at Hautebraye, even more exposed to artillery fire than the one at Vingre. It would be a nighttime, lights-out drive. By now, however, the mud had frozen, and between the moonlight, the flares, and the exploding shells it would be bright enough to drive in high gear.

There was no waiting at Hautebraye. In fact, Imbrie was to carry only one *blessé* on this trip, and the orderlies had him all ready for loading when Imbrie arrived. It was a ghastly case. Shrapnel had ripped open the man's torso, and he was raving deliriously. They had tied his hands behind his back to keep him from tearing his bandages open and pulling at the loose flesh. It was to be another slow and sorrowful trip to Compiègne for Imbrie, who could not tell, after he had arrived, whether or not his *blessé* was still alive.

Imbrie was so exhausted that twice he nearly fell asleep on his way back to Vic-sur-Aisne. By 1:00 he finally lay on the cold stone floor of the château, his infested sleeping bag pulled up around his shoulders, and drifted off into a deep, dreamless sleep. The French and German artillery awoke him at 6:30 the next morning. So, when his replacement arrived at eight, Imbrie was all ready to crank up Old Number Nine. Back at the quiet *cantonnement* in Jaulzy, at precisely 8:30 A.M., Imbrie sat down to a breakfast of tea, bread, and a lovely soft-boiled egg. Thus passed the first of countless 24-hour shifts for Robert Imbrie.[5]

Pity the fresh recruit, full of gush and flapdoodle though he be. The other drivers call him by his last name, if by anything at all, until he proves himself. The veterans might consent to sell him a regulation helmet and gas mask at a nice price; he'll discover later that both can be had free for the asking from the French Army. For ten francs, a recruit might be given the honor of subscribing to the *Bulletin des Armées*, and then find that the newspaper was automatically issued at no charge to all drivers and troops. Sooner or later, the brash, idealistic recruit will come to understand that, in truth, ambulance work requires little more than the ability to crank a car and steer it to where he is told. Once that realization sets in, the cakes or pastries, for which the money he had given the older recruits has been spent, will be brought to the drivers' tables, amid laughter, applause, and miscellaneous toasts thanking the recruit for his thoughtful gifts.[6]

An orderly pointed down the road toward the hill that was called *Le Mort Homme* (The Dead Man). The new man jumped into his ambulance and, working the hand levers, shouted, "How do I find the *poste?*"

"Can't miss it," the orderly yelled. "Go past two bad smells and turn left."[7]

April 23, 1915. Three o'clock in the afternoon. Rue d'Ypres, in the tiny Belgian village of Poperinghe, situated exactly between Ypres and the French border. Henry Sydnor Harrison, an ambulance driver from Charleston, West Virginia, more recently of Columbia University, waited near the train station and studied in amazement the swarm of human activity resulting from the previous day's battle, Second Ypres. There had been the surprise of poison gas, the temporary collapse of the Ypres salient, the Germans' press across the Yser — all accompanied by artillery bombardments "of a ferocity hitherto unequaled."

Harrison alone could see it. The soldiers were too preoccupied with arresting the German advance to spot what Harrison saw; the civilian refugees were too hysterical in their rush to the evacuation trains to look around. Everyone was caught up in some desperate activity — everyone, that is, except Harrison, who, as an American *ambulancier*, was neither in nor out of the war. Until orders to roll arrived, he was a mere observer, watching

> the new army [reinforcements] of England go up. Thousands and thousands, foot and horse, supply and artillery, gun, caisson, wagon and lorry, the English were going up. . . . Beautifully equipped and physically attractive — the useless cavalry especially! — sun-tanned and confident, all ready to die without a whimper, they were a most likely and impressive-looking lot.

Meanwhile, on his other side, another line of men, a group more somber and lugubrious, passed in the opposite direction: "The two streams actually touching and mingling, the English were coming back." Bloodied and beaten, the returning Tommies — at least those who were ambulatory — stumbled silently rearward, as the boisterous new Tommies advanced.

Then it occurred to Harrison: *it is all a continuous loop.* On one side "the cannon fodder going up" and on the other "the cannon fodder coming back. . . . These two streams [were] really one. These men the same men, only at slightly different stages of their experience."[8]

Charles B. Nordhoff spent New Year's Eve at a forward *poste* listening to the rats scampering about him. The new year, 1917, arrived in a splendid dawn: the sky a crystalline blue, and the sun shining down frostily on the silent battlefield. The inevitable explosions and machine-gun fire didn't begin until Nordhoff was brushing his teeth at a trough of icy water, and he was promptly called back. Three *blessés* needed to be taken to the evacuation hospital at once.

One of the soldiers was concealed in a roll of bandage wrappings and blankets, and lay motionless and mummy-like on his stretcher. In contrast, the two others were lively and talkative, although each had a smashed leg. Refusing stretchers, they clambered into the back and cheerily nodded good-bye to the *brancardiers* who had brought them in. One of the men bumped his bandaged leg and jerked back in reflex. *"Ça pique, mon vieux,"* he gasped to the alarmed Nordhoff, *"mais ça ne fait rien — allez!"* (That stings, my friend, but it's nothing — go!) And off they went.

At the hospital, the orderlies were hours behind, and they were not about to be rushed — not on this morning of New Year's Eve hangovers. Backed up behind a line of other ambulances, Nordhoff told his *blessés* that they would have to wait for the hospital book-keepers to catch up on their paperwork. As Nordhoff offered cigarettes to his two spunky passengers, the blood-stained roll of blankets on the stretcher began to move, and slowly a blanched face appeared. The man squinted at Nordhoff and the two other *blessés* and in a calm, gravelly voice, said, *"Oui, c'est une guerre de papier. Donnez-moi une cigarette."* (Yes, it's a war of paper. Give me a cigarette.) At that moment Nordhoff finally understood why in two-and-a-half years the French had not been defeated — despite Verdun, the Marne, Champagne, the Vosges, and other places that stood for inutterable devastation.[9]

The French battery was positioned below the embanked road leading north out of Verdun, and the Germans were trying to reach it with their large-caliber 210s. One shell landed in the middle of the road, just in front of one of Doc Andrew's drivers, who was on his way to a dressing station half a mile away. Another shell wiped out the remaining corner of a building across from the *poste* as he arrived. The *éclats* began to strike his car, so the driver jerked his brake lever back and, abandoning the Model T in the middle of the roadway, dashed for the underground dressing station.

A stretcher-bearer told him that the Boche, always systematic, were firing shells in batches of seven, between which there was a pause for several minutes. During one of these predictable intervals, the driver raced out to move his ambulance and caught a glimpse of a shadowy procession coming down a side lane through the dust raised by the shelling. There must have been a score or more of gray, dim figures, each bent over, pushing a two-wheeled canvas *brouette* on which lay indistinct forms wrapped in bloody rags. Waving to them, the driver shouted, "*Blessés!* Bring them over here!" He pointed toward the *poste.*

"*Non, ce sont les morts*" (No, these are the dead), came the ghostly reply. "*Il n'y a pas de blessés.*" There were no wounded.[10]

He had already been to the *poste de secours* at Haudromont several times that day before heading out for one last trip at 5:00 in the afternoon. The American section chief, William Yorke Stevenson, recommended he remain at the *poste* until midnight; the scuttlebutt was that the French infantry was going over the top just after sundown and there were sure to be some serious casualties. The middle-aged Philip Sidney Rice, whose bad heart had kept him out of the Spanish-American War, consented. Like all the other men of Section 1, he had absolute trust in Stevenson's knowledge and judgment.

The dressing station at Haudremont, about eight miles northeast of Verdun, was located as close to the front as automobiles could go, and it had been busy all day. *Brancardiers*, their jaws set and expressions glazed, had been continuously bringing in wounded from the front-line trenches. They paused only to duck into a makeshift first-aid shelter, where they might bandage the *blessé* they were carrying, or slosh a bottle of iodine on his wounds. Sometimes the shelling got so heavy the stretcher-bearers had to squeeze momentarily into an improvised *abri* (shelter) dug into the side of a hill or trench. Otherwise, the line of *brancardiers* was virtually unbroken as it wound down the communication trenches, which led directly from the front lines back to the *poste de secours* a few hundred yards away. There, a surgeon, working under the crudest of conditions, would perform whatever quick and dirty emergency surgery he guessed necessary. There, also, waited the American ambulances.

One of the drivers, Patterson, was just leaving with a load of *blessés* — three *couchés* in the back and one *assis* sitting in the cab beside him — when Rice arrived. Hanna went next. Then White left, but he got no further than the base of the hill when the German artillery began and his car stopped dead. As the shrapnel skittered and slashed around him, he and a fellow driver managed to transfer the wounded into another ambulance and speed away. Kitzburg's car was loaded next, and he took off down into the hailstorm of shrapnel.

Only Rice remained. He and a stretcher-bearer sat on a stone step outside the *poste*, smoking American cigarettes. Watching the shells land in the valley below, they surmised that the fighting at the front had to be heavy, in that no stretcher cases were being brought in. Most likely the *brancardiers* were holed up somewhere waiting for the artillery fire to abate. Finishing their smokes and seeing the German guns begin to close in on them, Rice and the stretcher-bearer stepped through the *poste*'s timbered entrance and felt their way down the steps in the dark.

In the tiny underground room lit stark white by a single carbide lamp, three military policemen were pinning a raving, struggling man to the floor, while a fourth tried to tape a gag in his mouth. *"Commotionné,"* one of the gendarmes said, looking up at Rice. "How you say? — shell-shocked. Fatigue of battle." Wedged into sitting positions, slumped against the wall, was a line of *blessés* in various states of consciousness. Beyond, a surgeon hunched over a makeshift table, snipping and cutting and dropping sticky things into a bucket at his feet. The stretcher-bearer brought Rice a cup of tea and returned to give the surgeon a few quick puffs on a cigarette. The struggling, shell-shocked man on the floor lapsed into a catatonic quiescence broken by occasional twitches and jerks.

It was only ten o'clock — two hours yet to sip tea, to watch the back of the French surgeon at his table, and think. Rice didn't like driving alone, although that was one of the reasons for the success of the AFS's Model Ts. The bigger, clumsier cars of the Norton-Harjes Red Cross units required two men, one as driver and one as orderly or guide. Having someone along, Rice thought, would make the work less nerve-racking. It would certainly be less lonely. Still, he had to admit that Doc Andrew's strategy of using the smaller, sprightlier Model Ts was working. Who was he to argue? He had been in France hardly a month — and at Verdun scarcely a few days.

Rice paced the room, stopping to peer outside every once in a while. The shelling continued. He studied the *médecin en chef*'s map and decided he wouldn't take the main road through Bras, even though it was shorter that way. That road had been heavily shelled, and Rice feared it would be impassable by now. Besides, someone said that gas had been released in the Meuse valley, which meant it would probably linger all night in the low areas around what was left of Bras. He decided he would take the back way, using the wisp of a road that weaved along a hogback above the gas — but beneath, or so he prayed, the crossing arch of artillery fire.

The midnight drive along the narrow hogback proved difficult indeed. Rice's car stalled twice, and each time, to get to the crank, Rice had to climb over the wounded man who was stuffed into the cab beside him and lift aside another who was clinging to the running board. Finally he made it, even though one of his cylinders had stopped firing altogether just when his Model T chugged and lurched into the *cantonnement* grounds. As soon as the car rolled to a halt, a group of *brancardiers* scurried about, transferring the *blessés* to other ambulances, which would take them to the proper hospitals. Dreaming vaguely that his car remained in motion and that he was still driving it, Rice slumped exhausted over the steering wheel for a few moments. Then, half awake, he tumbled out of the ambulance and staggered into the pitch-dark dining tent, tripping over a guy rope as he tried to light a match. From a cabinet Rice took a chunk of dry bread, a tin of sardines, and a half-bottle of *pinard*. Making his way to his cot, Rice dropped onto it, and, letting the victuals fall, went instantly to sleep. He had never lived through twenty-four hours like these in his entire life.

The date was July 20, 1917, a year after the German assault on Verdun had pretty much run its course. It was a decidedly unexemplary day. Although busy, dangerous, and at times nightmarish, the day was nonetheless routine. Ordinary. Typical. Perhaps therein lay the problem. By mid-September, Section Chief William Yorke Stevenson recommended that Philip Sidney Rice be hospitalized for burn-out, exhaustion, *commotionné* — call it what you will. The doctors in Paris diagnosed it as a mild case of battle fatigue.[11]

Later, in the autumn of 1917, the French began a massive offensive to push the Germans north beyond Fort Douaumont and Fort de Vaux.

Stevenson was still in charge of Section 1, and he found the roads around Douaumont to be a ghastly mess. It wasn't just the condition of the road surfaces, it was the sights and smells one encountered along them. French supply wagons were pulled by horses, and when a team got hit their corpses were left for days to lie where they fell. Moreover, a human body blasted by an artillery shell was seldom gathered up entirely. The terrain was littered with dead horses and bits of men attended by rats, flies, and other carrion-feeders.

Passing along the road to Vaux to help pull one of his men out of a ditch, Stevenson saw a boot lying in the road. Stopping to throw it out of the way, he picked up the boot and found part of a leg still in it.[12]

They tell the story of a driver who was hauling a *couché* to a hospital for the seriously wounded. Out of respect for the soldier's wounds, the driver proceeded down the road at a cautious pace. Meanwhile, in the back, the man had awakened and began sipping from a canteen, which someone had placed in his lap. He was soon feeling better, for, as they say, French canteens do not hold water. By the time the ambulance arrived at the *couché* hospital, the soldier, who was supposed to be recumbent and seriously wounded, was sitting up and feeling feisty.

When the hospital orderlies lifted the rear canvas, the soldier greeted them with a smile and a merry wave of the hand. He offered them a swig from his canteen and a drag on his cigarette. The officious orderlies, who were accustomed to dealing only with the most serious cases, dropped the canvas huffily. They chastised the driver for his obvious error and dispatched him to an *assis* hospital some twenty miles away, where less serious wounds were treated by, presumably, less able personnel. On the way, the soldier fell into a deep, boozy sleep. Since the *assis* hospital treated only ambulatory patients, the orderlies there were surprised to find a comatose form lying on a stretcher when they peered into the rear of the ambulance. The driver was admonished again and ordered to take the man to the hospital for *couchés*.

Having already wasted an hour trying to deliver his wounded soldier, the driver took off at top speed, indifferent to the jarring bumps and rattling washboard grade. The bouncing around eventually shook the soldier awake, and he began pounding on the cab and shouting loud, untoward comments about the driver's ancestry. He also resumed nipping on the canteen. The driver fumed at the prospect of carting this man endlessly back and forth between the two hospitals. He then stopped at the courtyard entrance of the *couché* hospital and used a tire iron to put his cursing patient firmly to sleep before the orderlies reached the car. They complimented the American driver for bringing them a proper *couché* this time.[13]

Christian Gross's first trip to the front at Chemin des Dames was a baptism by fire. For several nights he had listened to the sounds of the big guns, always starting up just after sundown and booming away through the night. He and his buddies were safely situated at the *caserne*, two miles away from the eye of the barrage. The call for them to roll came, surprisingly, well before noon. Ambulances there seldom worked during daylight hours, when the road to the *poste* was within easy view of the German trenches. Gross concluded that either there were *blessés* who required instant and major surgery or else the *poste* was packed with wounded men and they needed to make room for new arrivals.

A German barrage had begun and a roadside battery of French 75s was responding when Gross led the way to the *poste*. He raced past these deafening *soixante-quinzes*, which were pumping out 25 three-inch shells every minute or so. The sound alone could burst eardrums, rattle teeth, and blast a driver out of his seat. The *arrivées* (incoming) from the German 77s and whiz-bangs — a flat-trajectory, 88-mm shell — sprayed all around the trench side of the road as Gross's ambulance sped along. The earth seemed to be breaking loose with fierce eruptions of shrapnel, *éclats*, and clods of dirt and stone. Gross cocked his helmet down over his cheek and ear in protection, and kept his gaze straight ahead, trying to ignore the *arrivées*.

Wheeling to a stop in front of the dressing station, Gross left his engine running and ran stumblingly inside. He couldn't tell whether his unsteadiness was caused by the explosions or by his shaking knees. His forehead dripped perspiration, and he bit his lower lip to keep it from quivering. The bombardment had already inflicted massive damage. Arriving stretcher-bearers reported that in a single twenty-minute period — about the time it took Gross to drive from the *caserne* to the *poste* — two hundred men had been killed and one thousand incapacitated. Dozens of *blessés* needed to be evacuated. The surgeon on duty, though doing the best he could, had fallen hopelessly behind, and the moribund pile was growing. Several of the *blessés* had identical wounds: their chests or abdomens were ripped open, exposing slippery white tubes and pulsating red organs. A few men had bits of shrapnel driven into their crania; these fragments, Gross knew, would not kill them until the pieces were removed on some hospital's operating table. Wherever Gross and his fellow drivers looked, there was work to do, all of it desperate and some of it futile.

Back at the *caserne* much later that night, after they had gone to bed, Gross and his buddies — Mike Dailey and Milt Silver of Chicago, Bob Myers of Hyde Park, an Illinois Delt named Earl Swaim, and a Chicago Deke named Dave Annan — lay silently in the darkness. When someone said they must have all looked funny, driving with their steel helmets pulled down over the trench side of their heads like gol-durned cocky tin-horns, they all began to laugh. They laughed and laughed and laughed, though their voices shook in the wind like October leaves.[14]

Trench warfare, which was static and defensive, led to long-range artillery contests. To achieve the necessary accuracy, the cannoneers required spotters and communiqués, which gave rise to the importance of airplanes in the early days. The aviators soon extended their contribution to the war effort by dropping hand-held bombs and firing shots at troops on the ground. In response, some cannons were modified so they could fire at the aircraft, but nobody really expected to hit anything. A considerable delay elapsed between the pulling of the lanyard and the arrival of the shell at its projected target a mile or two away. Meanwhile, the plane had been twisting, turning, diving, rising, and freely following its own course at speeds of between 80 and 100 mph. The real function of antiaircraft fire was to keep the enemy planes high up in the air, where their pilots couldn't get a proper fix on the targets below.

However, at Pont-à-Mousson, where two or three hundred rounds were fired daily, a French antiaircraft unit set a record by bringing down three planes in a single day. The reputation of the

Pont-à-Mousson artillerists soared, even after it was discovered that only one of the downed planes had been German.[15] Three hits in such circumstances, after all, is three hits.

Coleman Clark's ambulance smelled. He hadn't had a chance to wash out the dried blood and other detritus from his previous trips that night, and he had one more trip to make to the *poste* before daylight. Shells occasionally hit the road, but as long as it was dark, the German artillerymen couldn't see the traffic and didn't know *when* to fire. So Clark figured he could make it, even though his path would be contested by teams of galloping horses pulling field pieces and heavy supply wagons. Under shell fire, these horses became virtually uncontrollable, wildly knocking everything — especially the light Model Ts — off the stone road and into the ditches of slime and mud. A shell hole, which could break an axle or spring a chassis, could be eluded even in the dark if the driver were sharp-eyed. But the horses, when maddened, could not.

Spotting a black shape in the darkness ahead of him, Clark slammed on his brakes. Getting out and approaching curiously, Clark fell back in horror when his eyes adjusted and he got a good look at the scene in the middle of the road: four dead horses, all in a heap, legs and harnesses twisted together in confusion. A fifth horse — alive — was tangled up among them, struggling in agony but unable to move, a leg visibly broken and blood streaming from its flared nostrils. Clark turned away. Ambulance drivers carried no weapons; he could give no merciful *coup de grace*. Off to the side Clark found the French driver, a crumpled, lifeless sack; and beyond him lay all that was left of the wagon, a few timbers and a couple broken wheels. It must have been a direct hit.

A passing lieutenant slowed his Fiat and gestured to Clark to clear the area, shouting that the road ahead had been blasted away. Clark reluctantly turned around and started back in the gray light of the breaking dawn. Shortly, a scene out of a Hieronymus Bosch painting began to materialize. Rising up out of the ditch of mud and slime, a group of eight or ten men crawled into the road. They were all badly wounded and their filthy wrappings and bandages were frazzled and slipping loose. One man had to be dragged along by the others, who seemed to be moving in soundless slow motion.

Clark stopped the ambulance. He didn't have room for all of the men, but as he loaded the *couché* in the back, the others came instantly to life. They rushed him, begging to be taken, each displaying his ghastly wounds, each voicing his pain. They pleaded and grabbed at him. They began elbowing one another aside, shouting in anguish, throwing themselves onto the fenders and hood of the ambulance. Clark knew he had to act quickly. He would have to choose arbitrarily. There was no time to deliberate, to assess and select, he told himself. He pointed randomly and said, "You, you, you, and you. Get in." The lucky ones scrambled aboard, shoving and kicking the others back and away, and Clark took off at once. He didn't look back at those he left behind nor hear their clamor.[16]

When Charlotte Read and an English counterpart drove off in their Fords that day in mid-May, they were about to become the first two women *ambulanciers* in the history of France to go to a front-line *poste de secours*. Read, an American nurse, was a driver for the Hackett-Lowther Unit (S.S.Y. 3), a British women's section attached to a division of the French Third Army. In May of 1918, the unit was assigned the duty of evacuating wounded from a *poste de secours* less than a mile from the German trenches, which was about as close to the German lines as any *ambulanciers* got, ever. "The wounded were brought in by stretcher-bearers," Read said later, "given first aid in the cellar [of a "ramshackle farmhouse"], and then put in our ambulances for us to rush back to a . . . dressing station, where they were changed into other ambulances, to be sent still further back."

The first trip to the front didn't particularly affect her. Sure, there was some shelling, and once she was so startled by a blast that she nearly jumped through her tin hat. Mostly she stood around waiting for the wounded to be brought in. Read took advantage of one of the long lulls to fetch some water from a French artillery unit down the road. That's when all hell broke loose. A German balloonist must have spotted her, for after she had walked about three-quarters of a mile, a battery of German 220s began to lay an intense barrage all around her, apparently in the hope of hitting the barracks, *poste*, headquarters — whatever from which this solitary woman must have come.

With the dirt flying and *éclat* slicing criss-crosses in the air above and beside her, Read raced back toward the battered farmhouse as fast as she could, "dodging in every direction according to where the shells fell." The last fifty yards were the most dangerous, for there was no cover, nothing but barren stone and hardpan between her and the brick-shielded cellar entrance. Read "hesitated for one second, took a deep breath and made one wild, desperate dash across that open space and slid on my stomach into our hole under the bricks just as a shell hit outside the entrance — missed by less than a second."[17]

Perhaps Richard Norton didn't think to object because this was new territory for him. Or perhaps he expected something appropriately illogical from Lieutenant Grillard and the French ambulance drivers — having met them the previous night and judged them to be "utterly stupid & unwilling & generally untrained." Then again, it could have been a matter of Norton's exhaustion. Whatever the reason, under normal circumstances, Norton would have found a way to ignore the order, which violated not only common sense but standard procedure.

Norton's Section 7 had been well baptized during the Champagne battles and, from what Grillard had told him, the roads leading north from Verdun to his new *postes* around Bras were passable. However, here, during the spring of 1916, there would be no daytime evacuations. That was the rule. German artillery fire was far too accurate and intensive during the daylight. All driving would be done at night without lights, period. Still, Norton's volunteers were eager to get back into action, and the French ambulance drivers they were to replace — Lieutenant Grillard's unit — were most willing to swap places with them. Perhaps, had Norton thought about it, *too* willing.

On the morning of June 12, 1916, several days before Norton's group was officially to take over the ambulance service in this sector, Lieutenant Grillard left a message for Norton, saying that he expected Section 7 to work the *postes* north of Verdun that evening. Most of Norton's men had spent the day moving up to this new position, so only a few drivers knew the roads and where, exactly, the *postes* were located. However, they responded to Grillard's call and worked through the night. Although the shelling had stopped, the night was nonetheless predictably hectic, with the usual number of breakdowns, lost drivers, and repeated trips back and forth to various hospitals. Norton and his men returned to their camp at 7:00 A.M. completely fagged.

The following noon, Norton was awakened by a messenger with an order — an order Norton later wished he had ignored. He was to send five cars to a *poste* outside Bras at once. Despite the fierce sounds of artillery fire to the north, Norton responded in reflex, calling for drivers immediately. Aware of the rule about daytime driving on the Verdun-Bras road, Norton was nevertheless deeply concerned about the French soldiers in such a deluge of shell fire. So, off his first three drivers went.

Lawrence McCreery left first, racing out into the hellish fire. Miraculously, he made it all the way to the dressing station and back with two slightly wounded *poilus*. Jack Wendell and Henry Hollinshed had followed him, but they were not as lucky. As they bounded over and swerved around the continuous explosions, their cars were eventually blown out from under them. Wendell took shrapnel in the back, and Hollinshed had his shoulder smashed. When Wendell and Hollinshed failed to return, H. C. Hoskier (Norton's assistant) set out to learn what had happened, telling an orderly to come out and find him if he weren't back in thirty minutes. Hoskier soon brought back word that the two men were trapped in debris outside Bras, and exposed to the incessant artillery fire. Norton had had enough. He refused to let the men who volunteered risk driving through the shelling to rescue their compatriots. "As you may imagine," he wrote his sister, "it was with very mixed feelings that I had to tell them I could not permit this."

Meanwhile, McCreery had collected a dozen or so *brancardiers* who knew the intricacies of the communication trenches leading to the *poste*. He persuaded Norton to let them go on foot to retrieve the two drivers. The shelling was as heavy in and around the trenches as it was on the road. One 210 smashed into the trench just behind McCreery's stretcher-bearers, killing one of them outright and wounding four others. But the group pressed resolutely on and by evening Wendell and Hollinshed were back in the triage hospital, being prepared for evacuation to the American Military Hospital in Paris.

In his report, McCreery noted that the French personnel at the *poste* had been struck speechless when he first drove up in broad daylight shortly after noon. The call for ambulances must have been a mistake, for they had issued no such orders. Nor would they even consider making such a request when Germany had dedicated itself to blasting all of Verdun and its environs to rubble.[18]

Richard Nelville Hall, twenty-one, the son of a University of Michigan professor and recent graduate of Dartmouth College, was killed about 2:00 A.M., Christmas Day, 1915. His car was struck by a shell as he was driving up Hartmannsweilerkopf beyond the Vosges in reconquered Alsace. Billeted at Moosch, Hall left for the *poste* at Thomannsplats just before midnight. His body was found by Robert Matter at 4:00 A.M.

Matter first spotted an unidentifiable crumbled mass about forty feet down a steep ravine. It turned out to be an ambulance, its chassis hopelessly twisted and roof and spare tires blown into a treetop. Further inspection revealed that the car belonged to Richard Hall, whose body Matter found a few feet away, lying on its side, the hands raised, as if they were still grasping the steering wheel. Death had been instantaneous. It is said that while Matter was investigating the scene, Hall's brother, Louis, stopped to offer assistance. Reluctant at that point to give Louis the news of his brother's death, Matter quickly assured him that he was merely stopping to attend to his brakes, and Louis drove on. Matter and fellow driver Allyn Jennings brought the body back to Moosch, and on December 26 a funeral ceremony was held in a small Protestant chapel five miles down the Thur (valley). Hall was buried with honors in the valley of Saint-Amarin, his *Croix de Guerre* pinned to the coffin. The gravestone inscription was direct and simple. It read: "Richard Hall, an American who died for France." Hall was the first American volunteer ambulance driver to die in the war.[19]

Edward J. Kelley of Philadelphia, newly assigned to S.S.U. 4, was killed September 25, 1916, on Hill 304 near *Le Mort Homme.* Kelley had been at the front only four or five days and Roswell Sanders had offered to show the recruit the dressing station at Esnes, to which they were assigned. It had been quiet for over a month. Some hundred yards from the *poste,* a random shell landed about ten yards ahead of them, the shrapnel demolishing the car's radiator and blasting into the cab of the ambulance. According to William W. Wallace's account, Sanders had pieces of metal lodged in his jaw and his skull, but he was able to stumble into the road, where he was rescued by driver Robert Gooch. Nothing, however, was to be done for Edward Kelley, whose brains were splattered all over the inside of the ambulance.

A. Piatt Andrew attended the funeral service, which was held in a small Catholic church at Blercourt on September 26. Until Kelley's death, his fellow drivers didn't even know the recruit's first name. Edward Kelley was the second American volunteer ambulance driver to die in the war.[20]

> To Gloucester days, and winter evenings spent in the old brown-paneled, raftered room, with its pewter lustrous in the candlelight; and the big, cheerful fire that played with our shadows on the wall, while we talked or read — and were content. Well — that peace has gone for a while, but these days will likewise pass, and we are young. It has been good to be here in the presence of high courage and to have learned a little in our youth of the values of life and death.
>
> — LESLIE BUSWELL[21]

Poster advertising a screening of the 1916 recruitment film
Our American Boys in the European War. (Courtesy William L. Foley Collection)

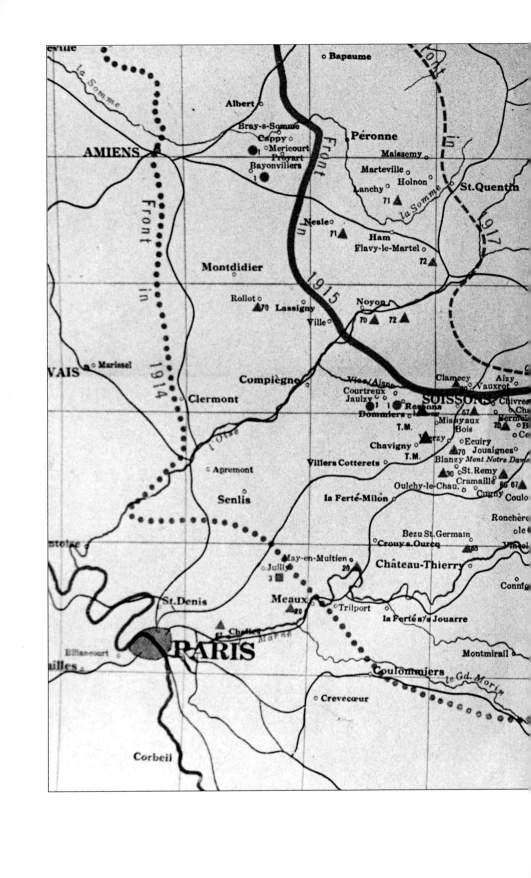

Map indicating the major areas of operation for the volunteer ambulance units in France, 1915–1917. *(Courtesy William L. Foley Collection)*

The Paris Squad assembled in front of the American Military Hospital (formerly the Lycée Pasteur), 1915. *(Courtesy William L. Foley Collection)*

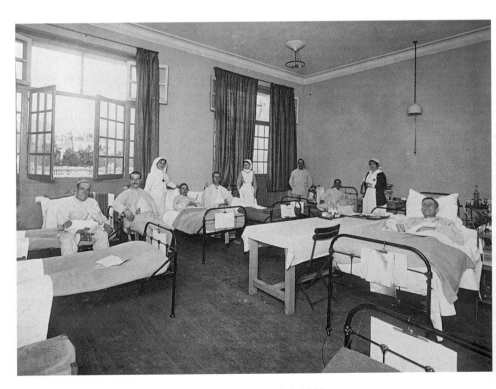

Interior view of a ward in the American Military Hospital, 1915. *(Courtesy William L. Foley Collection)*

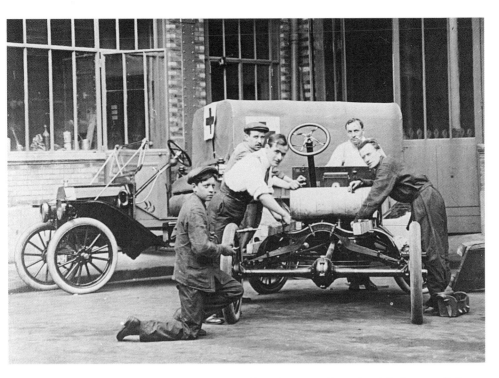

Assembling the second Ford Model T ambulance in Paris, 1914. Pictured at right in coveralls is Harold White. *(Courtesy William L. Foley Collection)*

Assembling vehicles 170 and 171 in front of the American Military Hospital, 1915. *(Courtesy William L. Foley Collection)*

Interior of the railroad receiving station at La Chapelle, 1915. *(Courtesy William L. Foley Collection)*

Herman Harjes standing next to one of his ambulances, 1915. *(Courtesy Alan Albright)*

Richard Norton, 1915.
(By permission of the Houghton Library, Harvard University)

A. Piatt Andrew pictured with Gabriel Puaux (left) and R. Puaux (right) in Paris, 1915.
(Courtesy William L. Foley Collection)

The American Volunteer Motor Ambulance Corps (SSU 7), 1916. Richard Norton is pictured second from right, front row. *(Courtesy William L. Foley Collection)*

Section ready to leave the American Military Hospital on January 20, 1915, for Dunkirk. A. Piatt Andrew is pictured fourth from left. *(Courtesy William L. Foley Collection)*

Mrs. Anne Harriman Vanderbilt, disguised
as a nurse, touring the front in 1916.
(Courtesy William L. Foley Collection)

Inspection tour of the front, 1915. At far left is
Waldo Peirce. Robert Bacon is in the fur coat,
and to his left are A. Piatt Andrew,
H. Dudley Hale, and Dr. Edmund Gros.
(Courtesy William L. Foley Collection)

Richard Nelville Hall (left), the first volunteer
ambulance driver to die in the war. Next to him are
his brother, Louis Hall (center) and Tracy Putnam.
All were members of of SSU 3.
(Courtesy William L. Foley Collection)

Loading Hall's coffin onto an ambulance, December 26, 1915. *(Courtesy William L. Foley Collection)*

Staff at the American Field Service Headquarters. A. Piatt Andrew is pictured at the center of the front row. To his right is Stephen Galatti, his assistant. *(Courtesy William L. Foley Collection)*

The Harvard Club of Alsace Reconquise. From left to right: Joseph M. Mellen, Luke C. Doyle, Stephen Galatti, Henry M. Suckley, Durant Rice, Arthur G. Carey, H. Dudley Hale, Lovering Hill, and Waldo Peirce. *(Courtesy William L. Foley Collection)*

Presentation of the
Croix de Guerre to
Arthur G. Carey and
H. Dudley Hale,
SSU 3, 1916.
*(Courtesy
William L. Foley
Collection)*

SSU 1 awaiting the call to action, Crombec, 1915.
(Courtesy William L. Foley Collection)

Members of the American Volunteer
Ambulance Corps, SSU 7, in Reims, 1916.
Behind them is a statue of Joan of Arc.
(Courtesy William L. Foley Collection)

Edward (Ted) Weeks, SSU 71, Verdun, 1917.
(Courtesy William L. Foley Collection)

Malcolm Cowley, TMU 184, 1917.
(Courtesy William L. Foley Collection)

Ernest Hemingway, 1918.
(Estate of Ernest Hemingway)

AFS volunteer Lloyd B. Seaver (SSU 19; later of the Lafayette Flying Corps) changing a tire, 1917. *(Courtesy Estate of Lloyd B. Seaver)*

Battlefield dead, 1917. *(Courtesy Estate of Lloyd B. Seaver)*

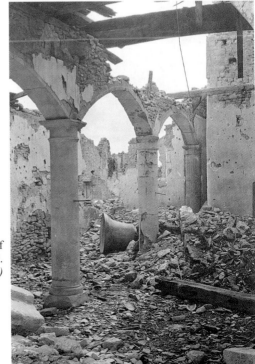

Photo showing destruction of the church at La Chalade, France, 1917. *(Courtesy Estate of Lloyd B. Seaver)*

Ambulance destroyed during fighting
in the Argonne, 1917.
(Courtesy Estate of Lloyd B. Seaver)

Group of *poilus* (French infantry)
in their trench, 1917.
(Courtesy Estate of Lloyd B. Seaver)

View of No Man's Land
showing what had been
dense forest, 1917.
*(Courtesy Estate of
Lloyd B. Seaver)*

Presentation of the first official American Flag by Arthur C. Kimber, SSU 14, 1917.
(Courtesy William L. Foley Collection)

William G. Rice and other drivers of Section 66 being signed up by recruiting officers of
the United States Army Ambulance Service, September of 1917.
(Courtesy William L. Foley Collection)

Testimonial awarded
to all members of the
American Field Service
following their service.
*(Courtesy William L. Foley
Collection)*

Section flag,
SSU 1/625
front and back.
*(Courtesy
William L. Foley
Collection)*

5

En Repos

Relatively little of the drivers' time was spent under fire at the front. William Yorke Stevenson calculated that an ambulance driver spent "some two-thirds of the time *en repos* (at rest), where, apart from the few scheduled runs, the periodical washings of the cars, and the putting them in first-class repair, [the driver] literally loafs."[1] *Repos* was a time when the drivers and their military units were stationed far beyond the sights and sounds and smells of the war. "The principal events of the day [during *repos*]," wrote the historian of Section 18, "were lunch and dinner."[2] One driver called it "the dullest monotony imaginable."[3] Another used the phrase "absolutely degrading," adding that "I think I'll go crazy if we don't get out of this soon."[4]

These periods of inactivity were designed for and highly prized by the *poilus*, who had exhausted themselves physically and psychologically in the trenches. They needed extended time for recuperation. The ambulance drivers, one might suppose, would equally enjoy a break from the horror and the pace of the war. After all, their schedules at the front left them precious little time to relax. Even light duty meant twenty-four consecutive hours on call at the front-line *postes*, with forty-eight hours back at the *cantonnement* (temporary barracks). Moderate duty, the most common, meant periods of twenty-four hours on call, twenty-four hours off. Heavy duty, such as the drivers experienced for weeks at a time at Verdun, the Somme, or in Flanders, usually required the drivers to be ready to roll at any time, whether they were asleep in their barracks, waiting at a relay station, or holed up in an *abri* somewhere near a *poste*. Actually, most drivers did seem to enjoy the respite of being *en repos* initially. "For a few days this is bliss," noted Philip Orcutt, a driver for Section 31, "but it soon becomes tiring again."[5]

Strictly speaking, some work took place during these periods. Cars had to be repaired and motors tinkered with. Uniforms required mending; a thank-you letter or two were to be written to stateside ambulance donors; a few perfunctory reports needed submitting. Once in a while, a driver would be called to transport a *malade* (a soldier who is sick rather than wounded) who had come down with the flu or a *blessé* who had wounded himself, say, in grenade practice. Sections also helped local hospitals with their jitney work. While Section 18 was *en repos* at Suzannecourt during the summer of 1917, for example, one ambulance each day was assigned to the hospital in nearby Joinville.[6] However, these modest tasks did little to relieve the overwhelming tedium.

Contributing to the drivers' boredom, no doubt, was their uncertainty about how long *repos* might last. There was no fixed time limit, in that the duration usually depended on the war. A section *en repos* could suddenly be called back to the front any time the French military wished. Conversely, the periods of rest could seem virtually endless. The American Field Service *Bulletin* of September 29, 1917 (no. 13) carried a letter from one AFS section that claimed the record for time spent *en repos*. Two weeks later, Section 9 submitted its log in challenge. The writer listed twenty-three French villages and towns, noting that his section had spent *repos* time "from one night to four months" at each of these sites. Further, the writer added that Section 9 had just gone two consecutive months "in which one *militaire* and two *civils* comprised the total of *evacués*." Harry Iselin, the commander of Section 12, felt the frustration too. He and his men were so demoralized by the inactivity that in mid-1917 they inquired about transferring to the Russian front.[7]

The ambulance sections did not have a choice about being posted *en repos*, or many of them surely would have declined the assignment. The contractual agreement between A. Piatt Andrew and Captain Doumenc of Joffre's *GQG* staff stipulated that the American ambulance sections were to be attached to, and were thus to be a part of, the French Army. Therefore, when the French Sixth Army unit that employed AFS Section 8 retired to La Veuve *en repos* at the height of the Verdun slaughter on June 2, 1916, Section 8 necessarily went along, despite the need for ambulances in Verdun at the time. Occasionally, a section might be spared the doldrums of *repos* by a last-minute transfer to a French unit that remained at the front. Alternatively, a section might enjoy both worlds by serving its period of *repos* close enough to the front to give its drivers some overflow work when the demand for ambulances exceeded the active-duty supply. As a rule, however, the French troops *en repos* spent their days in the tranquillity of the French countryside well behind the lines. The ambulance drivers affiliated with these troops, whether the drivers liked it or not, were posted there as well.

Unlike the French soldiers, whose *repos* time was spent in military activities such as drilling, bayonet instruction, and KP duty, the American ambulance drivers had no way to structure their time and were left to invent their own ways of passing the time. Most of the drivers proved fairly resourceful. Some ventured out on expeditions to gather souvenirs, such as valuable brass fuses from the German 77-mm shells. Also highly sought-after were shell casings, which could be hammered into *briquets* (cigarette lighters). A *poilu* would gladly trade his front-line souvenirs — helmets, knives, German medals — for a handsome *briquet,* especially if the American had filled it with hard-to-get *essence* (gasoline). The drivers' ostensible intentions were to smuggle these mementos to Paris and, with any luck, ship them back to the States. The smaller items, such as photographs, letters, war ribbons, usually got through, but the heavy trunks of fuses, shells, swords, and flags were routinely intercepted by customs agents. Such failure didn't inhibit the souvenir hunters, however, for their real, if subliminal, purpose was less to garner memorabilia than to find a way to pass the *repos* time.

The Americans even resorted to playing soccer against French and British footballers, suffering the predictable losses. Sections challenged each other to baseball games. The American Field Service *Bulletin* ran the scores and, at times, printed taunting accounts of the games written by the victors. In the heat of summer, men sent to remote areas, whose rivers and ponds were not contaminated, went for daily swims. In *Ambulance 464* Julien Bryan writes, "Today [June 9, 1917] we walked to the canal four miles south of the village and went in swimming. There were a couple of gun boats waiting here, to be sent up towards Prunay; and it gave one a queer feeling, emerging from a dive, to have this awkward steel monitor looking him in the face."

The most ingenious drivers *en repos* were surely those from Section 1, who were transferred from Triaucourt to a hilly, wooded campsite near Vaubécourt in early August of 1916. The day they arrived, they began organizing *sanglier* (wild boar) hunts.[8]

The long periods of free time enabled the Americans to get to know the French soldiers. Together they staged amateur theatricals and vaudeville shows, which sometimes featured the talents of *poilus* and French noncoms who had been professional musicians, singers, or actors in civilian life. The men also wrote and performed humorous sketches satirizing French and American politics or ridiculing German pomposity. Evenings of sing-a-longs were popular, the French never seeming to get enough of "Tipperary" nor the Americans of the *"Marseillaise."* Occasionally, French soldiers organized art exhibits in local barns or churches to display their front-line drawings and paintings.

Most drivers welcomed the opportunity to mix with the *poilu* and his officers, and the poet E. E. Cummings was no different. He and his friend Slater Brown spent virtually all of their free time with the French. Their fellow drivers, however, apparently resented such fraternization with the *poilus*, and Cummings believed the resentment contributed to his incarceration at La Ferté-Macé.[9] Cummings' section (21, a Norton unit) was headed by Harry Anderson, a garage mechanic from the Bronx. In *The Enormous Room*, a novel based on the diary notes he kept while imprisoned, Cummings says that he and Brown "didn't get on well" with Anderson. The friction, Cummings explained, was caused by "Mr. A's maintaining 'you boys want to keep away from those dirty Frenchmen' and 'we're here to show those bastards how they do things in America. . . .' "[10] More representative than Anderson's attitude was Leslie Buswell's: "I always try to talk with the soldiers (my French is improving, but still rotten) . . ." Typically, the outgoing Buswell spent Bastille Day, 1915, with an artillery battery and, after a few beers, was invited to stay for dinner, for which the French captain in charge of the battery contributed three bottles of precious wine. It was a merry get-together.[11]

The memorandum of agreement between Andrew and Doumenc signed in Chantilly stated that the American volunteers were to be governed by French military directives, laws, and command chains. These conditions made their position similar to the *poilus'*, in that the French soldiers and the American volunteers would serve pretty much on equal terms, ultimately subject to the same military authority. "The [ambulance] corps," James Muirhead wrote in *The Nation*, "is treated exactly as a French military corps, has to obey the same regulations and officials, and receives the regulation army rations (described as 'extremely good')."[12]

However, because they didn't hold military rank, the American drivers were neither enlisted men nor officers. They were simply *"militaires"* who wore uniforms with no insignia to indicate rank (although they were allowed to pin the red-winged symbol of the French Automobile Corps on their tunics if they wished).[13] Acknowledging the amorphous status of the volunteers, the French officer commanding Section 3 said in his original speech of welcome, "You are soldiers and non-soldiers, but I am going to pay you the greatest compliment in my power, by treating you as I would any French soldiers under my command."[14] The enlistment conditions of the *poilu* and the volunteer had one significant difference: the French were obligated to serve for the duration of the war, whereas the Americans signed on for a six-month term, after which they could re-up for successive three-month periods. The volunteers were also promised a seven-day leave *(permission)* during their first term.

Another condition of the agreement between Andrew and Doumenc specified that each American section was to be commanded by a French officer, usually a lieutenant, who would be chosen (theoretically, at least) with special attention to his knowledge of English, his familiarity with American ways, and his unflappable disposition.[15] Each commander was given a French staff, including a personal driver or two, a couple of noncoms (usually a sergeant and a corporal), and sometimes a cook. The staff managed the books, recorded the miles traveled, logged the *blessés* carried, tabulated the gasoline used, ordered supplies, and scouted out *cantonnement* sites. In short, the logistics of field operations came under the purview of the French.[16]

The French lieutenant in charge of an American section functioned primarily as a liaison between the French Army and the Americans. Orders were normally passed down from divisional headquarters to the lieutenant, who, in turn, handed them over to an

American *chef* (officially designated *commandant-adjoint*), who actually ran the section. Andrew appointed the American heads for the various AFS sections, and Richard Norton initially served in the field as the *chef* of his own Section 7. Later, when he formed additional units, Norton named other men as heads and returned to Paris to work out of his headquarters there. Herman Harjes, ever busy managing the Morgan-Harjes Bank and operating the American Relief Clearing House, kept close ties with Section 5, which was headed by Stephen Thorn for over a year and a half and then by Jack Philips. Once the Norton and Harjes corps were united under the aegis of the American Red Cross, Norton assumed overall command of field activities, inspecting and overseeing the work of the section heads, whereas Harjes carried out administrative duties in Paris.[17]

Andrew and Doumenc had also divided up the costs of the ambulance operations. The French provided gasoline, oil, tires, housing in the field, and the same pay as the *poilu*, alternatively described as one or five sous per day.[18] The drivers received a tobacco allowance, which most of them took in cash, pooling the money to hire someone to do the cooking — and scrounging — for the section. The American volunteers reportedly got "the same good food and generous ration that the French soldier receives."[19] The standard provisions were macaroni or rice or potatoes, coffee or tea, sugar, salt, 350 grams daily of canned beef [which the men called *"singe"* (monkey)] or sometimes horse meat, cooking grease, and raw red wine [affectionately known as *"pinard"* (bull's piss, according to one etymology)]. There were also large round loaves of bread. The loaves were about a foot in diameter, with the date of baking stamped on the bottom. Calling it "remarkable stuff," Julien Bryan noted that "it comes in freight cars from the interior and is usually two weeks old before we get it." One held the loaf against his chest and used a large, curved knife to cut it. After claiming that it was "about as palatable as soft pine," Bryan added that "it is supposed to be nourishing."[20] A typical breakfast in the summer of 1917, according to Bryan, included what the section's cook called "Quawcour Ats" (Quaker Oats) and stale bread and jam. About once a week they got a little butter, and less often a fried egg and a tiny piece ("a square inch") of ham. At noon on a typical day, Bryan ate "some rather tough Irish stew, which André [Tardieu] says he used to make for Baron Rothschild, with *pinard* and cheese for dessert." That night Bryan's section had "a three course meal with army bread soup, boiled lentils, and chocolate mush as the big item," as he writes in *Ambulance 464.*

While the French covered these costs, the American organizations and the drivers themselves met the remaining expenses. Andrew's American Field Service paid for board and lodging while the volunteers were in training or on leave. Like the Norton and Harjes sections, the AFS provided ambulances or trucks, spare parts, repair facilities, major maintenance work, and replacement cars. After affiliating with the American Red Cross, the Norton-Harjes sections occasionally received comfort kits of stationery, small items of clothing, reading material, and other tidbits. Each volunteer was responsible for his own uniform, clothing, and personal items, such as soap or sleeping bags. Except in emergencies or under special circumstances, the volunteers also paid for their own transportation to France and back. To cover these expenses, Dunbar Maury Hinrichs noted, "the American Field Service assured us that $300 was enough."[21] Hinrichs, however, budgeted a larger sum for himself, and was glad he did, since he had to buy a footlocker and some extra blankets after he arrived in Paris.

Repos afforded the drivers a fruitful opportunity to catch up on their correspondence. Many had kept notes of their routine activities, as well as their memorable ordeals, at the front, and the extended period of idleness allowed them to convert their notes into letters home, or pieces for newspapers and magazines. A few of the volunteers, such as William Seabrook, William Yorke Stevenson, and Emory Pottle, had been professional writers of one sort or another before the war.[22] Mostly, though, the volunteers had come straight from college or prep school, where they were used to casting their thoughts in written form. In addition to drafting analytic academic papers, the prep school boys and college men (in those days, before the general availability of the telephone) were also accustomed to maintaining regular personal correspondence. Before they went off to France, these young men were habituated to writing. They were eager to let the people back home know of their work and, insofar as possible, the state of the war.

In turn, the folks at home were eager to hear what the volunteers in France had to say, for reliable news of the war, not to mention the ambulance service, was virtually impossible to obtain. British and French military policy denied reporters access to the front.[23] When Mary Roberts Rinehart showed up in Cassel, some twenty miles behind the Ypres salient, to research a magazine article in early 1915, A. Piatt Andrew's friend René Puaux gallantly offered to take her around and serve as her interpreter. When he heard of Puaux's assistance, General Joffre sternly reprimanded the young officer for helping Rinehart, an act the general felt implicitly encouraged other reporters to venture into French terrain. "General Joffre," Andrew wrote his parents in 1916, "has allowed no foreign journalists at the front, and no French generals or officials have given interviews."

In regard to this policy, British Brigadier General S.L.A. Marshall noted that "there were no press correspondents; no one who understood, fully observed and was free to report what he knew."[24] Historian Liddell Hart described the policy as the "muzzling of the press — in Britain due mainly to Kitchener, followed by the equally stupid practice of issuing *communiqués* which so veiled the truth that public opinion became distrustful of all official news. . . ."[25] In his account of the 1917 campaign, *In Flanders Fields*, Leon Wolff offers several examples of misleading or fallacious news stories filed by well-intentioned but uninformed reporters who had no access to battlefield sources. "It is true," Wolff wrote in regard to a British and American news story that treated a bungled attack as if it had been successful, "that the correspondents billeted in Cassel were in a difficult position, both for observing and reporting. Censorship was rigid. Negative attitudes were frowned upon. . . . Measures were taken to keep the civilian writers in line."[26]

With the news of the war so poorly reported, letters from the American drivers found grateful and devoted readers hungry for firsthand news. Excerpts from their letters appeared in newspapers across the United States: in the New York *World*, the Boston *Post*, the Springfield *Republican*, the Detroit *Free Press*, and the New Orleans *Times-Picayune*. Magazines such as the *Atlantic Monthly*, *The Outlook*, *The Nation*, and *Scientific American* regularly carried pieces written by the drivers. Sometimes a particular driver's friends or relatives would collect his letters and print them as Christmas gifts, or submit them to a publishing house. Not all writers, however, wanted their words broadcast. "I'm not a bit keen on my letters being published in a

'Friends of France' [type of] book," Coleman Clark wrote his parents (March 20, 1917). "They were written for you and not for publication. . . ."[27] Clark's letters were eventually published posthumously.

Letters, newspaper pieces, and magazine articles notwithstanding, most Americans had little or no idea of the true state of affairs in the European war. After having served over a year at Mrs. Whitney's hospital in Juilly, Dr. James Judd returned to the States in October of 1916. "The American people as a whole," he wrote, "little realized the purposes of the war and the gravity of the situation."[28] After finding it relatively easy to raise money on the East Coast for ambulances, Dr. Judd spoke admiringly of the innate generosity of the American people, but he still maintained that "there was a woeful lack of understanding of the situation [in Europe]." However, he added, "if the realization of what the war meant was feeble in New York, it faded away [completely] as one went west."[29] Even after — perhaps *especially* after — the United States declared war on Germany, the American public seemed irritatingly naive in its attitude toward the hostilities overseas. "I am sore at the frivolous idea the country [has] toward the war," Coleman Clark wrote his parents on June 18, 1917. "I am sick of looking at picture after picture of women soldiers and Boy Scouts. Why don't the people as a whole over there realize the horrible thing that is in store for them?"[30]

Paul Fulcher took a more humorous approach to the misconceptions back home. In the American Field Service *Bulletin* of April 13, 1918 (no. 40), he pointed out that the letters he received from the States were full of hilariously mistaken assumptions. He had been sent, he claimed, a complete outfit of overseas caps, three inner tubes, and a rear spring for an unspecified Ford. None of the stuff could he use. Moreover, stateside writers assumed *their* letters were being censored, and they feared lest they let slip some secret information. Young girls asked Fulcher about "camp life" and sent along a personal copy of "The Emphasized Gospel of St. John." Some writers wanted to know if he could hear the guns, and virtually everyone asked to be remembered to their friends who were also in the ambulance service, as if all volunteers knew each other and intermixed daily. Perhaps the most famous (and funniest) lament of the home folks' misunderstanding of the true concerns of the American in the war is E. E. Cummings' poem, "my sweet old etcetera."

my sweet old etcetera
aunt lucy during the recent

war could and what
is more did tell you just
what everybody was fighting

for,
my sister

isabel created hundreds
(and
hundreds)of socks not to
mention shirts fleaproof earwarmers

etcetera wristers etcetera,my

mother hoped that

i would die etcetera
bravely of course my father used
to become hoarse talking about how it was
a privilege and if only he
could meanwhile my

self etcetera lay quietly
in the deep mud et

cetera
(dreaming,
et
    cetera,of
Your smile
eyes knees and of your Etcetera)

To the volunteers' dismay, some of the misunderstandings were caused
by exaggerated, melodramatic accounts sent home by their fellow
drivers. In another AFS *Bulletin,* David Darrah, for example, took

John Kautz to task for his collection of letters entitled *Trucking to the Trenches*. Darrah objected primarily to the book's factual inaccuracies. The title alone was misleading, Darrah claimed, since it implied that Kautz and the other camion drivers actually drove their trucks up to the trenches. "If anyone in the old camion service ever got to the trenches," Darrah noted, "it was because he was drinking."[31]

Kautz was in his late teens when he volunteered, which may account for the book's many patches of sophomoric effusiveness, but nonetheless his style sometimes aggrandizes a common inconvenience into a major deprivation. "It is a good deal more than seventy-two hours since I have slept or changed my clothing," Kautz wrote his parents on June 5, 1917 — failing to mention that he was still in residence in Paris at the time. He knew the martyr's role, too. In a letter prior to his leaving for the front, he pointed out that he had to write at that time because "out there, for the next two weeks at least, I shall be much too busy to write." No camion driver, of course, was ever that busy for two consecutive weeks, nor did any of them, except possibly Kautz, expect to be. Finally, after describing his decision to drive a supply truck rather than an ambulance, a choice that was urged upon him, Kautz noted with manifest self-centered forbearance that "[camion driving] is hard, grueling work, without honor or glory, but France needs us and I am glad to do it for the little while at least."[32]

Most of the drivers recognized that in this war they were mere supernumeraries. The real heroes were the *poilus* and the Tommies, the Algerian *Zouaves* and the mountain-conquering *Chasseurs Alpins*, the British Expeditionary Force's "Old Contemptibles," and the various Colonials (including Aussies, Canadians, and the Annamites of Indochina). As Robert Imbrie said, "[No one realizes] better than [us drivers] how insignificant has been [our] part compared to the real hero of this war — the obscure soldier in the trench."[33] Making a similar point, Richard Norton cautioned all prospective volunteers who harbored thoughts of glory: "Anyone who thinks he is coming out here to wander over the stricken field doing the Sir Philip Sidney act to friend and foe alike, protected from harm by the mystical light of heroism playing about his hyacinthine locks, had better stay home."[34] Well aware of the politics, monotony, and ubiquitous stupidity sure to frustrate the drivers, Norton wanted no pretenders to heroism. "This hero business will only win the volunteer the Order of the Wooden Cross [that is, a grave marker]."

The *poilu*'s quiet acceptance of the war's madness exemplified stoic self-control and dignity. "The thing that struck me most during my visit to France," Frederic Coudert said, "[was] the silence of the soldier. By that I mean his absolute freedom from bombast and high-sounding phrase."[35] The most celebrated statement about the war and lofty generalizations appears in Chapter 27 of Hemingway's *A Farewell to Arms:* "I was always embarrassed by the words sacred, glorious, and sacrifice and the expression in vain. . . . I had seen nothing sacred, and the things that were glorious had no glory and the sacrifices were like the stockyards at Chicago. . . . Abstract words such as glory, honor, courage, or hallow were obscene. . . ." The preponderance of the diaries and letters suggests that, like Hemingway and the French infantryman, the veteran drivers tried to avoid emotion-laden abstractions, relying instead on concrete details to convey their ideas and experiences.

The reluctance to employ flamboyant, abstract language did not mean the drivers' writings were mere lists of empirical details, devoid of sparkle or intelligence. Early in the war, Owen Wister, author of *The Virginian*, observed that the European conflict had prompted "people who are not trained writers to produce pages which have the quality of the very greatest literature. . . ." Having read dozens of letters from the volunteers, Wister concluded that "I have seen nothing whatever by any professional writer on the war that so touches the heights and the depths of emotion as did these private letters through their elemental, spontaneous simplicity."[36]

The intrinsic vividness of the details of war scenes enriched the volunteers' prose, no doubt, but their writing may not have been as spontaneously simple or artless as Wister suggests. For example, the following passage written by Carlos de Florez, one of Richard Norton's men, displays a well-chosen structural strategy:

> We walked back to the Pheasant [a bistro] for dinner, along the peaceful canal, where old men fish and little boys bathe, past the old church at Rossières with its over-crowded cemetery, where women in black with eyes that are red put fresh

flowers on fresh graves. They must be uncomfortable, these
soldiers, buried so close together, but even the cemeteries
were not prepared for such a war.[37]

The language here meanders with friendly ease (strained a bit,
perhaps, with the phrase "women in black with eyes that are red").
The tone mirrors the narrator's tranquil, absorbing stroll, the observations arranged in spatial sequence, set off by commas and flowing
together, like the "peaceful canal," in a long, fluid sentence. The
reader overhears, as it were, de Florez's quiet musing on the play of
presence and absence as his mind progresses from detail to detail.

The manner with which drivers such as de Florez wrote was
partially a consequence of the nature of their work. The ambulance
driver was not an anonymous functionary in a large military ensem-
ble. The drivers were allowed to retain individuality — in their dress,
their driving style, and even in the way they spent their *en repos* time.
The ambulance driver lobbed no shells at an unseen enemy, fired no
shots at faceless silhouettes. He dealt with individuals who required
individualized attention.

Another instance of the drivers' appreciation for detail appears
in a piece written by J. Halcott Glover. Fixing his eye on certain
particulars, Glover places them in a circular arrangement, highlight-
ing the grim irony observable daily in Pont-à-Mousson during April
of 1915.

> Old men dig in their gardens, women gather and sell vegeta-
> bles, girls stand in the evenings at their cottage doors, children
> run about and play in the streets, while often not more than
> two miles away, an attack may be in progress, and between
> the concussions of the cannon throwing their missiles from the
> hills over the village, can be heard the rattle of rifle-fire and
> the dull pop-pop-pop of the *mitrailleuses* [machine guns]. In an
> hour or two, scores, maybe hundreds, of wounded men, or
> lines of prisoners, will file through the village, and at any
> moment shells may burst over the street, killing soldiers or
> women indifferently; but the old man still digs in his garden
> and the girl still gossips at the door.[38]

The same violent contrast between the activities of peace and war was
noted by practically every volunteer. Typical is Stevenson's observa-

tion: "The country is zig-zagged with secondary and tertiary trenches and bristles with barbed-wire entanglements, but all around and in every direction the peasants are tilling the fields and the crops are growing."[39] The coexistence of the divergent activities of peace and war impressed visiting civilians as well. While on a tour of the front inspecting medical operations, Dr. Harvey Cushing noted that some of the soldiers had stripped bark and branches from trees to use as camouflage. He also noted that "alongside of them old men and women were working in the fields at their peaceful occupations." The first group was denuding nature, Cushing suggests, while the second was busy planting a crop, propagating nature. In addition, Cushing says, the old men and women in the fields were as "unconcerned as though the sound of cannonading and the drone of aeroplanes were a normal accompaniment of their day's work." Anne Vanderbilt, to cite another example, noticed a similar ironic juxtaposition when Andrew took her to the Verdun front in August of 1916. "What astonished me more than any of the apparatus of war," she wrote, "were the trailing vines and other wild flowers that covered these descents into hell [trenches leading to the *postes de secours*] as if they had been peaceful garden walks."[40]

The insights of volunteers such as de Florez, Glover, and Stevenson are accounted for to a large degree by Henry Sydnor Harrison and Malcolm Cowley, who first spoke of the ambulance drivers' unique perspective on the war. Harrison noted that "the ambulance-driver views the scene from a somewhat specialized angle. . . . He has extraordinary opportunities for viewing war as a thing at once of many parts [and] of a marvelous organized unity."[41] In *Exile's Return,* Malcolm Cowley, an AFS camion driver, develops a similar idea, which he calls the volunteers' "spectatorial attitude." Emphasizing their removed point of view, Cowley attributes a kind of detached voyeurism to the drivers, who, Cowley felt, were safely uninvolved in the war. "We ourselves were watchers. . . . The long parade . . . was a spectacle which it was our privilege to survey."[42] A brilliant literary critic, Cowley was not always reliable in his recollections and assessments regarding the war. For instance, his theory about Harry Crosby's life-altering trauma, when Crosby's friend Spud Spalding was hit by shrapnel and Crosby was spared, is based on a questionable reading of a letter Crosby wrote to his sister on November 23,

1917 (see Chapter Eight). Furthermore, in a chapter called Ambulance Service in *Exile's Return*, Cowley, who drove a supply truck and not an ambulance, maintains that "I have never attended a reunion . . . , if one was ever held." On June 8, 1918, however, the American Field Service *Bulletin* (no. 48) ran a story about the Boston Liberty Loan Parade, the night before which an AFS dinner was held. Cowley's signature is in the registration book. Moreover, despite his insistence that he had little to do with the AFS once he returned to the States, Cowley wrote a warm, richly detailed four-page reminiscence of the "Fourth of July 1917 in the Old T.M." for the AFS *Bulletin* of June 29, 1918 (no. 51), and in the summer of 1921, Cowley received an American Field Service fellowship to study at the University of Montpellier.

Cowley's claim that the drivers were mere spectators goes too far. They also pressed the flesh of the wounded; they knew the terror of the *obus* (mortar shells); they themselves suffered from shrapnel. In effect, the ambulance drivers were both in and out of the war. Theirs was not the point of view of the entrenched *poilu*, who was smack in the middle of the action and caught up in a struggle to stay alive. Neither was it that of the headquarters staff, who were notorious for remaining behind the lines and charting the progress of the war by means of graphs and maps.[43] John Keegan, author of *The Face of Battle* (1976), notes that Douglas Haig, British commander in chief at the time of the Battle of the Somme, and some of his fellow officers did not visit the front, believing the gruesome scenes there would unduly affect their judgment.[44] Similarly, Commander in Chief Joffre said, after he pinned a medal on a blinded soldier, that he should not be exposed to such unhappy sights because "I would no longer have the courage to give the order to attack." The drivers, however, were both intimate with the grim realities of the *poilu*'s world and could also trace the war's ironies with behind-the-line detachment.

The drivers' double perspective helped, at times, to mitigate their despair. Philip Orcutt's (author of *The White Road of Mystery*, 1918) description of an early-morning scene illustrates this very point.

> The trees are twice decimated, but the birds have stayed, and
> now they are waking and, overflowing with high spirits, sing

their message of good cheer. . . . Never has the song of birds
seemed more beautiful or more welcome, and, gladdened, we
listen while we may, before the slowly swelling thunder of the
guns, beginning their early morning bombardment, drowns
out all other sound.[45]

The soldier in the trench had scant opportunity to feel his heart
gladdened in this way, though moments of serenity were not entirely
denied the soldiers in the front-line trenches. Many have commented
on the poppy growing in the mud, but more often they were dis-
tracted by the voraciousness of the rats. The ambulance driver, who
lived miles behind the battered and barren front trenches, had a far
better chance of experiencing the uplift of a glorious sunrise or the
song of birds.

The dualities in a driver's day are also evident in a passage by
Kerr Rainsford, a driver working out of Verdun.

Minute after minute, crowded together, absolutely stationary,
loaded to the gunwales with sick and wounded, we waited for
the roadway to clear and for the next shell to strike. Beside my
wheels lay a horse still breathing but with both forelegs carried away at the body, and another lacking half its
head. . . . [Once moving], I took my load to an evacuation
camp at Fleury-sur-Aire, a long ride over smooth, empty
roads through a green and cheerful country, where flowers
grew in front of the cottages and women were. It was like a
month in the country.[46]

The world of the drivers turned in two directions.[47]

The moments of arresting beauty balanced the horrors, and,
overall, their writing tended to be marked by hope, by the feeling that
they were doing something positive. They rarely reached the degree
of fatalistic resignation the *poilu* displayed in his silent *c'est la guerre*
shrug. Only during the U.S. Army's attempt to militarize their units in
the autumn of 1917 did the volunteers display a widespread sense of
futility. For the American ambulance driver, little was ambiguous. He
seldom if ever had cause to question the sanctity of his work or its
intrinsic worthiness. Self-doubt was virtually unknown among the
drivers, since the nature of their work — to ease pain and save
lives — was indisputably noble. The ambulance driver was not

obliged to violate or compromise moral precepts. Indeed, far from provoking violence, an ambulance driver labored to alleviate its consequences. He did not operate within that nebulous zone of no-man's land that arbitrarily separated French flesh and blood from German flesh and blood.[48] *Esprit de corps* among the volunteers, a sense of shared background and experience, was very strong — except, of course, during *repos*, when the drivers were spared the feeling that they were helpless marionettes manipulated by mad puppeteers.

In contrast to the ambulance drivers' writings, characteristically upbeat and confident, stands the work by those who had done time in the trenches. British author Robert Graves' memoir *Good-bye to All That*, French author Henri Barbusse's novel *Under Fire*, and British poet Wilfred Owen's verse, for instance, are profound meditations on despair. Reviewing a collection of biographical and autobiographical sketches written by some Harvard drivers, Kenneth Murdock notes the volunteers' "frank joy in life and action tempered by serious purpose . . . ," which he contrasts with the disillusionment in John Dos Passos' *Three Soldiers*.[49] Dos Passos, Hemingway, and Cummings, who were drivers themselves, draw upon their own experiences in the war as a basis for some of their most caustic works to be sure. However, works such as Cummings' *The Enormous Room*, Dos Passos' *One Man's Initiation: 1917*, and Hemingway's *A Farewell to Arms* address arrogance, moral absolutism, inhumanity, jingoism, and sentimental egocentricity, transcending portraiture and biography in doing so.

Although a driver's writings may not be as timelessly universal as the works of Owen or Hemingway, his memoirs, letters, articles, and even journal entries nonetheless constituted a significant body of literature. Scattered throughout are remarks that bespeak a compelling need to put their experiences in writing. "I must write down the events of the last three days," Leslie Buswell noted, "for I suppose they have been the most tremendous ones I have experienced."[50] Like the Ancient Mariner, Job's messenger, or even Lazarus, the ambulance driver had come through some specific experience — of revulsion or exhilaration or excruciating tedium — with secrets to reveal, horrors and joys to relate, and powerful ironies to utter. Being *en repos* gave the drivers ample time to record and assess their sensations and observations. It gave them time to produce hundreds, if not thousands, of letters, newspaper and magazine articles, and preparatory notes for postwar memoirs. Thus, the otherwise empty weeks and months of *repos* afforded the drivers opportunity to work, to restore and rededicate themselves psychologically, and to write poignantly of their extraordinary experiences.

Yet, these were secondary activities, retrospective work. Being *en repos*, most of all, meant being out of the fundamental action. It meant not doing what one came over to do. It meant wasted time. Given the overwhelming emptiness and ennui of *repos*, the unusual behavior of the volunteers of Section 18 on August 6, 1917, made a peculiar kind of sense. After wasting away in idleness for a month, the drivers of this section learned on this particular day that they were being sent back to hapless Verdun — deadly Verdun, that most ominous, most perilous, most ruined and ruinous of battlefronts. They were overjoyed. "There was universal rejoicing . . . ," wrote the historian of Section 18, "[as] on a bright August day we took the road back to what we knew would be a wonderful experience if we lived to see it through."[51]

The Cars

"La Petite Voiture"
With apologies to Kipling

Oh! It's Lizzie this and Lizzie that,
And an "ugly hunk-o-tin,"
But it's *petites voitures* forward,
When the ranks begin to thin.

They say your system's lousy,
And you eat a lot of gas,
That your holler in'ards rattle
An' your joints are made of glass.
Oh! They say that you are 'opeless
And you're always in the way,
That your radiator's leaky,
That your guts is made of clay,
For: It's Lizzie this and Lizzie that,
And an "ugly hunk-o-tin,"
But it's *petites voitures* forward,
When the ranks begin to thin.

— NORMAN HUBBARD[1]

The car most commonly associated with the American volunteer ambulance drivers is Henry Ford's Tin Lizzie, the Model T. For good reason: it was a marvel of design and durability. The earlier Model N had been a success, but about 1906 Ford began to dream of a new car — one that would be easier to maintain and operate. In 1908, automaker Henry M. Leland amazed

the members of the Royal Automobile Club by ordering his mechanics to strip down three of Leland's Cadillacs to their component parts and mix them all together. Then, in front of the fascinated RAC members, the mechanics reconstructed three cars from
the pile of parts and drove the reassembled Cadillacs away. Leland
did not have long to enjoy his engineering triumph, however, for
that October Henry Ford unveiled the Model T, which eclipsed the
Cadillacs in terms of its simple construction and interchangeable
parts.

In those days, maintenance was primarily a matter of compen-
sating for wear and tear. Mechanics used babbitt and shims, and
sometimes even added sawdust to oil, to snug up joints, eliminate
bearing wobble, and quiet connecting rods. In search of a more
resistant steel, Ford contracted with a small company in Canton,
Ohio, to work on a special vanadium alloy. The steel finally developed
had ten times the tensile strength of any other metal being produced
in the United States at the time, including Carnegie's new armor
plating.[2] Because the stronger steel reduced wear on crankshaft,
camshaft, axles, differential gears, springs, and other high-stress
parts, Ford could claim a Model T would last for years — and it did.

Repairing an early automobile presented a related problem:
inexactitude. Few early car makers had the capability to mill and
grind their components to microscopic degrees of precision. As a
result, most spare parts varied considerably in their specs. They had
to be filed, hammered, bent, shimmed up, and pried into place — if,
that is, they fit at all. Housings, frames, and chassis sections required
retooling and heavy pounding to match up the holes and slots for
cotter-keys and bolts. Pursuing ever more exact machinery, Henry
Ford discovered the John R. Keim Mills of Buffalo, New York. After
a few years jobbing out his work to the Keim mills, Ford bought the
company in 1911 and moved its presses and personnel to Detroit the
following year. One historian, referring to its capacity and precision,
said, "No other plant in Detroit could match the vast Keim [machin-
ery]." An observer on the scene added that "each piece is machined in
a jig, so that every one is absolutely interchangeable."[3]

One of the Model T's most dramatic innovations, the casting of
the engine, also facilitated maintenance and repair. Pre-1908 Ford
engines, including those used in the models N, R, and S, consisted of

four self-contained cylinders bolted together, in-line. For his new car, Ford wanted all four cylinders enclosed in a single block. To achieve this, he proposed two castings: the block, which would contain the cylinders, and a head, which would be bolted to the block to cover the valves and form the top of the piston chambers. With the top sliced off, as it were, the cylinder sleeves and valve seats could be scoped and, if necessary, ground or polished to precision. To assemble the engine, the head was simply bolted into place, and the oil pan was attached to the block's underside. The engine's valves and upper cylinders, therefore, always remained accessible for regular service. The operator merely removed the head from the block, ground the valves or decarbonized the piston chambers, and then reattached the head. Similarly, the piston rods and main bearings were easily reached from below by removing a plate on the oil pan.[4]

The relative simplicity of maintenance and repair made the Model T especially appealing to the ambulance service, whose cars were in constant jeopardy from bad road conditions, continuous heavy-duty work, and enemy fire. "If a serious collision occurred," one ambulance driver said of his Model T, "two hours' work sufficed to repair it."[5] Late one afternoon, Frank Gailor's Model T was "slapped off the road" by a truck, and its rear axle and differential gears were smashed. After waiting for the spare parts to arrive, Gailor crawled under the car and had it up and running by midnight. "Thanks to the simplicity of the mechanism of the Ford, and to the fact that, with the necessary spare parts," Gailor wrote, echoing many of his fellow drivers, "the most serious indisposition can be remedied in a few hours."[6] The ambulance drivers were also impressed by the Model T's durability. Coleman Clark, for example, appreciated the toughness of his flivver: "Have more and more respect for a Ford," he wrote his parents during the Verdun campaign. "They go absolutely anywhere, and if treated right, they will last a long time." Clark's car had been donated by Mrs. W. K. Vanderbilt two years earlier, in September of 1914, and had been carrying out "the hardest work any car could do." Yet, as Clark's letter of August 4, 1916, maintained, its "engine is just as good as ever."[7] Also addressing the matter of a Ford's resilience, Julien Bryan wrote of a fellow driver's Model T bouncing off a tree and landing on its side across the road. The "rear wheels [continued] spinning around at a great rate, before [the driver] was able to shut off the motor." Eventually, a couple of French soldiers came along and helped set the Model T upright. The driver "thanked them and drove off as though nothing had happened."[8]

Arthur Gleason, a journalist touring the Verdun area, heard a similar anecdote from a driver named Jack Clark: "Yesterday, in a blizzard, [Clark's Model T] was blown off the road between two trees, over three piles of rock, through a fence and into a ditch. Three men and a horse removed her from the pasture, and she went on as ever."[9] Another driver, W. K. H. Emerson, told Gleason of his Tin Lizzie's ability to withstand duress. While trying to pass a camion on a hillside at night without lights, Emerson drove his Model T off the road and slid into a tree about halfway down the embankment. "Within ten minutes ten soldiers had lifted the machine and put it back on the road. . . . Nothing was wrong but the loss of one sidelight, and the car went better than before," Emerson claimed.[10]

Appreciating the durability of the Fords and the ease with which they could be maintained, A. Piatt Andrew decided to use the Model T almost exclusively in his Field Service. He wanted cars, he said, for which "stocks of interchangeable spare parts were always available. Uniformity in the type of cars used was a prerequisite of efficiency." Andrew therefore chose "at an early date . . . to limit our service to not more than two types of automobiles."[11] In fact, with a couple exceptions, nearly all of Andrew's men drove Model Ts. "We adopted the Ford motor [car] for the standard ambulances," he explained, "and in the years before the United States Government was lending its support to the Allied cause, we imported into France approximately twelve hundred such chassis."[12]

Andrew's decision to almost exclusively use Model Ts was not without its costs. For one thing, it meant that Andrew's drivers could not ship their personal automobiles over — even those volunteers who owned and preferred driving their own cars, and who could have afforded the shipping costs. Moreover, Henry Ford, who squandered millions on his "Peace Ship" fiasco, refused to give the ambulance service any financial break whatsoever. (Believing he could negotiate a peace among the belligerents, Ford outfitted an ocean liner, staffed it, invited selected friends and celebrities, and sailed for Europe. That was as far as his plan went. The ship docked in a Scandinavian port,

Ford became ill, no negotiations were conducted, and Ford returned home, having lost face as well as a small fortune.) "We received no favor or assistance from [Henry Ford] . . . ," Andrew wrote bitterly. "From him we could obtain not even the favor of wholesale rates in the purchase of cars and parts. . . . We were obliged to pay, not the dealer's price, but the full market price charged to ordinary retail buyers."[13] Several stateside auto dealers had offered to donate various new cars to the AFS at no charge, but Andrew, who was committed to the principle of uniformity, didn't want several makes of automobiles in his sections, and so he turned down their offers.[14]

Richard Norton, on the other hand, had no policy about the uniformity of automobiles in his sections. He welcomed whatever make of car a volunteer might bring along with him or a patron might donate. As a result, the Norton units at one time or another included a Panhard, Mercedes, Hudson, De Launey-Bellville, Mettallurgique, Peugeot, Cadillac, Rolls-Royce, Austin, Daimler, Italia, Sunbeam, and various Fords (Norton himself owned a Ford touring car). Heaven help the poor mechanics who had to master the workings of such a motley assortment of cars and who had to somehow fashion the necessary parts for each.

There were a couple of exceptions to Andrew's exclusive use of the Model T. Whenever Andrew had enough new recruits but not enough Fords to comply with a request to replace a section of French *ambulanciers*, the Americans ended up temporarily driving the Fiats the French section had been using.[15] The prospect of driving a Fiat initially appealed to Guy Bowerman: "We found 19 Fiats which carry 10 *assis* and five *couchés*. I believe we will like these cars much better than the Fords," he noted in his diary, "because they are larger and have a gear shift."[16] By the time he turned in his Fiat and picked up a Ford a couple of months later, Bowerman had modified his thoughts: "I really hated to leave old '821.' She was a darned good bus. But the Fiats are too heavy and burn too much gas. . . ."

Andrew's sections usually had one or two cars that were not Model Ts. The terms of the agreement between Doumenc and Andrew specified that an American section would consist of a minimum of twenty-two ambulances, a repair truck, and a touring car — as well as whatever vehicles were required by the French staff.[17] Although Andrew envisioned that most of the ambulances would be

Model Ts, he also felt that at least one of the vehicles should be a "two-or three-ton truck which could be made into a large motorbus ambulance for the carrying of sitting cases."[18] Thus, while Section 2 was still in its proving stage as Y Section at Pont-à-Mousson in June of 1915, Andrew sent them a large Pierce-Arrow. The section already had a Hotchkiss and nineteen smaller Model Ts in operation. The Pierce-Arrow and the Hotchkiss, however, did not make trips to the front. Instead, they were reserved for transporting *assis* from evacuation hospitals to nearby train stations, or to the base hospitals in inland urban centers.[19]

Not everyone liked the Tin Lizzies. Herman Harjes preferred Packards, Panhards, or other large models. Clarence Mitchell, who drove a Packard for Harjes, noted that "our machines are the admiration and envy of every French doctor that sees them. They carry six *couchés* and the stretchers run in on pulleys, which is a new idea here."[20] In a letter to Mabel Boardman, acting director of the American Red Cross, Harjes stressed his preference for cars that could hold "5 or 6 men lying down and as many as 15 to 20 sitting, with plenty of power to do quick evacuation work when fully loaded." Harjes conceded that there might be "certain localities where the light car [the Model T] may be more handy to get over bad roads," but, as he told Boardman, he firmly believed that "the best equipment . . . is a uniform make of strong big high powered cars."[21]

Neal Truslow, another Harjes driver, agreed that the flivver was overrated. "One constantly sees them [Model Ts] on the side of the road with broken axles, burned out bands in the transmission, bent radius rods, wheels dished and numerous other troubles that one never hears of in a heavier car. . . ."[22] Stephen Thorn, who headed Harjes' Section 5, also disliked the unreliability of the Ford chassis ("not sufficiently well built") and the tendency of Ford axles to bend or break.[23] Hemingway didn't like the Fords either. In *A Moveable Feast*, he favors driving his unit's Model Ts "over the mountainside empty, so they could be replaced by big Fiats with good H-shift and metal-to-metal brakes."[24]

Nevertheless, the Model T had far more champions than detractors. Although several drivers thought the steep, rocky terrain of the Macedonian Front north of Salonika too demanding for it, Coleman Clark found the car well-suited. "The particular virtue of the Fords,"

Clark wrote his parents,[25] "[is] that they can work in the most mountainous country, and on the most rotten roads, whereas the other big ambulances which the French use are very slow, cumbersome, and burn a great deal of gas. . . ."[26] William Seabrook agreed, adding that the Ford's ability to traverse practically any topography intensified the driver's sense of drama. "Our Fords could go over shell-pitted roads and torn terrain the heavy [ambulances] could not negotiate," Seabrook wrote, "so that we had the excitement, and honor, of working always as close up to the fighting as any vehicles could get."[27]

Even the French military authorities acknowledged the adaptability of the Model Ts. When Section 3, which had been working in the Vosges, was recalled to Paris to prepare for its transfer to Salonika, the *médecin en chef* of the Vosges campaign found himself "without his Ford cars to negotiate the steep hills and bad roads of that country, and it took him but a short time to realize that the large French ambulances were but a poor substitute." In response to the French commander's desperate calls for help, Andrew sent out a detachment of six Fords to the Vosges on 21 December 1916.[28] To cite another example: in early September of 1917, the American Field Service Section 1 received a letter from Captain Foix, a French Intelligence officer. "I herewith send you," Foix wrote, "two crates of [carrier] pigeons for General Riberpray's Division, whose headquarters is in the Carrière Sud. You would do me a great service [by delivering the pigeons], for our cars cannot go so far. . . ."[29] The English First Ambulance Section was working at the time alongside the AFS Section 1, and they too noted that "it would be impossible for [their] big cars (Rolls-Royces, Napiers, Panhards, and the like) to get up the Carrière Sud road."[30]

Its effectiveness notwithstanding, the Tin Lizzie was indisputably the most popular ambulance in France. "Always on the job, always efficient, the little car, the subject of a thousand jokers, gained the admiration of everyone," noted one driver.[31] The *poilu* preferred it to any other ambulance, no doubt because of its soft ride and speed. With the right grade and wind, the Model T could reach 55 mph, although its most efficient flat-land cruising speed was about 30 mph. However, as the war progressed and the worldwide demand for gasoline increased, the petroleum refiners began turning out poorer grades of gasoline, which resulted in a lower cruising speed (closer to 25 mph). Because of the reduced octane of the gasoline on the market, Ford had to decrease the compression of the Model T engines from 60 psi (pounds per square inch) — a 4½ to 1 ratio; 22 horsepower — to 45 psi (a ratio of 3.98 to 1; 20 horsepower).[32]

The ride was soft because standard equipment on the Model T included two transverse, semielliptic springs, which had to be modified to accommodate a large ambulance body. The back spring was reinforced and set on high perches above the axle, resulting in a soft, spongy, oversprung ride that the injured soldiers much appreciated.[33] In fact, William Yorke Stevenson noted that "many soldiers make it a point to salute the ambulances when they catch sight of [them] . . . , because they have heard of their quickness and comfortable springs. . . ."[34] Village children, especially, seemed fascinated by the strange-looking *petites voitures*. The "high stilted" axles and chassis gave the cars a ground clearance of ten and a half inches, and the extended rear overhang of the body made the car look like "an overfed June-bug."[35]

The degree of affection for the flivver, though, is nowhere so evident as in the drivers' comments about it. One driver said that by using *pinard* in his radiator, he had a better antifreeze than anything else available and, as a side benefit, after a few hundred miles the wine became almost drinkable. Another driver composed a parody of the Twenty-third Psalm, ostensibly deriding the Model T.

> The Ford is my car;
> I shall not want another.
> It maketh me to lie down in wet places;
> It soileth my soul;
> It leadeth me into deep waters;
> It leadeth me into paths of ridicule for its name's sake;
> It prepareth a breakdown for me
> in the presence of mine enemies.
> Yea, though I run through the valleys, I am
> towed up the hill;
> I fear great evil when it is with me.
> Its rods and its engines discomfort me;
> It annointeth my face with oil;
> It's tank runneth over.

> Surely to goodness if this thing follow me
> all the days of my life,
> I shall dwell in the house of the insane
> forever.[36]

It may be a psalm of complaint, but no Fiat driver ever bothered to gripe so amusingly about his car.

A more explicit example of poetic flattery is "Henry on the Grande Route," by Robert A. Donaldson, a driver for Section 70.

> You may take the Dago Fiat,
> The Renault, the Berliet.
> Just lead me to a Henry Ford —
> I'll swap you any day.
> These foreign speaking cars may sound
> All right to foreign ears,
> But they never can touch Henry
> In a hundred thousand years.[37]

Not all the spoofs were poetic. Using the genteel persona of "Reginald Vincent Spottiswoode II, Harvard '20," one driver submitted a "meditation" to the AFS *Bulletin* no. 70 (November 9, 1918). The Model T, he conceded, had "made a man of him." Back home, before his experience as a Ford driver, "Reginald" had never bothered to look under the hood of his car, and, predictably, his garage bills were of "prodigious proportions." Now, however, he "can change a tire in a foot of mud" all by himself, and he proudly claims to be able to tell "a commutator from a carburetor, a knock from a miss."

Overall, as a military ambulance, the Model T possessed many more advantages than disadvantages. The British and French, like Norton and Harjes, may have preferred ambulances that could carry four to six *couchés* or eight to ten *assis* at a time, but in reality things didn't work out that way. The *brancardiers* seldom brought the wounded to the *postes de secours* in such large numbers. To take advantage of their extra space, the non-Ford drivers were compelled to wait at the *postes* until a full or nearly full load of *blessés* had come in.[38] The waiting may not have been inconvenient or uncomfortable for the drivers, but it surely was for the wounded. When the *blessés* did arrive in large numbers, the shell fire, traffic, and surrounding chaos rendered the large cars annoyingly clumsy and slow. Unlike the speedy, darting *petites voitures*, the Fiats seemed like big, fat targets that needed five minutes and four lanes to turn around, and a clear, open straight-away to lumber down.

The Model T's scampering mobility was particularly evident during the height of the fighting at Verdun. The only active line of transportation at the time was the reinforced Voie Sacrée that ran between Verdun and Bar-le-Duc. Literally, *Voie Sacrée* meant "Sacred Way," but sometimes the phrase — or its paraphrase, *"la route sacrée"* — carried a markedly different connotation, something like "a damnable rotten road." A reporter for the London *Daily Telegraph* observed Model Ts at work during periods of intense traffic and virtual gridlock. The summer of 1916 saw two thousand fully loaded French camions and other cargo vehicles heading every day up to Verdun, and another two thousand trucks and wagons coming back empty — all at the same time on the dusty, rutted, and in places, narrow, Voie Sacrée. "Hundreds of lives would have been lost," the *Daily Telegraph* article stated,

> had it not been for the sections of the American Field Service stationed at Verdun. Equipped with small, light, speedy cars, capable of going almost anywhere and everywhere that the heavy French auto-ambulances could not go, the "rush" surgical cases were given to these American drivers. They were not given a place in the endless chain [of traffic], but were allowed to dart into the intervening space of sixty feet between the cars, and make their way forward as best they could. When an open field offered, they left the road entirely, and, driving across, would come back into line when they could go no farther and await another chance for getting ahead. They were able to bring the wounded down from Verdun often twice as fast as those who came in the regular ambulances, and always without . . . tying up for a single instant the endless chain of the four thousand [vehicles] of Verdun.[39]

The Model T was as widely celebrated for its adaptability as for its mobility and durability. William G. Rice served in the AFS two separate terms, driving a Model T during the first and a French Panhard the second. He tried to pass a convoy of camions in his Panhard one day, but couldn't make it. "In the attempt," he wrote, "we got hopelessly ditched." "Ah," he added, recalling his Model T days, "if it had only been a Ford!"[40] Andrew summed up the matter: the *petites voitures* "could work their way in and out among passing convoys. . . . They could travel over roads impossible to other motor vehicles . . . , climb the narrow zigzag mountain paths of Alsace . . . , [and] skim over and pull through the muddy plains of Flanders."[41]

The major limitation of the Model T, its size, actually turned out to be advantageous. Since the Fords were so small, they could accommodate only a driver, whereas the larger cars used two men, a *chef* and a *sous-chef*.[42] The Norton and Harjes sections, which used relatively few Model Ts, assigned thirty-five to forty men to each section of twenty or so ambulances. Neal Truslow counted twenty-two cars and thirty-five men in the Harjes Formation in mid-1916, "including two mechanics who attend to all repairs, though the drivers are expected to keep their cars in shape as far as possible."[43] Edward Coyle, a volunteer in the Norton-Harjes corps (after the merger), noted that American Red Cross sections required forty men to operate some twenty ambulances.[44]

Andrew's AFS corps, in contrast, averaged fewer than twenty-five American volunteers for the twenty-two cars that typically constituted each section.[45] The small number of men in each section tended to build a sense of camaraderie. "The sections," Andrew wrote, "were more like large families than military formations. The officers and men whether French or American . . . [called] each other by familiar names rather than by formal titles."[46] Also, with fewer men to provide for in each section, Andrew gained considerable savings, in terms of the operating costs per car.

However, this economy exacted a price from the AFS drivers. Driving an ambulance in the best of times was stressful work, but for the volunteers who drove alone, the anxiety level could be particularly high. For example, after learning that his Fiat, which he drove with Ned Weeks, was to be traded in for a flivver, Harry Crosby was concerned about the exchange. "The only trouble about a Ford section," Crosby wrote his father a bit apprehensively, "is that there is only one man to a car which necessitates one's being 'solus' a good deal of the time. However, I guess I can do it as well as anyone. Hundreds in other sections have to drive alone, so why worry?"[47]

The Model T proved uniquely cost effective because a Ford's list price was considerably lower than, say, a Packard's. Besides, a Model T buyer could purchase the chassis by itself. That is, you could buy the engine, frame, wheels, and suspension system, and build your own body to mount on the chassis. James F. Muirhead calculated the average cost of an outfitted large car such as a Packard for the Harjes Formation to be between $2,500 and $3,000. Model T estimates varied, but the top-end figure most commonly cited was $1,600 total. This included the cost of the chassis, shipping it, building a customized body, and maintaining the car for the first six months. In 1916, the standard Model T touring car, body and all, cost $360 FOB Detroit. The chassis by themselves were even cheaper, of course, and their price fluctuated little, in that they were nearly identical for all body styles throughout the Model T years. The AFS's Model Ts needed customizing as ambulances anyway, even when a donor shipped over a complete, ready-to-drive Model T sedan. Moreover, because it took up less cargo space than a complete car and weighed less (1,000 pounds as opposed to 1,500), the Model T chassis was significantly less expensive to ship.

Nothing was wasted. The wooden frame for the body, various seats, and lockers were fashioned from the crates the chassis were shipped in. The carpentry was done by Kellner et Ses Fils, whose shop was located in Billancourt, a suburb on the southwest edge of Paris, where the AFS operated a repair park.[48] Richard Norton also hired the Kellners to customize his various vehicles, although in January of 1917 Norton was alarmed to discover that the shop had been contracted to build fifty airplanes for the British and 250 for the French. The Kellners assured him they would continue accepting jobs from him and the AFS.[49]

In early 1916, some major changes were made in the AFS ambulances. Originally, the rear of the ambulance body, where the *blessés* were carried, was covered with canvas that had been stretched and lacquered. The canvas proved light, but was difficult to clean and disinfect. Worse yet, it offered little relief from the wind, dust, and winter cold. The first to get the new model that May was Robert Imbrie, who praised its "all-wooden body and electric [head]lights." Stronger and more stable than canvas, mahogany was now used for the entire body, a change that made the car much heavier and more costly to customize. Although the electric headlights were a big im-

provement over the messy carbide version, they had a major draw-
back too. Wired in series from the magneto on the flywheel, the 9-volt
lamps dimmed and brightened as the engine's speed changed. (The
magneto's output varied from 8 to 28 volts, which meant that low
rpms barely lighted the lamps, whereas high rpms could produce so
much current that the bulbs would burn out.) These disadvantages
notwithstanding, "with some slight changes [Imbrie's] car was the
model adopted thereafter for all the ambulances."[50] Most drivers,
incidentally, continued using rolled canvas windshields to screen out
some of the dust and cold, since glass was dangerously susceptible to
shattering. Rolls of canvas also remained in use to cover the cab's
open sides, where the factory-installed bodies would normally have
had doors. Actually, the "door" on the driver's side of the standard
issue Model T was a dummy, since the hand lever was in the way. The
Model T was the first major automobile, incidentally, to use a left-
hand drive. Ford decided to place the driver on the left, it is said, for a
couple of reasons: two drivers meeting could stop and talk with each
other; more importantly, lady passengers could exit from the cab
away from traffic and directly onto a sidewalk, without having to slide
across the front seat.

The AFS drivers painted their ambulances slate blue ("war
gray," some called it), stenciled their registration and section numbers
on both sides of the car, and added large Geneva red crosses to the
ambulance body just behind the cab and on the roof. On the sides of
the cab, the sections painted their logos, the most famous of which
was probably Section 1's Indian head designed by the French painter
Jean Tardieu, who based it on the U.S. five-dollar gold piece. The
cars were not complete without a number of handmade boxes and
storage lockers, the smallest of which was a narrow box placed inside
the cab next to the driver. This box typically held spare spark plugs,
tire chalk, chains and rope, and a small steel envelope containing the
car's papers — usually an *ordre de mouvement,* a permit to enter and
remain in the military zone; an identification card; and an authoriza-
tion for acquiring gasoline. On the left running board rearward sat a
large side-locker for tools, extra inner tubes, a pump, and a canvas
bucket. Beside it was strapped a canister of extra water. Four cans of
reserve gasoline were fastened to the right rear-side of the ambulance
body, along with an additional can of oil and one of kerosene. Once

the AFS began using wood rather than canvas for its cargo areas, the drivers could strap one or more spare tires onto the roofs of their ambulances.

The Model T's ambulance compartment accommodated two stretchers on the floor and another centered above them. The third stretcher was slid in on rails hinged to the ceiling's cross-beams. When not in use, these rails were swung over and strapped flush to the sides, and seats were installed to accommodate four *assis*. Thus, the AFS ambulance was officially designed to hold three stretcher or four sitting cases. However, the Model T could actually hold three *couchés* or four *assis* in the back, and three more *blessés* squeezed in up front. "In an emergency," Andrew noted, "as many as ten wounded men have been carried at one time, the inside of the car being crowded to its capacity, and the foot-plates [running boards] and mud-guards [fenders] serving as extra seats. . . . The driver seems almost buried under his freight."[51]

Each section had at least one mechanic to make major repairs, though the drivers were expected to carry out the basic maintenance of their Fords. "We have one paid mechanic — an American — in each section," Andrew wrote, "whose business it is to diagnose the difficulties . . . and to show the men how to correct these difficulties." Such an arrangement, Andrew explained, worked quite well because "almost every American boy knows something about automobiles, and [because] the cars we use are of simple construction. . . ." Thus, "the individual driver . . . oils, greases, and repairs his own car."[52]

Although easier to maintain than most other cars, the Model T presented an imposing list of upkeep items. There were at least twenty high-friction areas that required regular greasing or oiling. For example, the hub cup on the fan needed to be filled with grease every fifty miles, the spindle bolts (on the tie rods) were to be lubed every hundred miles, the commutator required oil or Vaseline every two hundred miles, the steering post bracket had to be oiled every five hundred miles, the differential was to be checked and filled with grease every six hundred miles, and so on.

The engine required even more frequent and demanding attention. Since the oil was distributed by a splash system, rather than an oil pump, the oil level was supposed to be checked at least once a day. This efficient and simple system exploited the eccentric shape of the crankshaft and the motion of the piston rods. Splashing into the oil in the pan at split-second intervals, the crankshaft and rods splattered oil over the bearings and other high-friction parts. However, the bearing hardest to reach by the splash method, the front main, was the bearing that invariably required the most oil. Two petcocks were positioned on the rear of the oil pan, one above the other. The driver crawled under the car and opened the top petcock. If oil flowed out, the oil level was too high, and the engine was likely to carbon up. If, on the other hand, no oil came out of the top petcock, good. The driver then opened the lower one. If oil came out, the oil level was just right. But if no oil flowed from the lower petcock, the level was too low to achieve the necessary splashing effect.

The drivers didn't seem to mind the repair and maintenance work — even those who had seldom before gotten their hands dirty. For instance, Leslie Buswell, a former actor with no discernible mechanical aptitude, was amazed at his own proficiency. "Yesterday I discovered that the main backspring of my car was broken and I had to replace it," Buswell wrote. "Imagine me on my back all day, working like a madman. . . . I managed it all right, however, and so feel myself quite a mechanic."[53] One driver shrugged off the work as little more than baby-sitting, "cleaning plugs and cylinders, tightening nuts and bolts, oiling and greasing, washing our little cars just as though they were a lot of dirty kiddies."[54]

The diaries most frequently mention problems with the Ford's commutator, tires, and spark plugs. Particularly susceptible to dirt and wear, the commutator was a timing device that worked in synchronization with the pistons and, at just the right moment, sent the low-tension magneto current to the coils (each spark plug in the Model T had its own coil). Tires and inner tubes could also be exasperating, as Edward Weeks recalled: "We mounted the jack on wooden blocks . . . and attacked the flat with two thin-tongued tire irons." After prying the tire off the rim and removing whatever nails or sharp stones had caused the flat, Weeks "replaced the tube, cursed the tire back on the rim, and finally inflated the new tube with a hand pump."[55]

The spark plugs seemed to have a predilection for fouling up on the road when the shelling was heaviest. A Model T could limp along pretty well on three cylinders when the load was light, but the slower the speed, the more it was exposed to shell fire. Understandably, the driver preferred to pull the car over and take care of the spark plugs as soon as he could — and then get the hell out of there. Kerr Rainsford, for example, was chugging and lurching in from Dead Man's Corner to Verdun, when "three large-calibre shells passed overhead." Nevertheless, he decided to stop in the middle of the bombardment to change a clogged spark plug and refill his boiling radiator.[56]

Radiators tended to boil over because the cooling system, like the oil system, involved no pump. To circulate the water or antifreeze, the Model T used what Henry Ford called the "thermosyphon method," a cooling process based on the principle that hot water rises. As the water in the cooling jackets around the cylinders was heated, it rose and flowed into the top of the radiator. There, the water was cooled by the air rushing through the radiator, aided by a fan. The cooled water then cycled back down into the lower water jackets at the base of the block, where the pistons firing in the cylinders heated the water up again. And so it went. The method worked well in most instances, but during slow, heavy pulls, when the engine was working hard and the car's speed minimized the air flow through the radiator, the water would begin to boil, the steam escaping out the overflow tube and leaving less water in the cooling jackets. So, the engine got hotter yet and still more water boiled away.

A driver's inexperience could also contribute to the overheating of a Model T engine. The Ford had two levers beneath the steering wheel: an accelerator, which administered the gas and controlled the car's speed (there was no gas pedal on the floor), and a lever for retarding or advancing the spark. As a driver increased the speed of the car, he advanced the spark, but if he overdid it, the engine would ping or knock. Conversely, when his speed decreased, as on a steep grade, the driver had to retard the spark. However, if he cut it back too much, the engine overheated.

Inclines that were especially steep posed another problem for the Model T driver, again because Ford had designed the car to be as simple as possible. Just as there was no oil pump and no water pump, there was no fuel pump. The gasoline tank was located under the driver's seat, at a level higher than that of the carburetor, which allowed for a gravity feed from the tank to the engine. Going up long, steep grades, however, reversed the gravity flow, since the car's incline put the tank lower than the carburetor. On such occasions, shrewd drivers would simply turn the car around and back up the hill the rest of the way. Such a technique led some drivers to conclude that the Model T had more power in reverse than in low. Although the transmission ratio slightly favored reverse, the real reason a Model T's engine might die while trying to get up some particularly steep hills in low was the placement of the fuel tank.

Starting a Model T was always an adventure. When a piston fired and the engine began turning over, the driver leapt into action, setting the gas and spark by adjusting the levers on the steering column and switching the ignition from the battery over to the magneto — meanwhile praying that his sputtering engine wouldn't die on him. It was essential that the driver learn to crank the car without wrapping his thumb around the crank handle. Should a driver's grip be full and firm and his elbow locked, the engine's kick (the sudden reverse motion of the crank when the pistons failed to fire) could sprain or break his wrist, or worse. James H. McConnell's diary for November 18, 1915, recorded a typical incident: "B— broke his arm cranking his car this morning. He will be out of commission for three weeks, so the surgeon who set it informed him."[57]

The biggest challenge of all faced by the Ford driver was learning to operate the Model T's amazing gearless transmission, which involved maneuvering three foot pedals and a hand lever. E. B. White once described the planetary transmission as "half metaphysics, half sheer fiction," affectionately noting that it generated "a certain dull rapport between engine and wheels."[58] "Orchestrating them [the lever and the three pedals]," one historian wrote, "was an acquired art, rather like playing the organ. The whole body was engaged. But once mastered, all sorts of tricks became available. . . ."[59] The hand lever had three positions. Pulled back, it engaged a perfunctory brake on the wheels, primarily intended for keeping an already stopped car from creeping forward. Straight up (or slightly forward), the hand lever kept the transmission in neutral. Pushed all the way forward, it launched the car into high speed.

The left pedal, when partially depressed, released the transmission bands, putting the car in neutral; when pressed fully to the floor and held there, the same pedal activated the low-speed bands. One could always spot a Model T driver who worked the mountain districts by the hole in his left shoe, as Preston Lockwood observed. Watching a fellow driver work on his car at a *poste de secours* in the Vosges, Lockwood noted, "He is on his back tightening bolts underneath his car, and a hole in the left sole of his projecting shoe tells of hours with the low speed jammed on, for this is the way we have to drive down as well as up hill."[60]

The right foot pedal operated the transmission brake, possibly the single greatest weakness of the Model T. The brake bands in the transmission were notorious for stretching and wearing out, and ambulance drivers soon learned to use low whenever possible to lessen the strain on this brake. Driving in mountainous terrain, Luke Doyle noted that "we must run our motors in low speed or we use up our brakes in one trip."[61] But low speed, which produced higher rpms, was not always a viable option, as Doyle admitted under different circumstances: "We did not dare to use our low speed for fear the Boches would hear us. . . ."

The center pedal, when pressed to the floor, put the car in reverse. When everything else failed, reverse could be used as a brake. Waldo Peirce learned this lesson the hard way. Peirce's diary records his experience driving in the Vosges above Moosch in November of 1915. "Brakes loose as empty soap-bubble," he noted, using clipped, telegraphic syntax.

> Endless convoy of mules appeared at bottom of hill. Tailenders received me sideways or full breach — couldn't stop — didn't think to put on reverse, so did some old fashioned line-plunging. Heard cases crack, men swear, mules neigh, but heard no brake taking hold. Tried to stop later, but only succeeded in doing so by dragging against bank. . . . Car rubbed along like an old elephant scratching its cutlets, and padlocks, keys, tools, side-boxes removed like flies.[62]

The next day, making a similar trip, Peirce wrote: "brakes refused to work — used reverse successfully — no mules slaughtered or even touched. . . ."

Despite the fits and starts the ambulances gave their drivers, in the final analysis the cars were their protectors and providers. "The car," Arthur Gleason observed, after spending several days watching the Norton, Harjes, and AFS drivers at work in Verdun,

> becomes a personality to the man at the wheel. . . . It isn't just any old car. . . . In that particular car you have carried 500 wounded men, you have gone into the ditch, stuck in the mud, and scurried under shell-fire, shrapnel has torn the cover, and there is the mark of a rifle-bullet on the wheel-spoke. You have slept at the wheel and in the chassis. . . . You have eaten luncheons for two months on the front seat. . . .[63]

As a sign of their closeness to the cars, the drivers gave them pet names such as Maude, Old Number Nine, Hunk-o'-Tin, and Elsie. Richard Norton named his touring car Lucille, and the Mercedes in his section was called Gabrielle.

"It is difficult," Robert Imbrie felt, "for one who had not led the life to appreciate just what his car means to the *ambulancier.*"[64] It is his only home for days, Imbrie noted, adding,

> he drives it through rain, hail, mud and dust, at high noon on sunshiny days, and through nights so dark that the radiator cap before him is invisible. Its interior serves him as a bed-room. Its engine furnishes him with hot shaving water, its [fenders] act as a dresser. He works over, under and upon it. He paints it and oils it and knows its every bolt and nut, its every whim and fancy. When shrapnel and shell *éclat* fall, he dives under it for protection.[65]

The driver entrusted his life, as well as the lives of the wounded he carried, to his car. Proud, too, he was of his Model T, Packard, Sunbeam. "No millionaire in his $10,000 limousine feels half the complacent pride of the ambulance driver," Imbrie said, "when . . . he has at last succeeded in inducing it to 'hit on four' and with its wobbly wheel clutched in sympathetic hands he proudly steers its erratic course."[66]

CODA

You may reflect on an *ambulancier*'s mechanical knowledge, his
appearance, morals, religion, or politics, but if you be wise, reflect
not on his car.[67]

Part III
The End of Something

7

Politics, Motives,
and Impressions

The hardships of the war, the tedium
of *repos*, and the temperamental demands of the early automobiles
were not the only challenges American volunteer ambulance drivers
faced during the first two and a half years of the war. Despite their
selfless dedication, the volunteers were hardly regarded as heroes by
the American public, which was unsupportive of the volunteers and
unsympathetic to their work. Indeed, during the first years of the war,
90 percent of Americans was estimated to be disposed against any
involvement, voluntary or not, in the European conflict.[1] Government policy regarding the war also tended to isolate the volunteers.
Reciprocally, the drivers' firsthand experiences on the battlefields of
France distanced them psychologically from the indifferent American
public and resolutely neutral United States government they had left
behind. In short, the various American ambulance corps serving
overseas from late 1914 to mid-1917 were pretty much on their own,
compelled largely to fend for themselves.

Even the premier relief organization in the United States, the
American Red Cross, failed to be of much help to the volunteers
during this period. Experienced drivers such as William G. Rice
preferred the YMCA, which operated a number of canteens and
hospices, to the ARC. "The YMCA is doing great work here," Rice
wrote from Aix-les-Bains, "at least [its] work gives everyone that
comes here a great time. . . . If the Red Cross spent its money half as
well, I'd not begrudge it the millions it has raised by pretenses."[2]
Greayer Clover also contrasted the efforts of the ARC with "the

wonderful work [of] the YMCA," noting specifically that "a YMCA girl is the only one here allowed to talk to men. Nurses and Red Cross-ers are forbidden to converse with [us]."[3]

It wasn't just moral support or friendly companionship the American Red Cross failed to provide its drivers. Prior to the U.S. declaration of war on Germany in 1917, the American Red Cross supplied only one major consignment of ambulances to France. The ARC supposedly shipped seventeen Fords — twelve donated by Yale and five by Harvard[4] — to Herman Harjes, its official representative in Paris, in the late spring of 1915. By the time the Yale-Harvard Fords arrived, the French Army (in accord with the agreement set up by A. Piatt Andrew and Captain Doumenc) had revoked its restrictions on American ambulance drivers.[5]

In May, with his corps of Packards and Panhards rumored to be going to the front (and perhaps having heard that the ARC was about to come to the aid of his section with some new Model Ts), Harjes decided to petition the American Red Cross for formal affiliation. He cabled the ARC on May 21, 1915, requesting its official sponsorship, specifically asking for permission to issue Red Cross identification cards to his drivers. By carrying these ID cards, Harjes' drivers could not be mistaken for spies, and thus would be protected from hostile interrogation, imprisonment, or worse, should they happen to fall into enemy hands, which was a distinct possibility now that they were allowed to drive to the front lines.

The right to use its name was the ARC's preeminent contribution to its ambulance sections before 1917. In its letter of June 4, 1915, granting Harjes' request for formal affiliation, the ARC cited the terms of Chapter 3, Article XI, of the Geneva Convention and added four additional conditions: one regarding personnel, one concerning passports, and one detailing the proper use of the Red Cross flag. The fourth condition was the most succinct: "It is understood that the American Red Cross is not responsible for the financial support of [the ambulance corps]."[6]

True to its disclaimer, the American Red Cross made only one significant monetary contribution to its ambulance sections in the first two and a half years of the war. In late July, 1915, it gave Harjes $2,500 to "be used in getting the wounded as rapidly as possible to where they may receive proper treatment away from the front." Two weeks later, the ARC closed its overseas hospital units, and Acting Director Mabel Boardman wrote Harjes explaining that the action was a financial necessity. Boardman's letter also informed him that the ARC was forwarding a final $500, which had been donated specifically for the use of his ambulance section.

No more funds were sent.[7] On January 30, 1917, Harjes wrote Eliot Wadsworth, vice-chairman of the Central Committee of the ARC, to say that he had enough new volunteers to add more sections, but that he needed money. "We have only about $20,000 to keep up [the current] work," Harjes told Wadsworth. Simply to maintain his present operations, he added, would require $100,000. "Anything you [the ARC] can do for us," Harjes implored, "will be very greatly appreciated." Harjes' request met with silence, and he never again appealed as directly for funds from the ARC.[8]

The ARC may well have been financially strapped at the time. Later, on May 1, 1917, shortly after the United States declared war on Germany, President Wilson named a War Council to organize a massive ARC membership and fund-raising drive. In the next six months, the ARC grew from 486,194 members to over 5 million, and the number of local chapters increased from 562 to 3,287.[9] Prior to the declaration of war, however, the ARC had been a relatively small, unsettled, and underfunded organization. "The Red Cross seems to have been in a state of upheaval" during the period before the U.S. involvement in the war, observed Amy Owen Bradley, who drove for the American Fund for French Wounded.[10]

In that all of the volunteers' daily requirements were furnished by the French Army, the ARC deemed that the ambulance corps required only "partial support," as one ARC historian called it.[11] Harjes' drivers received no salary other than what they received from the French Army, augmented a few cents a day by Harjes; and, their uniforms came with the job, covered by Harjes as an out-of-pocket expense, as were the additional salaries of the section's cook and mechanic. Harjes' volunteers, like the others, were responsible for their own transportation to and from Paris.[12] Consequently, the ARC could rationalize that Harjes' "Red Cross" unit needed merely to have its rations "supplemented occasionally by Red Cross issue" (usually "comfort kits" of personal items such as shaving materials, tobacco, soap, washcloths, games, magazines, mufflers, stationery, and other goods donated by members of local ARC chapters). That is to say, despite its professions of partial or occasional support, the American Red Cross offered little real aid — financial or otherwise — during 1914–1917.

Contemporary politics figured in the ARC's limited assistance to its Norton-Harjes ambulance sections.[13] Operating field hospitals or providing doctors and nurses was easily justified, when the ARC could afford it. This type of work was clearly humanitarian and nonpartisan: wounded people of whatever nationality needed care. However, sponsoring a corps of young men serving near the front lines as adjunct members of the French Army was another matter altogether.[14] The ARC had learned a bitter lesson during the Boer War. Clara Barton had permitted a group of men from Chicago to form an ambulance corps in the name of the American Red Cross to aid the Boers, persuading the British to allow this Red Cross ambulance unit to pass through their lines. To Barton's astonishment, once the Chicagoans reached the Boers' camp, "the so-called Red Cross representatives promptly dropped their brassards and joined the Boer fighting forces."[15] The British were understandably livid, and the ARC was sorely chastened and thereafter closely monitored.

The international headquarters was not the only administrative agency to concern itself with the impartiality of the ARC. Another was the White House. Since the President of the United States was, *ex officio*, the titular head of the American Red Cross, Woodrow Wilson had direct oversight of the Red Cross's activities. Wilson's unremitting advocacy of neutrality before 1917 meant the ARC had to be strictly neutral, and could not display any overt favoritism. Wilson publicly insisted on neutrality from all American organizations and citizens "in fact as well as in name . . . in thought as well as in action."[16] Committed by Wilson to strict and manifest neutrality, the American Red Cross was effectively prohibited from aiding its Norton-Harjes ambulance corps, who were *de facto* members of the French Army.

Although Wilson's policy of neutrality was apparently endorsed by the vast majority of the American citizenry, it produced some rather curious, if not hypocritical, consequences. For example, colleges and universities that had made a practice of bringing over visiting professors began to consider political balance, rather than academic expertise or needs, as a primary qualification. The Amherst faculty, while deploring "the inexcusable blunder of Germany's entry into neutral Belgium," nevertheless had to ensure that its series of Monday-morning lectures was made "by representatives of the various warring nations."[17] Phillips Academy at Andover, which had been inviting German professors to its campus since 1910, halted the practice in 1915. German academics were suddenly no longer welcome. Trying to remain ostensibly neutral, Andover did not publicly voice its anti-German bias, which was surely intensified when General Leonard Wood visited the campus on November 12, 1914. General Wood, a notorious pro-Allies hawk whose presence on campus would seem to belie the pretense of impartiality, was a guest of ex-Secretary of War and influential Andover trustee Henry L. Stimson, and thus was not only welcome on campus but was allowed to give his standard anti-German speech.[18]

An even stranger consequence of Wilson's call for inviolate neutrality involved Ellery C. Wood, one of the very first volunteer drivers. Wood wrote to the *Yale News* in the autumn of 1914, pointing out the need for ambulances. As a result, $9,200 was raised at the Harvard-Yale football game that fall, a sum sufficient to buy twelve Ford ambulances, which were turned over to the American Red Cross for shipment overseas. According to Wood, "We hoped they [the Fords] would all go to France and England, but Mabel Boardman of the Red Cross decided to split the gift to three for France, three for England, three for Germany, and three for Austria."[19] Thus was the Red Cross's — and Wilson's — insistence upon impartiality to be served. Boardman's efforts, however, failed. Letters acknowledging delivery of the cars came from the St. John Ambulance Association in London and from the *Croix Rouge Français.* The three cars bound for Germany may have made it — Wood never found out — but he heard that "the Austrian [ambulances] were captured on the high seas and went to Britain."

From the very outbreak of war in 1914, President Wilson's official response cautioned against siding with the efforts of Belgium, France, Britain, or, for that matter, Germany and Austria. Wilson's "Proclamation" of August 4 cited the U.S. Penal Code of 1909, from which he inferred eleven "forbidden acts" his policy of political neutrality proscribed. Most of the eleven acts pertained to aiding and abetting the quarreling nations, but two in particular applied to the general public and, more specifically, to any Americans who might be entertaining ideas about volunteering to serve abroad. Wilson claimed that the Penal Code implicitly prohibited any U.S. citizen from "enlisting or *entering into the service of* either of the said belligerents . . ." and from taking "part, *directly or indirectly*, in the said wars . . ."[20] [my emphasis]. As the days passed, Wilson kept up the beat. In his address to the Senate on August 19, 1914, he railed against any "transaction that might be construed as a preference of one party to the struggle before another. . . ." In a speech to the Daughters of the American Revolution (April 19, 1915), Wilson noted that "we cannot afford to sympathize with anybody or anything except the passing generation of human beings." So it went.

These words — this policy — ran directly counter to the beliefs of many young college men, who were aroused by a sense of duty and inspired by friends, professors, or alums to go to the aid of France. Wilson's insistence upon neutrality contravened as well the passion of other men and women who were horrified by stories of German atrocities in Belgium. The policy also affronted those who detested the political arrogance of Kaiser Bill and were, at base, Anglophiles or Francophiles. It also frustrated the instinctive yearnings of still other adventure seekers, who saw themselves racing motorcars, or flying biplanes across the fields of Champagne, or marching in the ranks of the French Foreign Legion, which was now for the first time called upon to fight on the home soil of *La Belle France.*

William Seabrook was one of the volunteers who commented most bitterly on Wilson's policy of neutral detachment. Older than most of the other drivers, Seabrook had left his family and a successful advertising business to join Andrew's American Ambulance Field Service. In his memoirs of those days, Seabrook reflected upon Wilson's attitude.

> President Wilson had publicly deplored the action of such few, scattered, misguided American youth as had volunteered, while most of their families and the general public felt pretty much the same about it. . . . [They] considered that the Americans, mostly youngsters, who had joined the [Lafayette Escadrille], the Foreign Legion, or the American Ambulance

> Field Service ... were adventurers, freaks — or at best
> young, misguided idealists.[21]

Like Seabrook, drivers were at times openly contemptuous of
Wilson and his insistence upon strict neutrality. They made fun of him
in the skits they wrote and performed during entertainment nights *en
repos*. They referred to the shells that didn't explode — the duds that
did nothing — as "Wilsons." Even A. Piatt Andrew, according to one
of his drivers, "never missed a chance to knock ... Wilson."[22]

Sidney Howard, who became a successful dramatist and screen-
writer after the war, was also enraged by the President's inaction.
Writing to his mother just before he joined the ambulance service in
early 1916, Howard said, "I wish I knew of some means whereby I
could do this Wilson damage politically."[23] The longer Wilson insisted upon America's impartiality, the more Howard steamed. In a
letter of October of 1916, having served several months in the AFS,
Howard described President Wilson as "a stubborn politician [with-
out] the courage to say one strong word — [or] to do one strong
thing." Referring to the upcoming election, Howard wrote his mother
that a change *had* to be made in American war policy. "Bitterly as I
have come to despise Woodrow Wilson [during these] two years of
the war," Howard noted in his letter, "I cannot conceive a continuance
of his — even his cowardly patience."

Most volunteers, however, simply ignored Wilson's words and
followed their own promptings, letting their actions speak for them.
"Every time a man volunteered," William Yorke Stevenson noted, "he
carried with him the hopes and sympathies of all his relatives and
friends; and as the [ambulance service] grew, so did the pro-Ally
sentiment grow by leaps and bounds in the United States."[24] Their
letters home gave voice to their point of view. While the U.S. government was "hesitating and those in authority were proclaiming the
necessity of speaking and even thinking in neutral terms," Andrew
wrote, the AFS volunteers were "writing [about their experiences]
and agitating in terms that were not neutral. . . ."[25] The volunteers'
letters had effect, sometimes immediate and sometimes delayed. According to Coningsby Dawson, writer of several effusive books on the
war, the impact of the volunteers' example was widespread: "The
American college boys [who] had won a name by their devotion in

forcing their ambulances over shell-torn roads [and those in] the American Flying Squadron . . . stirred, shamed and educated the nation."[26] Noting that the volunteers' letters were often printed in local newspapers, Henry Sleeper observed that "when the time came for us to make a general campaign for men and cars [throughout the country], every town where such early publicity had been given, proved doubly ready to cooperate."[27]

Given Wilson's rhetoric and the public sentiment in favor of neutrality, the young men who volunteered for overseas ambulance work had to be strongly motivated, or so it might seem. Yet, their motives proved to be as varied in kind and intensity as the volunteers themselves, and were not always a consequence of political or philosophical considerations. Some of the men, such as the fictional characters at the end of Dos Passos' *42nd Parallel* who signed on as a lark one drunken night, were oblivious to politics and prudence. Like Dos Passos' characters, these volunteers believed the war would be short, and they wanted to see the action, in Dos Passos' words, "before the whole thing went belly-up." Such was the feeling of Edward Weeks as he waited for his passage overseas. Although it was hardly his only or most compelling motivation, Weeks "longed to get into the action before it was over."[28]

Many of the very first volunteers were simply seeking instantaneous adventure. Robert Imbrie, an early driver for the AFS, wrote:

> At the outbreak of the war the restless ones of the earth flocked to France, drawn there by the prospect of adventure. . . . The ambulance [corps] attracted its share of these characters. . . . There was an ex-cowboy from Buffalo Bill's Congress of Rough Riders, big game hunters . . . , a former 4th Cavalryman, a professional Portuguese revolutionist, a driver of racing cars, . . . an All-American football center. . . ."[29]

Confirming Imbrie's observation, a survey by Paul-Louis Hervier of the first American volunteer ambulance drivers counted among the total "young athletes spoiling for some way in which to expend their energies" and "roving spirits in search of adventure."[30] When the poet Emery Pottle wrote his alma mater, Amherst, calling for volunteers, he appealed to the more adventurous students by describing the glories and dangers of serving in the ambulance corps.[31] The romance of driving a motor-ambulance for a noble cause with considerable risk had an irresistible appeal for many young men. "We were romantic," noted Dunbar Hinrichs. "Surely being romantic is no sin."[32]

However, the drivers soon learned that the romance was only skin deep. "An American ambulance driver," Lansing Warren noted, tongue-in-cheek,

> is a fellow who comes to France to save Humanity. But by the time he has been on the western front for a couple of weeks, his efforts in this pursuit have been concentrated on one integral portion of the whole in the animated endeavor to save himself.[33]

Of a more serious nature were the drivers' letters that attempted expressly to disabuse prospective volunteers of the notion that ambulance driving was glorious fun. Whereas many letters played up the dramatic excitement of pounding battered cars through darkness and shell fire, other letters stressed the back-breaking aspect of the ambulance service, its tedium, and the depressing futility of the endlessness of the war. "When I write you about what we have done," James M. White told his brother (the letter was excerpted in the New York *Sun*), "I . . . want you to know that this work is no play, and far from being an occupation of the 'semiheroic rich.' "[34] John Masefield, the British poet who visited the front in late 1916, reported that "this war will perhaps be remembered for the monotony and the patience behind the lines."[35] Arthur Gleason's best-selling *Our Part in the Great War*, an account of his visit to Alsace and Verdun in 1916, described ambulance driving as "hard, unpicturesque work, with an occasional fifteen minutes of tension."[36] In a direct effort to caution the men who had inquired about joining his brother's ambulance corps, Eliot Norton responded with a form letter that contained this candid warning: "[An *ambulancier*] must realize that sometimes a [driver] has, for quite a period of time, very little to do: the result is that the time hangs heavy . . . and accordingly a volunteer must be a man of good disposition, possessed of self-control."[37]

Most new volunteers respected such warnings and understood,

at least in the abstract, that ambulance driving could be boring, tedious work. "I want you to realize," Coleman Clark wrote his parents prior to sailing for France, "that I do not look upon [driving an ambulance in France] as a sight seeing trip, mixed in with a lot of adventure, but I appreciate the hard labor it will be."[38] By the time Mrs. W. K. Vanderbilt visited the sections at Verdun in August of 1916, there were few purely adventure seekers left in the ambulance service.

> I do not believe that a sense of adventure was the impelling motive in most instances. They did not look the part of the soldier of fortune who gives his loyalty light to any cause. . . . [They] have arranged to give six months to the cause of France and her allies, because they believe in France and the things for which she and her allies are fighting.[39]

Serving the cause of France was indeed a motive commonly mentioned in the volunteers' letters and journals. Yale student Greayer Clover, who lost his life in the war, wrote his parents that he wanted "to serve — serve the country [France] and the cause." By joining the ambulance service, he wrote, "I will be really serving and doing something worth while."[40] Coleman Clark felt the same way: "I feel that France needs men badly right now, and that I ought to go right away."[41] Ralph Ellington, a member of a group of volunteers from Amherst, was prompted by a similar desire — "to share in her [France's] struggle for freedom, liberty and equality."[42] In his collection of verse, *Turmoil*, Robert Donaldson also pledged that "her [France's] hard-fought battle is our cause of right. . . ."[43]

The aspiration to serve the French cause was not the only factor in these men's decision to volunteer. L. D. Geller, a former director of the American Field Service Library and Archives, believed that one of the men's primary reasons for volunteering was their sense of historical indebtedness to France for its support in 1776. After studying the various manuscript material in the library and archives, Geller concluded that

> certainly adventurism provided some motive for going overseas to join a foreign army years before the United States entered the war. Humanitarianism also was a motive. But, by

and large, the historical idealism of repaying a debt to France for its role in the American War of Independence and the defense of French culture and civilization against the perceived barbarism of the invading force, were uppermost.[44]

The idea of repaying a historical debt was especially popular in Andrew's American Field Service. Andrew stressed America's historical obligation in the articles he wrote, in his welcoming addresses and other occasional speeches, and even in the certificates he issued each driver. Other volunteers echoed Andrew. "These men," Philip Orcutt noted in the preface to his book *The White Road of Mystery,* "feeling that America owed a debt to France, banded together to form the original American Ambulance Service."[45]

Not all volunteers, however, shared this view; William G. Rice, for one. During a funeral service Rice attended, the minister "brought in, as usual, the notion that we are making return for the Revolutionary services of Lafayette," Rice wrote in a letter home, *"which is not the least my notion."*[46] Indeed, memoirs, journals, and letters from the various American ambulance organizations indicate the volunteers' motives were hardly singular or fixed. Some men, in fact, didn't know why they joined. "I have asked other Americans why they volunteered," Edward Coyle (a Norton driver) said, and "in no instance did any of them give a solid reason. . . ." Their answers, he decided, could be summed up as a collective "Damifino." Coyle admitted he didn't even understand his own reasons for volunteering. "I must have talked myself into going," he confessed, going on to explain that one night at dinner with a friend he simply blurted out his intention to sign on with Richard Norton.[47] Assessing the veracity of what people claim to be their motives is, at best, dicey business. One may be inclined to believe Coyle, for instance, when he admits that he and most of the men he talked to didn't know why they volunteered. Yet, what seems like candor may in fact be false modesty or a psychological ruse of some sort. On the other hand, the claim by some men that they were repaying Lafayette for his contribution to the American Revolutionary War may sound a little too highfalutin. More to the point, this analogy does not hold. Americans had several previous opportunities (for example, 1798, 1848, 1870–1871) to repay its debt to an embattled France and didn't bother. Further, to serve on behalf of France in 1914 aided the preservation of the status quo. In effect, by going to France the volunteers were acting to maintain the established culture and nineteenth-century geopolitical systems of France and England. Lafayette's efforts, in contrast, aided the American colonies and their desire to free themselves from the geopolitical establishment of the period. Although a person's professed motives are often confused and sometimes virtually unreliable, the cause people think or claim moved them to action can be as revealing and significant as an unstated or subliminal motive.

Whatever moved the drivers to volunteer in the first place, their feelings about their work and its worth nearly always changed after they had spent time driving ambulances or camions for the French Army. If the drivers had no specific incentives before, or if their intentions were abstract and idealistic, the volunteers soon developed very firm and explicit motives. Personally, Stevenson "[doubted] if more than half the men go over to France from really altruistic motives," pointing out, however, that "later on France gets a sort of grip on you ... and one begins to want to stay and to 'see it through'. . . ."[48] Julien Bryan also acknowledged that he had undergone a major emotional transformation during his tour of duty.

> I went over, as did so many of the others, with the object of seeing war at first hand and of getting some excitement, as well as being of some service. . . . But having arrived in France and learned of some of the terrible things which had been done by the enemy and what the French people had gone through . . . , our point of view was altered, and we were ashamed of our primary object in offering our services.[49]

More extreme was the case of James R. McConnell, who volunteered for the ambulance service because he didn't want to miss "the opportunity of a life-time." He considered the war "the greatest event in history," and he itched to be a part of it, "not just as a sightseer, looking on. . . ."[50] McConnell's passionate involvement intensified the more time he spent in France. "As happened in the case of so many other young American volunteers," wrote the historian Edwin Morse in his discussion of McConnell and others, "interest in the war as primarily a great adventure was gradually replaced ... by an absorbing desire to be of substantial assistance to the French people. . . ."[51] Prompted by his new — and increasingly fervent — dedication to the French cause, McConnell grew disdainful of ambulance driving. It wasn't enough for him; it was too passive; it did nothing to deter, drive back, or destroy the German invaders. McConnell concluded that "it was plainly up to me to do more than drive an ambulance."[52] So, this dedicated, gifted, and popular young man joined the Lafayette Escadrille; soon thereafter his plane was shot down, and he was killed.

Although the transformation was not as all-consuming for most drivers as it was for McConnell, virtually every driver described his experience as bringing about some major change in his outlook on life. "If it [the war] ever ends," Carlos de Florez pledged, "how I shall live! The hours I have squandered, the pleasures I have ignored, no longer will they escape me. . . ."[53] Or, to cite the cooler words of Andrew: "No man can pass through such an experience unchanged."[54] Malcolm Cowley also acknowledged a shift in his perspective. "Not that my soul has been transformed with wonder," he wrote his friend Kenneth Burke, "but just that I have been drawn out of my fixed orbit." Cowley advised Burke that the war "is the great common experience of the young manhood of today, an experience that will mold the thought of the next generation, and without which one will be somewhat of a stranger to the world of the present and the future."[55]

A volunteer's particular transformation was sometimes a result of the psychological impact of the war's horrors, about which many drivers were open in their letters and journals. While waiting to go to the front, Sidney Howard was assigned to take an ambulance to the Paris train station at La Chapelle. "Our train — my first," he wrote his sister (July 12, 1916), "made me a Pacifist for life." After describing the scene in ghastly detail, Howard noted that "one expects to be affected in some wise by horrors. But this is all too matter of fact and too inutterably [sic] appalling to turn the stomach. It's the head that is turned. . . ." When chlorine was first used in Flanders, the ambulance drivers were the first noncombatants to witness the horrible effects of the gas. One driver noted that his sense of pity and revulsion escalated to a new level.

> Trains rolled in filled with huddled figures, some dying, some more lightly touched, but even these coughed so that they

were unable to speak coherently. . . . These sufferers from the new form of attack inspired in us all feelings of pity beyond any that we had ever felt before. To see these big men bent double, convulsed and choking, was heartbreaking and hate-inspiring.[56]

In addition to their introduction to man's inhumanity to man, many of these young drivers were suddenly made aware of their own powerlessness. "You realize," Julien Bryan wrote, "how absolutely weak and helpless you are when a load of dead are brought in, some with arms and legs gone, others with heads and trunks mixed together. . . ."[57] However cocky and invincible a volunteer might be when he signed on, after working a few days out of the Verdun *postes*, for example, he was surely a changed, more humble, man, perforce made more aware of man's mortality. "Those of us who used to laugh at danger have stopped laughing," a member of the AFS Section 8 said. "We don't come back any longer and tell each other . . . how close this or that shell burst to our car — it is sufficient that we come back."[58]

The transformation of a driver's outlook somehow became evident in his very appearance. "One half of the boys were wearing poilu trousers and poilu shoes," Stevenson noted, describing a line of American *ambulanciers* slogging down the Voie Sacrée from Verdun. "Some had on helmets," Stevenson observed, "and all had a week or two's growth of beard. Every one was covered with mud, and the cars were all smashed up as to headlights, fenders, radiators, and also covered with mud and dozens of *éclat* holes. . . ."[59] *As out, so in*, one might say.

The shock of the war's horrors and the lessons of their own helplessness and vulnerability notwithstanding, the volunteers often spoke rhapsodically of their time in the ambulance service. "The great hours of my life," one driver called this period.[60] William Yorke Stevenson considered his ambulance-driving days as "ten months of the most interesting, and, I am almost tempted to say, the happiest, months of my life."[61] Even A. Piatt Andrew, having been an assistant professor at Harvard, a high government official, and a candidate for Congress, felt a change in himself. "I can truthfully say," he confessed after only one month as an *ambulancier*, "that I have never been more interested in life. . . ."[62]

Epitomizing this transforming effect are the words of Reginald Nöel Sullivan, a devout pacifist. Independently wealthy, Sullivan was an accomplished singer, was fluent in French and German, and was a frequent prewar visitor to Paris, with many socially and culturally influential friends there. Sullivan, in other words, was a self-assured and worldly young man when he volunteered. His term in the AFS convinced him, however, that his life before the ambulance service had been little more than a busy, insubstantial, social and artistic whirl.

> I hope nothing I have said [Sullivan wrote home] would lead you to believe that I am unhappy or bored here. On the contrary I am very well and feel I will some day look back on these days as some of the very happiest of my life, for they have afforded me a wonderful lot of solitude in which to analyze my chaotic life. . . .[63]

The experiences of the young American volunteers, to be sure, were indelibly instructive, but perhaps even more impressive for some of them was the conduct and bearing of the French soldiers, the *poilus*. "People at home think that we are making tremendous sacrifices to . . . do this work," Julien Bryan noted. "But they [our sacrifices] are nothing compared to those which the simple, uneducated poilu makes."[64] Over and over the American volunteers mention the selflessness, courage, and resilience of the *poilu*. "We [drivers]," William Seabrook said,

> had our own occasional casualties, worked a good deal of the time under shellfire, occasionally in gas, but the risks we ran were nothing compared with those of the [*poilus*] who were doing the fighting. . . . We were intensely aware of this difference.[65]

The views of Bryan and Seabrook were hardly unique. Sidney Howard's assessment was virtually identical, although he expressed it more succinctly: "One and all the 'poilus' are noble souls."[66] Using abundant anecdote and detail, Charles Nordhoff set forth a similar view. "One becomes very fond of the French soldier," he said, pointing specifically to the "interesting traits," hidden talents, and general toughness of the *poilu*.[67] Robert Imbrie made the point unequivocal: "No man can have served with [the *poilus*] without having grown stronger through their courage, gentler through their courtesy, and nobler through their devotion."[68]

A volunteer's admiration for the *poilu* sometimes generalized to include the French population at large, for their endurance and personal sacrifices. In September of 1916, while serving his first term in France, Coleman Clark spoke of "my intense desire to stay on to do my part, which seems so little when I see poor, uneducated soldiers give and do so much."[69] A little over a year later, Clark's sympathies had broadened. "I could not easily express the feelings of admiration I have for France," he wrote, adding his own disclaimer.

> When I mention France, I do not mean the corruption in her government, the life at Paris, or the ordinary Frenchman's limited views on everything not French. I think of the people as a whole, which the ordinary American knows nothing about; *their suffering and determination, still bound to win after 3 and a half years* . . . [my emphasis].[70]

J. L. Rothwell underwent a similar expansion of his feelings. "If I respected the French before I came over here," he said, "that respect is now multiplied many times." Commenting on the almost stoic acceptance by the French of the unrelenting, arduous demands of the war, Rothwell noted, "If anything goes wrong or any personal pleasures [become] hardships, it's 'Pour La Guerre' [in the French mind], and is all right."[71]

In his book *No Man's Land: Combat and Identity in World War I*, Eric Leed notes that "the learning experience of war . . . equips the individual with a kind of knowledge that could be called 'disjunctive' rather than integrative. What men learned in the war set them irrevocably apart from those others who stood outside it."[72] A similar observation could be made about the noncombatant ambulance drivers, who sensed that they had been uniquely educated by their experiences. Once engaged in ambulance work, most drivers evolved a view of the Red Cross, Wilsonian neutrality, the nature of the war, or the character of the French people that contrasted sharply with the public sentiment they left behind in the States or the often naive notions to be found in letters from home. "America," a camion driver named H. Byrd noted in a May of 1917 letter to his parents, "is absurdly ignorant of . . . this great war. It is a tremendous and grim thing, and the sooner America realizes it, the better."[73]

Even after the American Army had been deployed in France, the ambulance men believed they were of a different cast of mind than their fellow Yanks, who were only newly involved in the war. Describing the traits and outlook of a veteran *ambulancier*, AFS driver Robert Donaldson wrote that "the ambulance man knows the poilu's faults, but he also knows his multitude of virtues, and refuses to have him run down, or called a 'frawg' by doughboys who [think they] won the war by their own single effort." Pointing out the difference between the popular American disposition, as represented by the army's doughboy, and that of the *ambulancier*, Donaldson says:

> When some chesty individual proclaims that we done it all, and the poyloo never was no good anyhow, you are likely to hear [the ambulance man] stating the evident truth that the poilu is the finest soldier of the war.[74]

Disjunctive or not, the impact of the drivers' work produced new and transforming sensations; sometimes ghastly, sometimes mind-numbingly dull. Whether of terror or tedium, these new sensations altered the drivers' attitudes toward the war, their fellow man, and their own lives — reshaping, or clarifying, or intensifying their sense of themselves and what they valued. In one of his articles describing the nature of the ambulance service, A. Piatt Andrew tells of a Harvard graduate who had been out of college for over a decade. During the years since his graduation, the Harvard man had been living "an idle, care-free life, playing bridge and doing the social functions." When Andrew spoke to the man, who had recently joined the ambulance service, he asked the driver about his profession in private life. "I have never done much of anything, sir, up to the present," the Harvard grad replied. "But I doubt when the war is over whether I shall ever be happy doing that again."[75]

8

Some Female Drivers
and
Other Noteworthy Volunteers

The complete history of American *ambulanciers* in the Great War will never be satisfactorily told because a significant part of the record is incomplete: that involving the work of female American volunteers. American women who drove ambulances in France usually got there by sheer force of their ability, ingenuity, and resolve, and yet their extraordinary work is seldom treated in detail in either public or private accounts of the war.[1] One notice concerning a military unit, for example, ran in the AFS *Bulletin* (no. 65) of October 5, 1918, under the headline, "Lady Ambulanciers Win Praise."

> Woman's section Y.Y.U. 2, which has been performing *corps d'Armée* evacuation to S.S.U. 711 has been highly praised for their work. The boys say they are speedy and courageous.

That's the entire quotation. No further mention of Y.Y.U. 2, or any other women's unit, appeared in the AFS *Bulletin* (First Series), which ran from July of 1917 to May of 1919. Other references to female American *ambulanciers* appear here and there in various documents but are like this one (which the Sam Spades of the decade would have dismissed as "cold leads": allusions; incomplete, casual, and impossible to trace further). Still, sparse though the evidence may be, many women did in fact swap their stateside lives for a term of ambulancing that was largely without exhilarating moments.

To suggest that World War I revolutionized cultural attitudes toward women, however, would be misleading. The war did not suddenly license the American woman to contribute freely and directly, howsoever she wished, to the war effort. Despite the claim of Barbara Steinson that the women who served "in relief and preparedness activities . . . were not dominated by men,"[2] strict, if unwritten, Victorian rules of conduct that still governed the lives of most American women at home about the turn of the century remained largely intact for those who served overseas. As Ellen S. More has said about female doctors who volunteered for hospital work, "Wartime conditions seemed an ideal setting for women to take their places beside their medical brethren and leave their Victorian manners behind. Yet, their claims to equality went unheeded. . . ."[3]

May Sinclair offered a firsthand account of what it was like to be a female volunteer in her *Journal of Impressions in Belgium* (1915). Rebecca West's review of this work by Sinclair, a highly respected English author, described it as "largely a record of humiliations,"[4] and so it is. The men whom Sinclair encountered assumed she had volunteered for the fun and adventure of watching men in danger. "He began," Sinclair said of one man, "by asking if we women enjoyed going out [on duty] with the Field Ambulance; he supposed we felt very daring. . . ."[5] Sinclair, in fact, felt useless: "I don't know where I come in," she confessed at one point. "They called me the Secretary and Reporter, which sounds very fine. . . ."[6] However, there was no reporting to be done, and to be "eating Belgian food . . . [while] doing nothing for the Belgians" disturbed her deeply. "We are not justifying our existence," she said, referring to herself and the other four women in her group. "We are frauds," she concluded, adding that "there was no earthly reason why I should have come, and none whatever why I should remain."[7] Shortly thereafter she was sent to England on an errand, and she stayed there.

Despite Sinclair's feeling unwanted, British women were far more welcome as contributors than their American counterparts. As the war progressed during 1914–1915 and the number of casualties multiplied, British men who had been driving ambulances for rear-line hospitals were needed by the army to carry *blessés* at the front lines. The British began using women as drivers to handle rear-line jitney driving in British sectors. British records show that in April of 1916 Mrs. Graham Jones, who had been driving an ambulance since the early days of the war, was put in charge of the first autonomous British women's ambulance unit. Assigned to a large base hospital (1,300 beds) in Northern France, Jones had thirteen women driving for her, sometimes transporting *blessés* 130 miles a day.[8] In addition, by mid-1916 the Women's Auxiliary Army Corps had formed a motor branch under Miss Christobel Ellis, who had driven an ambulance in 1914 for the French Red Cross. Significantly, there are few accounts extant of American women drivers that compare with the material in Barbara McLaren's 1917 book or Sinclair's "journal of impressions."

Americans got a detailed portrayal of a female driver — British, of course — and the circumstances of her work in Ruth Wright Kauffman's article, "The Woman Ambulance-Driver in France," which appeared in a popular American magazine in 1917.[9] Kauffman's article focused on a resourceful and resolute driver who "had her own car and had been running it for years." Riding in the car with Kauffman were two passengers, "rosy cheeked young women returning from a fortnight's leave to England," whom Kauffman recognized by their uniforms as VADs, initials she erroneously assumed to be short for Volunteer Ambulance Drivers. Actually, VAD stood for Voluntary Aid Detachment, a service organization that came into existence in 1910 to augment the work of the British Red Cross and the St. John's Ambulance. Originally intended to include both men and women, a VAD in practice consisted nearly exclusively of women, primarily because of the shortage of available men. Originally, the initials VAD referred to an entire unit, but inevitably the twenty-three or so individuals in a detachment came to be known as VADs. In addition to serving as aides to nurses, VADs performed general service duties such as cooking, store keeping, and secretarial work (McLaren, pp. 56–57). Catherine Barkley in Hemingway's *A Farewell to Arms*, for instance, was a VAD working for a Red Cross hospital in Milan.[10]

Despite her misunderstanding, Kauffman was impressed with what she learned about female *ambulanciers* during this trip. Citing but one fortnight of activity, she noted that her driver's unit had completely evacuated two ambulance trains, and had transported 2,115 *couchés* and 719 *assis* cases some 8,718 miles — in the process, loading three hospital ships. The colonel in command of the section of drivers told Kauffman that he "should feel a lot safer with those young [English] women than with most men."[11]

Few American female drivers ever got such favorable press or respectful attention as Kauffman's driver, even from other women. When Esther Lovejoy and four others went to inspect an American Red Cross canteen at Pont-à-Mousson and other operations thereabouts in December of 1917, the driver who hauled them over the battered and exposed roads was deemed a "brave little girl and as pretty as a picture" (Lovejoy's words). If "her driving was not such as to inspire confidence," Lovejoy and her entourage nonetheless encouraged "our little chauffeuress" as much as possible because "women ambulance drivers were still on trial in the war zone."[12] These brief and patronizing remarks were all that Lovejoy offered about the solitary young American who daily drove the dangerous and battle-scarred countryside south and east of Verdun. Lovejoy didn't bother recording who this woman was, how long she had been driving the tortuous roads of Lorraine, or why she had taken such a job in the first place.

As a rule, American women tended to make their contributions indirectly: through the numerous relief agencies they founded and supported.[13] Whereas most of these organizations sent money and supplies to representatives who were stationed in large cities overseas, a notable few dispatched their contributions to the very verge of the battlefields. One of these latter was the American Fund for French Wounded, the largest emergency relief organization formed specifically for the European War. The AFFW began work in April of 1915 under the aegis of a larger English relief outfit, but by December the American unit had grown so dramatically that it spun off as an independent organization, with its own distribution depot in Paris and with the energetic and influential Anne Morgan as its treasurer.[14] In all, there were over fifty American international relief organizations, in which some 90,000 women had served by the end of the war. Three hundred forty-eight of the women who worked overseas died, mostly from influenza, typhoid, and other diseases.

Although A. Piatt Andrew's American Field Service hauled some of the AFFW's supplies and donations to the three thousand-plus evacuation and base hospitals,[15] the American Fund for French Wounded had its own corps of drivers, all women. According to Paul-

Louis Hervier's early records, "Miss Caspairs, Miss Arnold, Miss Anny [sic] Bradley, Miss T. Dunham, Miss Hart" all drove for the AFFW.[16] Amy Bradley, whose letters were published in 1918 under the title *In Back of the Front in France*, began delivering AFFW-donated supplies in "Lizzie," her gray Model T, to the numerous Parisian hospitals in November of 1916. In a matter of weeks, Bradley's experience made her an expert driver and mechanic: "There's nothing that I don't know about 1914 Fords by now," she wrote.[17] As her skills became recognized, she was sent on longer junkets. For instance, in March of 1917 she was assigned a Red Cross car to deliver comfort kits[18] and reclining chairs to two hospitals at Concarneau, on the coast south of Quimper; and the following May, Bradley and two other AFFW relief workers made a journey to Verdun, a trip truly rare for women. Overall, however, Bradley's duty tended to be delivery work, carting around supplies and doctors and VIPs. "For the last four days," she noted in the winter of 1917, "I have been driving Dr. Alice Brown, of Winnetka, Ill., on her rounds of dispensary work. She visits six towns, each twice a week. . . ."[19]

Bradley was a graduate of the Winsor School in Boston, and following the war she and other Winsor School alumnae who had served overseas were invited to submit accounts of their experiences. Bradley and several other Winsor grads had driven for the American Fund for French Wounded, including Mrs. H. C. Force (Anna Greenough), who drove for the AFFW from July of 1917 to July of 1918, and Cynthia Wesson, a driver from June to September of 1917.[20] Mrs. P. D. Lamson (Alice Daland), an AFFW driver from July to October of 1916, saw the work pretty much as Bradley had seen it, primarily as delivery, or jitney, duty.

> Our daily job was first to see that the particular car entrusted to each one of us was kept in running order, then to take it over across the river to the headquarters of the committee . . . , find out from the order book what our deliveries were to be, look up the hospitals, etc. on our maps of Paris, get our bales and bags into the cars and start away as quickly as we could.[21]

Elizabeth Ayer, another driver for the American Fund for French Wounded (November of 1917 to May of 1918), echoed Lamson and

Bradley: "My work consisted in taking boxes and bales of supplies to hospitals, both inside and outside of the city. . . ."[22]

Few other accounts of female American drivers are as detailed as Bradley's letters or the material from other Winsor School alumnae.[23] Much more typical is this unfinished, intriguing reference from Paul-Louis Hervier's *The American Volunteers with the Allies*:

> Mrs. Bartlett Boder, who in America sings under the name of Mary Carter, also insisted on playing a useful part. In February 1915, dressed in khaki, she drove a huge wagon over the roads of France for the British commissariat; some months later, at her own request, she was put in charge of a motor-ambulance.[24]

Although Boder/Carter was a celebrity, and apparently one of the first American women to serve, no account of her work as an ambulance driver has been found.

Although offering some bits of information, the most common references to women who drove ambulances tend to be, like Hervier's, sketchy and fragmented. For instance:

> Katherine Stinson has received attention as a post-war pilot for the American Red Cross, but she went overseas initially as an ambulancier, although virtually nothing is known about her ambulance-driving days.[25]
>
> Elizabeth Remsen Thomson, who, according to her daughter, knew "all about automobile engines," is implied to have driven an ambulance in the war.[26]
>
> Mrs. Oswald Chew (Ada Knowlton), one of the founders of the Women's Overseas Service League, accepted a post with her husband in a French hospital unit at Ressard-sur-Metz in November 1916. The following year, after a short-course in automobile repair, she joined the *Service des Automobiles* in Le Mans, where the work proved arduous — which is about all the record shows.[27]
>
> Mrs. J. Borden Harriman (Florence Jaffray Hurst), a friend of President Wilson and a member of his Federal Industrial Relations Committee, drove a local ambulance on weekends for the American Red Cross in connection with Walter Reed

Hospital.[28] In August 1918, she was asked by the ARC to go to Paris as second in command of a large unit of women drivers doing jitney work in Neuilly. Harriman gives this unique experience in only one of the 350 pages in her 1923 memoirs.[29]

The American Women's Hospital, formed by female doctors who had been turned down by the all-male U.S. Army Medical Corps, had its own section of women ambulance drivers.[30] The work of Helen Douglas (later, Mrs. Guy Mankin) as an ambulance driver for the American Women's Hospital was celebrated as a mark of her character when she started working in local, state, and eventually national politics after the war. Helen Douglas graduated from Rockford (Illinois) College in June of 1917 and, according to her biographer, immediately volunteered to drive an ambulance for the American Women's Hospital. Because the minimum age for the work was 24 and Douglas hadn't yet turned 23, she fudged on her passport application and listed her year of birth as 1893, which still didn't make her old enough for an overseas post. After working a year at the headquarters of the American Women's Hospital in Washington, Douglas finally got to France, arriving on November 9, 1918 — two days before the Armistice. Nevertheless, she still had plenty of ambulance work to do, given the typhoid, influenza, and pneumonia rampant among the civilian population.[31]

The *New York Times* occasionally mentioned women who were headed for France to drive ambulances.

> Leilah Pugh will sail for France to offer her services to the American Ambulance Corps as a driver. She is a sergeant in the Motor Corps of the National League for Women's Service and has met the requirements of the Police Department as a motor driver. Since war was declared against Germany, Miss Pugh has been aiding recruiting in NYC and rendering other volunteer services with her automobile [*New York Times*, 6/2/17].

> Miss Janet Boland Sutherland, who is forming a Women's Ambulance Unit for service in France, announced yesterday that her organization is practically completed, and that her volunteers, each of whom will furnish, equip, and drive her own car, are receiving daily training. She will have at least

fifty women enrolled, according to present indications. Miss
Marjorie Bond of Malden, Mass., who offered her services
yesterday, wishes not only to go to the front herself, but to
organize an entire New England unit similar to Miss Suther-
land's. [Ibid.]

American women are needed to drive ambulances in France,
and it is the intention of Miss Ethel Drake . . . to recruit a
number to assist them [Drake and an Englishwoman, Mrs.
Mary E. Symons] in their work. Miss Drake heads the
ambulance service on the Drake Section Sanitaire. . . . [She]
is an American [who] went to France in 1914 and took up
work among the French wounded. . . . "We must be very
particular about the type of women we bring back [to
France] with us," said Miss Drake. "They must possess two
preeminent qualities, they must be of the right physique
and with a well-balanced mental equipment. Again, they
must be financially able to pay all their expenses. It is to
be a strictly volunteer work and there can be no financial
return for labor. We want women between the ages of 25 and
55; they must be in the pink of condition, and must have
poise and that essential capacity for individual action at the
right moment. We want no neurotic women nor women to
whom the romance of the cause is the first appeal. . . ."
[Ibid., 5/5/18]

Yet again the information provided by these fragmentary departure notices is all that exists regarding these women or their
work.

The absence of a detailed record is particularly lamentable in the
case of Zella de Milhau, at one time a well-known Long Island artist.
On September 19, 1916, the *New York Times* reported that de Milhau
sailed "Saturday on the *St. Louis* . . . , [taking with her] an ambulance
which she herself will drive on the evacuation line." Nearly forty
years later, her obituary in the *Times* (3/5/54) noted that de Milhau
"received the Croix de Guerre and the Gold Medaille de la Reconnaissance for valor at the front." These two brief citations constitute
the extant public information about her work as an ambulance driver
in France.[32]

Perhaps the only female American driver besides Amy Bradley
whose experiences are amply documented was Mary Dexter, thanks

to her mother's decision to publish Dexter's letters. Called "protean" for her many talents and multidimensional career,[33] Dexter was in demand virtually everywhere. Shortly after the outbreak of the war, she signed on to manage the kitchen and work in the wards at the American Women's War Relief Hospital in Paignton, South Devon. In May of 1915, Dexter was offered a job driving a motor van in Belgium, delivering food and supplies to hostels and refugee camps. When her abilities as a nurse became known, she was given a post with the Ambulance de l'Océan (the DePage Hospital) at De Panne, Belgium.

Many of the men Dexter took care of suffered from shell shock, a relatively new phenomenon caused by the improvements in artillery technology and by applying the massive bombardment tactics of sieges to trench warfare. In an effort to find ways of treating this mind-crippling disorder, Dexter returned to England in May of 1916 and began studying applied psychology at the Medico-Psychological Clinic in London. After over a year in the Clinic, Dexter grew impatient and in September of 1917 postponed any further study in order to sign up with a British ambulance section, the Hackett-Lowther Unit. Hackett, an Irish woman who had received the Croix de Guerre, ran the unit's canteen, whereas Loupie Lowther, an Englishwoman commissioned a second lieutenant in the French Army, oversaw the automobile operations, using her own bulky six-cylinder Wolseley as an ambulance.[34]

While awaiting repairs on the Chalmers she had been promised, Dexter prepared for and passed her driver's and mechanic's exams. In late October the car was still not in working order: "The Chalmers is not ready," she wrote her mother, "so I am to drive a new car, a G.M.C. (American). . . ."[35] There was further delay until the scuttlebutt finally promised movement: "Tomorrow," she wrote her mother on November 15, 1917, "I must get into my overalls, and give the G.M.C. a thorough oiling to be ready for the run to Cagny" (where the Hackett-Lowther Unit was to be stationed).[36]

Located just south of the Somme, near the point where the British and French trenches hooked up, Cagny was a busy village when Dexter arrived. "There are heaps of women driving for the English army, and for the French," she observed, adding that

> an American woman spoke to me in the street yesterday
> who has been chauffing for the French near Amiens for
> some months. But there are none [women drivers] who
> are actually driving ambulances attached to an army, go-
> ing up to the postes des secours, and under fire, as we
> shall be.[37]

Despite her expectations, Dexter didn't get to the front-line *postes* on this tour. In fact, in late January the unit was posted at Evacuation Hospital 16 at Creil, which put Dexter and her section even farther away from the trenches. Accordingly, when she learned that her medical associates in England were swamped with work and wanted her back, Dexter was understandably tempted to abandon ambulance driving altogether.

She decided to stay at Creil, however, where she performed some of her most demanding and courageous work.[38] Preparing for their spring assault, the Germans bombed and shelled Creil continuously from February 6 to 10. Dexter worked steadily through the bombardments, driving her GMC — of which she had grown particularly fond — day and night. During the bomb attacks of mid-March, Dexter proved again to be indifferent to danger. She risked her life constantly in her efforts to pick up wounded and deliver them promptly to the Creil hospital. Situated in a railway station, the evacuation hospital was a dreary, unhappy place used not so much to treat patients ("very few dressings are done here," she wrote) as to identify those who stood a chance of being saved. It was "not a hospital with beds," Dexter explained to her mother, "but a Salle de Triage, where the patients come in from the front and are sorted out and sent on to different hospitals. . . ."[39] The largest group of *blessés* she dealt with was destined for the hospital's moribund ward, a fact she fails to reveal to her mother.

On May 12, 1918, Dexter learned that her unit was finally to go to the front. Her excitement was barely containable. Although she could specify only that she was "somewhere in France," a few days later Dexter and the rest of the unit were headquartered near Compiègne, as close to the trenches as any ambulance section.[40] "I wish I could tell you about [a visit] right up to the very front lines," she wrote ecstatically on May 24, conscious of the French censor. "Very few women have yet been so close to that part of the lines," she noted proudly, "and the soldiers stared at me open-mouthed."[41]

Dexter's joy was to be short-lived because her back, which had been bothering her for months, had grown much more painful. "I can't do any walking to speak of," she admitted to her mother in her letter of May 24. In addition, Dexter's sixth month was to end the following day, May 25, 1918. Either she had to re-up for another term, which her back pains discouraged, or return to England, where she herself could receive treatment from specialists while she resumed her work with shell-shock patients. "I *hate* to leave before the coming [Allied] offensive," she wrote emphatically. Dexter returned to the London psychoanalytic clinic in early June of 1918, denying herself any more trips to the front. Leaving when she did, Dexter missed out on receiving the Croix de Guerre awarded collectively to the Hackett-Lowther Unit; she also was not around for the medals and citations distributed to individual drivers at the close of the war.[42]

In contrast, the exploits of the American men who volunteered to drive ambulances in the Great War, especially those who later gained some fame, have been recounted in hundreds of memoirs, biographies, and histories. Indeed, some of the men celebrated for their service as *ambulanciers* didn't drive ambulances at all.

When the huge Euro-Disney theme park opened outside Paris in April of 1992, several U.S. newspapers carried stories about Walt Disney's long-standing devotion to France and to the French people. Offered up in evidence was Disney's work as a volunteer ambulance driver in the Great War. Observing that "Walt Disney's own French connections proved useful to the company's publicists," the *New York Times* pointed out that Disney had served "here [in France] as an American Red Cross driver during World War I."[43] The San Francisco *Chronicle* chose to quote Roy Disney, an executive in the Disney organization, who maintained in his opening-day speech that his uncle Walt "had been a decorated World War I ambulance driver 'only a few miles from here on the Marne River.' "[44] However, according to Walt Disney's biographer, Richard Schickel, Disney did not drive an ambulance in France during the Great War. In the summer of 1918, Disney hoped to join the U.S. Navy, as an older brother had done, but he was too young. In fact, Disney did not turn seventeen until December — and the minimum age for the Navy was eighteen. So, in the autumn of 1918 he applied to the American Red Cross, whose minimum age for its ambulance service was seventeen. Although he was only sixteen, Disney asked his mother to complete and sign the necessary ARC papers, which he altered to make himself old enough for the ARC. The Red Cross accepted him as a driver and sent him off for training. To his dismay, Disney was still in the staging area in Sound Beach, Connecticut, when the Armistice was signed in November. In other words, Walt Disney never did drive an ambulance in the war. However, shortly after the November cease-fire, Disney did go overseas as a driver of a small truck that belonged to an ARC canteen in Neufchatel (France). While working for the canteen, Disney proved to be especially adept at painting insignia and camouflage on cars and camions, a talent that made him some money and persuaded him to go into commercial art when he got back to the States.[45]

Dashiell Hammett's purported career as an ambulance driver has also been stretched. Rather than join a volunteer ambulance unit, Hammett enlisted in the U.S. Army, which, in June of 1918, assigned him to its Motor Ambulance Corps. Hammett himself used to tell of wrecking an ambulance and injuring several people, though military records do not mention the incident. Actually, Hammett's bouts with the flu kept him in various military hospitals on and off for nearly the entire period, until the Army discharged him in May of 1919. He never got overseas.[46]

The African-American painter Henry Ossawa Tanner has also been erroneously identified as a volunteer ambulance driver during World War I. In a biographical essay issued in conjunction with a 1991–1992 exhibit of Tanner's paintings, Leigh Jackson of the Philadelphia *Daily News* states that during World War I Tanner "left painting temporarily to drive an ambulance in war-torn France."[47] Moreover, the chronology that accompanied the Tanner exhibit proclaimed that during the years 1917–1919 "Tanner work[ed] for the American Red Cross in France as an ambulance driver."[48] In fact, the 58-year-old Tanner served in the ARC, but not as an ambulance driver. In 1917, Tanner proposed to the American Red Cross that he start a vegetable farm on the grounds of its hospital at Vittel, the village near which he and his wife were living at the time. The convalescing soldiers, Tanner suggested, could do most of the gardening themselves, yielding fresh produce for the ARC to distribute among its numerous hospitals. Tanner's plan was quickly approved, and he was officially made a lieutenant and attached to the ARC's Farm Bureau. His farm produced potatoes, carrots, asparagus, and other vegetables, as well as some livestock. In October of 1918, Tanner resigned his post to take a more amenable position as an artist in the ARC's Bureau of Publicity.[49]

The novelist and short-story writer Louis Bromfield left Columbia University before completing the spring term in 1917 and "enlisted in the Army Ambulance Service," as his biographer notes, "in order to get overseas sooner."[50] As a member of the army, Bromfield should be distinguished from the drivers who volunteered for the private ambulance units of A. Piatt Andrew, Richard Norton, and Herman Harjes.[51] The term *enlisting* suggests an action different from "volunteering." For one thing, "enlisting" can imply less freedom of choice. When the Selective Service Act was passed by Congress on May 18, 1917, for example, it specified June 5 as the day of registration for all American men between the ages of 21 and 30. This bill encouraged, if not subtly coerced, draft-eligible men to enlist rather than to wait to be drafted. As one army driver put it, "Better 'went' than 'sent.'" When Bromfield enlisted in May, the option of joining the volunteer ambulance sections was still open. It remained open until October of 1917, at which time the sections were absorbed into the American military. Further, at the time Bromfield signed up, the Red Cross was also accepting volunteer drivers for its units in France and Italy. So, although he drove an ambulance during the war, Bromfield did his driving for Section 577 of the U.S. Army Ambulance Corps, and not for any of the volunteer units.

Notwithstanding those who have been wrongly identified as volunteer ambulance drivers, many other American men who subsequently achieved varying degrees of success, mainly in the arts, were true volunteers. Waldo Peirce, for example, joined the American Field Service's Section 3 in November of 1915. The section was billeted in the Thur (valley) town of Mollau, in the Vosges. That

winter Peirce (1907) and other Harvard alums in the section donned
their fur coats and formed "The Harvard Club of Alsace Reconquise"
to celebrate Harvard's football victory over Yale.[52] A large and rau-
cous man who later became an award-winning painter,[53] Peirce was a
favorite among his fellow drivers, particularly for his ability to keep
them "in stitches with his 'Comptes Drolles' [sic]" and his hilarious
parodies of the sycophantic personnel in the Transportation Committee in Neuilly.[54] Struck several times by shrapnel, Peirce was once hit
over the heart, the *éclat* tearing through his heavy winter coat and
ripping into a leather wallet, which he carried in an inside breast-
pocket, where it finally stopped.[55] Peirce's rebellious nonconformity,
referred to obliquely as his "Latin Quarter existence," got him quietly
dismissed from the section in the summer of 1916.[56] However, on
November 3, 1917, according to AFS *Bulletin* no. 18, Peirce was back
in Paris as an enlisted man in the U.S. Army.

Another flamboyant driver was Harry Crosby, a poet and publisher of some importance during the decade following the war. The
scion of a well-to-do Boston family ("Uncle Jack" was J. P. Morgan),
Crosby sailed for France in early July of 1917 aboard the *Espagne*. His
carriage and demeanor thoroughly impressed his fellow passenger
Edward Weeks (who after the war became editor of the *Atlantic
Monthly*). Crosby "was brimming with life," wrote Weeks, voicing an
opinion he would never abandon, "and when he laughed his lips had a
mischievous curl."[57] When they were assigned to AFS Section 71,
which consisted of Fiats rather than Fords, Crosby invited his new
pal Weeks to be his co-driver. During the following months and a
subsequent period near Verdun driving a Ford solo for S.S.U. 29,
Crosby was shaken by the gruesome scenes around him.[58] Returning
to the States with a Croix de Guerre and a Field Service Medal in
1919, Crosby enrolled at Harvard and took an accelerated "war
degree" in 1921. But life in the United States and on Beacon Hill
proved too staid and suffocating for the newly zealous sensualist, who
opted for Paris with his equally adventurous wife, Caresse, and her
two children.

Robert Hillyer, a Harvard classmate of E. E. Cummings' and
John Dos Passos', and a fellow contributor to *Eight Harvard Poets*,
sailed for Paris on May 19, 1917.[59] Hillyer was awaiting assignment
at the Norton-Harjes headquarters in Paris when his college buddy

Dos Passos showed up on July 2. By the end of the month, Hillyer's section (S.S.U. 60), which also included Dos Passos, was sent to a holding station in Châlons-sur-Marne before moving on to the tiny village of Erize-la-Petite on the Voie Sacrée, several miles behind the front lines. To amuse themselves in "the damndest godforsakenest hole I ever landed in" (Dos Passos' words), the two friends tried writing alternate chapters of a long philosophical novel.[60] Except for a couple of tough weeks at Verdun, Section 60 was shuttled from one small, dormant village behind the lines to another during Hillyer's tour of duty. When the unit was faced with militarization in September of 1917, the pacifist Hillyer — his first published work was an antiwar poem in *The Masses* (February 1917) — chose to resign from the ambulance service and return to the States rather than join the army.

By coincidence, James N. Hall's piece, "Carnot's Story," and Charles B. Nordhoff's set of "Letters from the Front" appeared in the *Atlantic Monthly* of October 1917. The two men were both serving in France at the time, but they didn't know each other. Hall was a pilot in the Lafayette Escadrille, and Nordhoff had come to France as an ambulance driver in December of 1916. When his term as *ambulancier* expired in June of 1917, Nordhoff joined the Foreign Legion and was granted his request to be assigned to the Lafayette Escadrille.[61] Yet Nordhoff and Hall, the one a fresh trainee and the other an experienced pilot, still did not meet. Only after the Armistice were the two author-pilots finally brought together, when Dr. Edmund Gros of the American Military Hospital hired them to edit a stack of official records, informal notes, bios, letters, and journals into a two-volume *History of the Lafayette Flying Corps*. A decade later, Nordhoff and Hall published their immensely popular novel *Mutiny on the Bounty* (1932).

Having had two plays produced in 1916 (*Standards* and *Servant-Master-Lover*, both flops), John Howard Lawson sailed for France on the *Chicago* in June of 1917. Aboard ship Lawson met John Dos Passos, another dedicated pacifist. "I had joined the volunteer ambulance service," Lawson said simply, "to avoid the draft."[62] Serving in the same Norton-Harjes section (S.S.U. 60) as Dos Passos and Robert Hillyer,[63] Lawson found new creative inspiration and was soon spending his abundant free time working on what would be his

first successful play, *Roger Bloomer.* Most of Section 60 refused militarization that September and thus were ordered to return to the States,
where they would face the draft. Lawson, however, hid out in Paris for
a few weeks before signing up with the American Red Cross, which
was seeking volunteers to drive in Italy. In November, Lawson and the
new ARC unit, which also included Dos Passos, made the long, exacting drive to Milan via Marseilles, only to discover upon arriving that
the ARC officials in Italy insisted they trade in their light Fords for
sturdy, dual-wheeled Fiats. While driving in Italy, Lawson and a few
other drivers began to voice their pacifist sentiments with increasing
intensity — until they were summarily discharged from the Red
Cross. Lawson made his way to Rome, where he got a job "doing
publicity for the same Red Cross that had just dismissed me forever."[64]

Writers Julian Green, Ramon Guthrie, William Seabrook, and
Sidney Howard all served in A. Piatt Andrew's American Field
Service. Green, who spent most of his postwar career in France
writing highly successful novels in French, drove for S.S.U. 33.
When the unit was faced with militarization, he, like Lawson and Dos
Passos, opted to drive for the American Red Cross in Italy. Ramon
Guthrie, who served in two AFS sections (3 and 9), finished out the
war in the aviation corps, before launching his career as a poet and
professor of French (Arizona and Dartmouth). In 1915, William
Seabrook, one of America's most popular writers from the late 1920s
to the early 1940s, left his wife and a thriving advertising business to
drive an ambulance in France as a member of S.S.U. 8.[65] Gassed at
Verdun, Seabrook was invalided out of the war with a Croix de
Guerre. Sidney Howard, who was to receive the Pulitzer Prize for
drama in 1925 *(They Knew What They Wanted)*, had to wait in Paris
nearly six weeks in the early summer of 1916 for a front-line assignment. Frustrated and dispirited, Howard considered switching to a
Harjes unit, until a spot opened up for him as a driver in an AFS
section, S.S.U. 3, which was stationed in the Vosges. Howard became
so committed to ambulance work that when his term expired in
December of 1916, he re-volunteered for an AFS unit being formed
to go to Salonika in frozen, forbidding Macedonia.[66]

Malcolm Cowley, whose astute insights and criticism would profoundly affect twentieth-century American literary history, went to

Paris in May of 1917, intending to sign up to drive an ambulance for
A. Piatt Andrew's American Field Service. When he got there, however, he and other new arrivals were urged to drive French army
trucks for the Réserve Mallet.[67] Andrew assured the men that switching out of ambulance work would not jeopardize their "status as
gentlemen volunteers."[68] Cowley relented and spent two months
waiting for his assignment, which turned out to be in T.M.U. (Transport Militaire) Section 526. His tour of duty included an extended
stint hauling munitions up from the battle-scarred Aisne toward the
sad Chemin des Dames.

The practice of putting new ambulance drivers in truck sections
had its genesis in April of 1917, shortly after the United States
entered the war. With America now on the side of the Allies, there
was nothing to keep the AFS from providing drivers for French
munitions trucks — something the AFS would not have been allowed
to do during the U.S. policy of neutrality.[69] Furthermore, the AFS
happened to have a surplus of volunteers and a shortage of ambulances at the time.[70] The AFS's shortage of ambulances had several
causes: the U.S. Army had reserved most of the cargo space on
transatlantic ships; the French shops that once constructed ambulance bodies for the AFS were busy building airplanes and tanks; the
renewed U-boat activity sank many transport ships (for example, the
S.S. *Orleans*, which went down in July of 1917, was carrying fifty
Model T chassis and three cases of parts for the AFS). So, Andrew
put the proposition to a unit of mostly Cornell volunteers who had
just arrived: would they be willing to drive French army trucks rather
than AFS ambulances? "They gave us overnight to think about it,"
recalled E. H. Pattison. By May 8 the Cornell Unit to a man had
accepted camion duty. "In the first place," Pattison reasoned, "our
ambulances would not have been ready for a long time. . . . In the
second place, this Service is no more dangerous than the ambulance. . . . And it would be very hard to refuse our services when the
French say they need us. . . ."[71] As the Cornell Unit went, so went
subsequent sections: A unit from Andover consented to driving
trucks instead of ambulances, as did a unit from Berkeley, a
Dartmouth unit, and even a so-called Bastard Unit, which included
men from Yale, Harvard, Williams, Columbia, Chicago, and other
colleges and universities.

Switching from ambulance driving to munitions delivery, however, was not easy for many volunteers and, despite Andrew's urgent pleading, a number of them rejected camion duty.[72] For one thing, driving a munitions truck required that a volunteer agree to a change of purpose. He would not be performing the humane service of attending to wounded soldiers; he would become a direct contributor to the fighting, a combatant, as it were, and accordingly his vehicle could not display the protective Geneva red cross. Those volunteers with individual or institutional sponsors covering their expenses felt compelled to get permission before switching to munitions work. Finally, those who did agree to the new duty had to convince people back home of the rightness of their decision. "I sincerely hope that in case you do not favor my action," one young man told his parents, "that you will refrain from too severe a criticism until I can get home and explain [my decision] comprehensively. . . ."[73] Another member of the Cornell Unit, H. Byrd, made a similar plea: "Please do not criticize my action [he wrote to his parents]. It would be unfair to me, for no one in America has the knowledge that he must have before making any conclusions. It isn't what we came to do, but it is the thing to do."[74]

Duty in the Réserve proved at times to be dangerous and formidable.[75] It called for "courage [and] initiative in the emergencies which constantly occur," according to Martin Samson of the Cornell Unit, who insisted further that "there is nothing humdrum in driving under artillery fire."[76] After returning from a conversation with some of the *camionneurs*, ambulance driver R. N. Sullivan conceded sympathetically that "they have really had a very hard deal of it and looked worn out with hard work. The trucks," Sullivan observed, "are fearfully heavy to drive. . . ."[77]

Other drivers, however, felt that too often camion duty proved tedious and uninspiring. "As a general rule," Pattison wrote, "we load up in the afternoon and then go and wait behind some hill or in some wood where the Boche sausages [lookout balloons] can't see us, until dark, and then go to the depot and unload."[78] Even Sullivan, though speaking in sympathy, noted that the camion drivers "were often kept waiting for eight and nine hours in ammunition parks with nothing at all to do."[79] After several weeks working near the *camionneurs*, William Rice concluded that "the very fact that they work in convoy instead of individually necessarily makes [camion driving] decidedly less interesting" than ambulance driving. "And of course," Rice added, "ambulances go nearer the front than these great ammunition-carrying trucks."[80]

Whether their work was regarded as dangerous or dull, the camion men were nonetheless proud of their direct involvement in and substantive contribution to the war effort. *Camionneur* Dunbar Maury Hinrichs convincingly maintained that by delivering troops and war supplies to the battle zones, the Réserve Mallet "did more to help win World War I than all the ambulance men who ever served. . . ."[81] In the final analysis, the numbers show that most American ambulance volunteers could hardly refuse the French request for camion drivers. When it was absorbed into the U.S. Army at the end of September of 1917, the Réserve Mallet had grown to sixteen T.M. units and over 800 men, all in a matter of five months.

E. E. (Edward Estlin) Cummings' career as ambulance driver fell into two equal parts: three months as a driver (in Paris for a while, lost and loose, but mostly *en repos* with Section 21, bored and bitter) and three months in prison, fascinated and inspired.[82] Cummings decided to volunteer for Richard Norton's ambulance corps on April 7, 1917, the day after the United States declared war on Germany. The Norton family home, where Richard and Eliot grew up, was near the Cummings' home in West Cambridge, a fact that probably prejudiced Cummings in favor of Norton's corps. His decision to join, however, was also triggered by his pacifism and fear of the draft. He chose, he said, "to do something I want to do . . . , versus being forced to do something I don't want to."[83] So, on April 18 he sailed for France out of New York on the *Touraine*, aboard which he met and became close friends with William Slater Brown.

On the boat train to Paris, Cummings and Brown got separated from the other volunteers, who got off at the wrong stop. Finding their way to the Norton-Harjes headquarters at 7 rue François Premier, the two friends left their names and temporary addresses, and merrily set off to sample the City of Light. For the next five weeks they heard nothing from anyone, so they lived like carefree tourists exploring Paris: scouting out the parks, sitting in cafes, surveying nightclubs, attending concerts, inspecting museums and galleries, and — in Cummings' case — falling hopelessly in love with a prostitute.

Eventually the Norton-Harjes staff caught up with them, and Cummings and Brown were dispatched to Section 21, a unit of fifty men and twenty cars, Fiats and Fords, stationed in the quiet Noyon sector. With little military activity to occupy them, Cummings and Brown spent many hours with the *poilus*. Such conduct earned them the ridicule and contempt of the other American drivers who, nominally officers, disapproved of fraternizing with the French foot soldiers — even if the intermingling enabled one to practice his French or get the latest dope about, say, the officially hushed-up mutinies in the eastern Aisne sector. For Cummings the contempt was mutual, in that he found the drivers in his section to be "just the same people we left America to avoid."[84]

Slater Brown's candid letters to his friends back home, intercepted by the censors, aroused the suspicions of the French authorities. On a Sunday late in September, Brown and Cummings were taken in for questioning by the Noyon *ministre de sûreté*.[85] Cummings was about to be dismissed, free and clear of all charges, when he was asked a final, perfunctory question: Did he hate the Germans? "No," he responded, honestly but imprudently. Despite Cummings' attempt to clarify his position — "I like the French very much" — the interrogation resumed with new vigor. The authorities decided to keep the recalcitrant Cummings in the Noyon jail until they figured out what to do with this man who would neither incriminate his friend Brown nor admit to hating Germans. After three days in the local jail, Cummings was taken to the Dépôt de Triage, an internment camp in the town of La Ferté-Macé about a hundred miles west of Paris. This Dépôt was a cold, dirty complex of three former seminary buildings, including a converted chapel, and a surrounding seven-foot stone wall. Every few months an examining commission came by to pass sentence on the imprisoned men and women. Those judged innocent of espionage or treason were freed or deported; those still under suspicion were sent to a concentration camp; and those considered guilty were handed over to military authorities for trial. For the next three months, all spent in this grim, dank prison, Cummings had *"the time of his life."*[86]

Meanwhile, Richard Norton, Cummings' parents, and the U.S.

State Department worked to secure his release. According to the entries in his diary, Richard Norton learned from Herman Harjes on September 18 that Cummings and Brown had been tried and "may be put in an internment camp." On September 28, Norton heard that Cummings and Brown had been kicked out of Section 21, although one of the drivers told Norton personally that presumably Brown got in trouble for an article he wrote for a college newspaper and "Cummings as Brown's friend was tarred with the same brush." On October 4, Norton talked with the Red Cross people and tried to find out what happened to Brown and Cummings. Either the Red Cross had no information, or they stonewalled him. Three days later (October 7), Norton discovered that Cummings and Brown were "being kept by the French under surveillance." Norton's next — and final — entry regarding the matter appeared on November 9, 1917. Norton had just seen the papers containing the charges against Cummings and Brown. Cummings, the documents showed, was guilty only of being a friend of Brown, whose letters quoted the *poilus'* unflattering opinions of their officers and the conduct of the war. Preoccupied with other pressing matters, Norton did not propose any action on behalf of Brown or Cummings, nor did he mention the matter again.

Norton may have lost interest early, but Cummings' father and the ambassadorial staff persisted. As the letters and cables flew back and forth between Cambridge, Washington, and Paris, Cummings was happily studying and making notes about his fellow inmates. Moved by his sympathy for them, he kept a journal in which he captured their sometimes fetching, sometimes frightening, ethnic and personal idiosyncrasies. (This journal served as the basis of his 1920 novel *The Enormous Room.*) The examining commission finally showed up and determined that Cummings should be set free — but not allowed to leave the country. On December 18, however, before this sentence could be administered, a telegram signed by both the Ministry of the Interior and the Foreign Office arrived at La Ferté-Macé. The wire directed that Cummings be released at once and sent directly to the American Embassy in Paris. Then, three days before Christmas of 1917, Cummings boarded the *Espagne* and sailed for New York, an exonerated and free man.

★

In the autumn of 1916, John Dos Passos passed through Bordeaux on his way to Spain. He was shocked by the number of crippled and maimed ex-soldiers he saw.[87] When his father's death took him back to the United States in January of 1917, Dos (as everyone called him) began planning his return to Europe as an ambulance driver for the Norton-Harjes corps. After setting his affairs in order, Dos Passos sailed for France in late June, sensing "a strange break with everything past" and describing himself as "a fiercer pacifist-at-any-price than ever."[88]

When he reached Paris, he was sent directly to the Norton-Harjes training camp at Sandricourt and assigned to S.S.U. 60, the unit that included his new friend Jack Lawson and his college pal "Bobby" Hillyer. Although Section 60 spent most of its time in small villages well behind the lines, for two hellish weeks at the end of August the men were stationed at Verdun and endured gas attacks virtually every night. Nevertheless, Dos Passos wrote, "It's queer how much happier I am here in the midst of it than in America, where the air was stinking with lies and hypocritical patriotic gibber[ish]."[89] When his section was pulled out of Verdun on September 1, Dos Passos wrote his friend Dudley Poore, who was driving for Andrew's AFS, that "curiously enough I adore la vie militaire, apart from my [pacifist] convictions. It's been a long orgy of food and drink with intermittent excitements of shells and assorted horrors."[90]

Having refused militarization in September, Dos Passos was released from duty in mid-October and headed for Paris. When he heard that his old writing buddy from Harvard, Cummings, was being held by the French for some unspecified crime, he tried desperately to track him down. Failing to contact Cummings, Dos Passos then signed on with the American Red Cross, which was sending a unit of volunteer drivers to Italy.[91] While working for the ARC in Italy, Dos Passos continued unabashedly to proclaim his pacifism and generally to irritate his American Red Cross superiors. Although they did not dismiss him as they had Jack Lawson, they did refuse to renew his appointment when his term expired in June of 1918.[92] His appeals to the American Red Cross officials in Rome were of no avail, and when he traveled to Paris to present his case directly to the ARC's European headquarters, he was again denied.

Dos Passos was therefore a man without assignment, and to be in Paris without demonstrable affiliation with some relief agency or military organization was dangerous indeed. The U.S. Army had made the city off-limits to all ambulance drivers who had refused militarization, and the MPs that enforced this policy were, according to one observer, "the toughest, most unreasonable, rudest, and two-faced MPs that ever walked two and two down any street, any-where." To clinch his point, the writer added, "God damn them."[93] Under a headline reading "American Idlers Rounded Up in Paris," the *New York Times* of November 23, 1917, reported the U.S. Army's policy of deporting those who refused militarization. Citing a story that appeared in the Paris *Herald* (Nov. 23, 1917), the *Times* of November 22, 1917, noted that over 200 former ambulance drivers had been discovered in Paris by American military authorities, who took the men's passports and ordered them to "enlist in some branch of the active service" or else "be sent back to America, where they would be dealt with as the circumstances warranted." The article added that "the French authorities will be asked to cancel their [the ex-*ambulanciers*'] residence permits." Dos Passos knew of the policy and its harsh terms, for his diary of February 18, 1918, had noted that *"today we heard of the first case . . . of a man sentenced to death by court martial for refusing to undertake military duty, when drafted and assigned"* (his emphasis).[94] Dos Passos knew that unless he joined the army, an option he had twice rejected, he had no choice but to return home, particularly in that the Red Cross officials told him that if he tried to travel to Spain or Switzerland, they would have him arrested. So, in late July of 1918 John Dos Passos left Europe and sailed for New York, visions of antiwar novels a-dance in his head.[95]

Ernest Hemingway's active service for the American Red Cross lasted from June 4 to July 8, 1918, but he was in the ambulance corps for no more than half of those five weeks. Hemingway's unit, Section 4, operated out of Schio (Italy), a town some fifteen miles north of Vicenza. Because of the relative inactivity of the Schio sector, only three of the unit's cars were put on call each day.[96] Section 4 used mostly Fiats (it had seventeen of them, and only six Fords), two men usually assigned to each car, who traded off the driving. In other words, with only three cars out each day and two drivers per car, no one — including Hemingway — in Section 4 did much ambulancing that June. Hemingway understandably termed the operation "the Schio Country Club."

Eager to see more action than the Schio Country Club afforded, Hemingway left the ambulance service sometime prior to June 22[97] and volunteered to run a front-line, rolling canteen for the Red Cross. Supposedly, Hemingway was to drive around distributing comfort kits and minor items to Italian soldiers entrenched along the Piave (River). However, there was no canteen vehicle at Fossalta, where Hemingway was posted, nor any further instructions about what to do. Itching to get to the front and mingle with the soldiers — despite the enemy troops across the river — Hemingway decided to bicycle to the trenches, packing whatever cigarettes, chocolate, and post-cards he could scrounge up.

About midnight on July 8, an Austrian trench mortar "reformed [him] out of the war," as he says about a wounded and disillusioned character in one of his stories. Hemingway had crawled up to a forward listening post to distribute his cigarettes and chocolate when an incoming five-gallon tin canister hit, the explosion flinging slivered bits of steel rod and shards of flatmetal every which way. Despite the shrapnel that riddled his legs and torso (277 pieces, to be exact, according to Hemingway's count),[98] Hemingway picked up a wounded soldier nearby, slung him over his shoulder, and hobbled some fifty yards before machine-gun fire blasted his right knee. He managed another hundred yards before collapsing. The stretcher-bearers got the immobilized Hemingway to a *smistamento,* the Italian equivalent of a *poste de secours,* from which he was taken by ambulance to a field hospital near Treviso. On July 17, Hemingway arrived by train at the Red Cross base hospital in Milan. After spending the next several months recuperating in Milan and the surrounding country-side, the 19-year-old Hemingway boarded the *Guiseppe Verdi* on Jan-uary 4, 1919, and sailed out of Genoa for New York, wearing a handsome Italian cape and carrying a superfluous cane.

Thus, Ernest Hemingway, who received his wounds and conse-quently earned his medals as a canteen runner, became perhaps the most celebrated ambulance driver of World War I. The truth to tell, he had driven an ambulance only once or twice at the most — and, as geometricians say,[99] QED.

9

Militarizing the Gentlemen Volunteers

Once the United States joined the war in April of 1917, militarizing the American volunteer corps presented no apparent problems for the plan's architects in Washington. Militarization would merely make an administrative transfer of the Norton-Harjes and American Field Service ambulance sections into the U.S. Army Ambulance Service. The AFS camion units would go into the Transport Division of the Quartermaster Corps, and all drivers would be converted into army personnel. Simple.

First, though, one diplomatic matter had to be taken care of. Because the volunteers were currently aiding French troops in the battlefield, Washington was anxious about appearing arbitrary or uncooperative in transferring them into the American Army without French approval. Consequently, American officials used diplomatic channels to ask French officials if they themselves would publicly request the United States to militarize its volunteers. The French hesitated. Trying to break the deadlock, Eliot Wadsworth, Chairman of the American Red Cross, cabled Herman Harjes in April to ask for his assistance: "Anything you can do to get French Government to make request will be helpful."[1] Still there was no response from the French. Worse, when French *maréchal* Joffre traveled to America that spring, he openly urged the United States not to take the volunteers away from his embattled divisions.[2] Finally, a compromise was reached and the deadlock was broken. The U.S. Army would go ahead and militarize the volunteer corps; then it would immediately reassign the sections back to the French.[3] The drivers themselves approved of this solution, for they preferred to remain attached to the French Army. With this diplomatic obstacle overcome, militarization appeared headed for a smooth implementation, and the policy was formalized on May 26, 1917.[4]

Taking over the volunteers was not an urgent or critical matter for the American officials. To be sure, the ambulance corps had much to offer: experienced drivers, cars and other equipment, and on-site training camps and repair parks. Nevertheless, U.S. military authorities figured they didn't really need the volunteer sections, in that by the end of May the army had begun building its own corps of drivers, hundreds of whom were already in training at its camp in Allentown, Pennsylvania. At the time, the American Expeditionary Force was not close to being ready to sail for Europe, so the Yanks would not see hostile action, or need ambulances, for several months. In Washington, that is, militarization was not only treated as a simple, straightforward matter, but decidedly a back-burner affair.

In France, the prospect of militarization evoked a more passionate and immediate response. When word reached Paris in April that war had finally been declared, A. Piatt Andrew was overjoyed. "What we have longed for during these two long years at last came true . . . ," he said. "Driving down the Avenue de l'Opéra, I nearly ran over a man, my eyes were so dimmed by tears. At last!" he exclaimed. "These are great days."[5] The very existence of the American Field Service was a testament to his desire to help France, and the early rumor about militarization excited him. With America in the war, the transfer of his volunteers into the American Army was, to Andrew's way of thinking, a logical and propitious next step. Militarization, he felt, would truly enable the AFS "to attempt great work."[6]

The men in charge of the American Red Cross ambulances, Herman Harjes and Richard Norton, on the other hand, did not like the plan. "Have seen Harjes and Norton," Andrew wired Henry Sleeper in late April, "who don't want their services militarized. . . ."[7] They didn't budge from this position. Two months later, Norton and Harjes discussed the matter with Major Grayson Murphy, who served on President Wilson's War Council, making it clear that they did "not believe in having them [their ambulance corps] taken over by the U.S. army."[8] When Colonel Kean, the man in charge of implementing the army's policy, arrived in Paris the following August, he reported to American Red Cross officials in the States that "Harjes is quite reluctant to see the [ambulance] service militarized . . . , [although] he has been very pleasant about it."[9]

Less congenial was Richard Norton, who was against the idea of militarization from the start. On June 18, 1917, Norton had a talk with Harjes about Red Cross matters: "Harjes told me that the Commission intended to ask me to take charge of all the ambulance divisions." Such a statement would have been precisely what Norton had wanted to hear, for he liked the idea of being in charge and was good at it. He may well have taken Harjes' statement to heart and thereby invested his hopes and ego in the prospect of heading the ambulance divisions. If Norton truly did believe what Harjes had reported, the decision to turn the volunteer sections over to the army must have sorely disappointed him.

Part of his displeasure may have stemmed from the misleading or deliberately ambiguous information from Washington. As strange as it may seem, until the end of July, Norton did not know, or refused to believe, that the program to militarize his and the other volunteer sections had been formally adopted on May 26. On Thursday, July 12, an ARC officer in Paris happened to mention that he had received "a telegram saying all the authorities in Washington were agreed that the Red Cross should be militarized." Yet, for Norton, this news was not definitive, for it spoke of the Red Cross in general, which may or may not have included the Norton-Harjes ambulances, and the form of the operative verb, *should be*, did not predicate any action.

Neither had anyone told Norton's brother, Eliot, who was the stateside fund-raiser and recruiter for the Norton-Harjes units. Replying to a July 13 letter from Wadsworth of the ARC, Eliot Norton wrote, "Of course you understand that if the Sections were militarized and men given pay, the whole nature of the Sections would change."[10] Eliot's conditional *if* indicates that he apparently believed militarization still to be a negotiable issue. In a letter to Henry Davison a few days later, Eliot Norton speculated on some of the potential effects of militarization. "Richard would undoubtedly feel badly, and if he steps out for good and all — as I hope he will *in case the Sections are militarized* — he will have made his mark . . ."[11] [my emphasis]. For Eliot, clearly, the issue was not entirely closed.

Stepping out for good did indeed enter Richard Norton's mind, even though, like Eliot, he didn't believe the final decision had been made. On July 30 Norton met with Harjes and Majors Murphy and Perkins to discuss "a cable [Murphy] had just received, saying *Col. Kean was on his way from America to take command of all the R.C. ambulance service.*" The cable's import, here underscored, surely seems straightforward enough, but Norton and the others were puzzled by its implications. "They [Harjes, Perkins, and Murphy] don't know what it means," Norton observed, sensing something ominous, "but it looks as though it was exit time!"[12]

Colonel Jefferson Kean, a military man assigned to the American Red Cross, had been detached from the ARC early in the summer of 1917 and returned to the army, specifically "to take over and militarize all of the Norton-Harjes sections and the American Ambulance units."[13] When Kean arrived in Paris on August 20, Norton was away at the front with three of his sections, which were working the battlefields around Hill 304, Le Mort Homme, and up beyond Verdun. Norton returned to Paris on August 22, after nearly two weeks in camp with his battle-weary drivers, and contacted Colonel Kean. A meeting was scheduled for the following day, for Norton was eager to meet this man who, according to rumor, had come to Paris with "an absolutely cut & dried scheme which will utterly destroy our existing organization."[14]

The next afternoon, a few military and ARC officials, including Harjes, witnessed the face-to-face meeting of the two principals: Colonel Jefferson Kean, a proud, slow-talking Southern gentleman with military composure and self-assurance, calmly but firmly intent upon taking command of men he did not know and managing an operation he had never seen, aware that he had the support of Wadsworth and Davison, the top men at the ARC, and of General John J. Pershing, the head of the American Expeditionary Force (AEF); and Mr. Richard Norton, with his stiff, unyielding New England bearing, monocled, ever candid, uncowed by military trappings, having just come in from two weeks spent with his beloved gentlemen volunteers among the mud and bodies and blood of the Verdun sector, still reluctant to accept Kean's takeover as an irreversible *fait accompli.*

This meeting, which proved a decisive one for Norton and his men, took place on Thursday afternoon, August 23, 1917. Norton was finally confronted with the undeniable fact that "Col. Kean," as he noted resignedly in his diary, "has been authorized to take over our service & the Field Service." In the face of this news, Norton silently concluded that he would have to step down, although he wasn't yet ready to announce his decision. When Kean offered him a commission as a major in the U.S. Army Ambulance Service that afternoon, "I [Norton] said I must think it over during the night, though I knew perfectly well what my answer would be."[15]

Nor was the session entirely pleasant for Colonel Kean. Although he did most of the talking, Kean impressed no one with either his general intentions or specific plan, which, as he set it out that day, was that the volunteer drivers would be made privates and continue as drivers in the U.S. Army Ambulance Service, for which they would receive a private's standard wage of $36 a month. The section leaders would be commissioned as lieutenants and retain their position as heads of ambulance sections. A captain would be placed over each group of five sections and majors over groups of fifteen sections. Above them would be a few lieutenant colonels, and at the top of the heap would be Colonel Kean.[16] No one deferred to his authority; no one seconded or applauded his proposal. Indeed, he seems to have revealed how little he understood the situation. "Col. K. seemed much surprised," Norton observed, "that we did not greet his plan with cheers. He is plainly very ignorant of the true conditions." That evening, Norton talked the matter over with his aides, who to a man "were exactly of my opinion, that the time had come for us to withdraw."[17] The men asked Norton to submit their resignations along with his the next morning.

The conversation in Kean's office on Friday morning, August 24, was clipped and icy.[18] When Kean read Norton's letter of resignation, the Colonel blanched slightly and expressed the usual regrets, politely voiced in his cordial Southern drawl. Kean then asked Norton to suggest a replacement, and Norton handed him his aides' letters. He had no recommendation, he replied, because his entire staff was resigning. "This is a very serious matter," Kean said, and the meeting was over. Norton wrote in his diary that night: "Perfectly obvious he [Kean] has no notion of what the service is or of how it should be run."

One of the intrinsic flaws of Kean's plans did not show up until well after the army's plan was in place. In the American Army, the ambulance corps came under the Medical Service, and doctors were placed in command of cars, drivers, mechanics, and supplies.[19] Clearly, the U.S. Army was unaware of the changed nature of warfare. In previous wars, when hauling the wounded meant long, slow trips in carts pulled by mules or horses, it was advantageous for the teamsters to have medical training, and for the administrators of this type of transport service to be concerned about medical requirements. However, the advent of speedy motor-ambulances, which could get the wounded back to care centers in much less time, required of the drivers mechanical, rather than medical, aptitude. As William G. Rice observed, the *ambulanciers* trained under the Medical Service at Allentown "were not taught to drive and were not taught French, the two things that make them useful here [in France]."[20] The French Army, by contrast, put its ambulances under the command of the Automotive Service, which functioned much like the modern motor pool and provided transportation for all branches of the French Army, including the Medical Service. "Surgical and medical training had, therefore, no part to play in the ambulance service in France," Andrew noted. Rice agreed that doctors were wasted in the administration of an automotive corps. "In the French Army," Rice said, "the men in command of French automobile sanitary sections know nothing of medicine and everything of automobiles."

Norton's resignation did not end the dispute between the two men. Actually, the friction between Norton and Kean was just beginning to heat up. "He [Col. Kean] is a perfectly pleasant person to deal with, being a gentleman and a southerner," Richard Norton conceded to his brother, Eliot, the day after turning in his resignation. Unfortunately, Norton added, "he has come with an entire misapprehension as to the work here. . . ." Norton then itemized for Eliot the problems he thought Kean had overlooked. Essentially, Norton felt, the authorities in Washington and their emissary, Kean, did not understand "that the whole plant of cars, men and material could not be turned over to him [Kean] at once, lock, stock and barrel."

Among the problems Norton mentioned was one involving his own Section 7, which had originally been, and still remained, incorporated under the laws of England. Militarizing it, Norton claimed, would be a violation of international law, just as would seizing any

English corporation and handing it over to the U.S. Army. Another difficulty concerned the Goelet ambulances used at the Sandricourt training camp north of Paris. Goelet and others, Norton ventured, might not want the ambulances and other material they had donated specifically to the Red Cross, a nonpartisan charity, taken over by the American Army.

In addition, Norton suspected that his carefully screened drivers, whom he sincerely felt to be exemplary in ability, dedication, and conduct, "would not want to be hurled in with the type sent from Allentown [the army's training camp]."[21] Aside from the snobbishness implicit in this remark, there was some legitimate concern. The Allentown men were notoriously ill-prepared for ambulance driving, in that the emphasis of their training had been on "boot camp" activities. When Lansing Warren met his first Allentown trainees, he was surprised that "they had been given rifles and bayonets and were coached in the manual of arms. They drilled and learned infantry tactics. They had never seen an ambulance . . . , and several did not know how to drive a car."[22]

Norton also believed that Kean had not fully considered the limited terms of the volunteers' contracts. Having signed on for six months under the special conditions of the ambulance service, some volunteers might not be able to stay on for the duration of the war, as the army required. Others, by virtue of their age or physical condition, simply might not qualify for the American armed services. For any number of reasons, converting the volunteers into military personnel would not be a simple, straightforward matter. Nor would it be advantageous, Norton concluded, for his drivers to accept militarization. "In fact," he said, "as the whole spirit will be changed [I] cannot advise them to [transfer into the army]."[23]

Norton's strongest objection to militarization pertained to what he called the "volunteer spirit." When one driver complained about having paid his own way to France, as volunteers were obliged to do, only to be drafted into the army, Norton replied that there was "a far deeper and more important reason [for objecting to militarization]: The volunteer spirit will absolutely leave the work." Norton's notion of "the volunteer spirit" is difficult to pin down, but in his letter to Eliot, he suggested that it resulted from giving the volunteers "scope for the use of their intelligence." Norton apparently felt that because the act of volunteering intrinsically presumed a man's thoughtful dedication, a volunteer could safely be allowed to make his own considered decisions. He did not have to be ordered about. Such respect endowed the *ambulanciers'* lives in France with a special cohesiveness, a certain communal *élan*. The volunteer ambulance corps was, to Norton, rather like a gentlemanly service club. Instead of raising funds for widows and orphans, its members performed ambulance duty in France.[24]

In addition to the letter to his brother, Norton wrote a second letter the day after he resigned. This one was intended only for his section leaders, but it reached other eyes and ultimately sealed Norton's fate. In his typically forthright manner, Norton alerted his section leaders to many of the same problems he had raised with Eliot. Once the volunteers had officially transferred into the U.S. Army Ambulance Service, Norton said, they could be recalled from their duty with the French and, if the army chose, arbitrarily ordered to any part of the world. Although literally true, this statement was perhaps unnecessarily alarmist. Norton tended to dispose his drivers against militarization: "I myself were I a young man," Norton said, "would not think of doing it [accepting militarization]." Never one to disguise or suppress his views, Norton wanted his men to understand what he thought they were in for. He felt obliged, therefore, to observe that after militarization, "there will be none of the volunteer spirit left."[25]

Colonel Kean didn't get his hands on a copy of this letter for nearly a month, but he made up for the delay by showing it immediately to General Pershing. In the letter, Norton had said that a militarized driver "will henceforth . . . be nothing more than a mere private." General Pershing was offended by that final phrase, which he felt demeaned his troops. "Saw Perkins," Norton scribbled breathlessly in his diary on September 26, "who said there was the devil of a row over our men not going into the ambulance service & that Pershing was very mad at some of my private letters which Riggs & Stelle had got from men in the sections & given to Col. Kean who had shown them to Genl. P. The latter was particularly mad at my speaking of *'mere privates.'*" Pershing was never to let Norton forget his denigrating phrase.

Norton was told again of Pershing's ire the next day: "Late in

P.M. called by Harjes down to his office owing to telegram from Pershing who is up in the air owing to my reference in a private letter to 'mere privates.' " Although he had worked closely with Norton, Herman Harjes wasn't aware of Norton's "most unfortunate" letter until Kean and Pershing alerted him to it. However, it angered him as well, and on September 28 he wrote the section's leaders, saying that Norton's letter "has my strongest possible disapproval." Harjes' opinion, however, did not carry its usual weight. Harjes had accepted militarization in August and was commissioned a major in the army's ambulance service, but he transferred almost immediately to the infantry, where he served as chief liaison officer of the AEF. Section leaders were therefore skeptical of Harjes, particularly when he made claims such as "I [Harjes] am satisfied that it [ambulance duty] is one of the best services which we can render. . . ." Harjes himself, after all, apparently got out of the army's ambulance service as soon as he could.

Colonel Kean's response to Norton's letter was one of simple outrage, although its intensity was rare for this Southern gentleman. Convinced that the letter was deliberately hostile in its substance and tone, Kean railed about Norton to virtually everyone he could think of who held a position of influence. Having brought General Pershing's wrath down upon Norton, Kean wrote ARC Chairman Wadsworth to say that Norton had shown a "malevolent desire to break things up." The Colonel added that "Major[s] Murphy and Perkins are thoroughly disgusted with him," although Norton's diary suggests their reaction was somewhat less extreme. Moreover, Kean wrote Wadsworth, "General Pershing is thoroughly enraged."[26] In November, Kean grumbled to Mabel Boardman, who was still affiliated with the Red Cross, about "the evil example and counsels of Mr. Richard Norton."[27] To Henry P. Davison, the man who chaired President Wilson's War Council, Kean complained that "Mr. Norton's conduct has been both underhanded and unpatriotic. General Pershing has applied to it stronger adjectives and expletives."[28]

Someone pressured Norton to write his section leaders another letter retracting, or at least modifying, his criticism of the militarization plans. Kean told Wadsworth that "Majors Murphy and Perkins made [Norton] write" it, but Norton never mentioned the matter. In any case, Norton did send a follow-up letter to his section leaders on September 16, using a formal, unpersuasive voice: "Every one of us must help in every possible way to make this transference as easy as possible." Instead of recanting, Norton was simply more diplomatic: "There are, of course, questions in the transference of the volunteer organization to Colonel Kean which are complicated by the rules of our government and the rules of the French."

Norton's private fury was equally as intense as Pershing's and Kean's and, as a matter of principle, he could not allow his convictions to go unvoiced, although Norton's audience was now pretty much limited to his brother. The Colonel, Norton told Eliot, was "utterly out of place." Impossible to pin down and agonizingly slow to act, Kean displayed a hopeless ignorance of the circumstances of the war, Norton said. "I have never seen a job worse thought out, or more miserably handled than the one which Col. Kean is trying to manage," he wrote Eliot. "His whole tone," Norton said, "is that it is unpatriotic of them [the drivers] not to enter *his* service."[29]

Norton was not just making this stuff up. Like many military men, Colonel Kean was a stickler for details and, at times, capable of mind-boggling pettiness. Take, for example, the day Norton asked him to sign the release papers that would allow two of Norton's drivers to go home. One had a broken leg and the other suffered from "several large wounds." Both men were therefore unable to complete their terms as volunteer drivers and, further, their injuries disqualified them from transferring into the army. However, Kean refused to sign the releases.[30] He advised Norton that the drivers first "ought to be examined by an army surgeon as he didn't believe the certificates given by French doctors." A few days earlier, Norton had inquired about militarizing a driver who had lost two fingers at Verdun. Kean said he could not allow the man to transfer into the army "if his wound prevented him from using a saber."[31]

Although strict in dealing with others, Kean seems to have been more lax about his own obligations and promises. During the afternoon meeting on August 23, Kean announced that all section leaders who agreed to be militarized would receive commissions as lieutenants. A few weeks later, however, Norton learned that Kean "today told one of the oldest and best of our leaders that he could not promise this at all, and that generally speaking, all the commissions in the service were to be kept for men coming from America."[32] Norton was not the only one to complain of Kean's duplicity.[33] Alden Rogers and

his fellow *camionneurs*, for instance, had been assured that militarization would not alter their job trucking supplies and munitions to the
front lines. Yet, two days after most of the drivers in Rogers' section
had agreed to be militarized, they were moved to a camp behind the
lines at Soissons. Weeks passed before they saw front-line duty
again.[34]

Colonel Kean's oversights and inconsistencies were not the only
causes of the dissatisfaction with the militarization program. The
army's recruiters, particularly the first ones who went out to enlist the
volunteers, also provoked antimilitarization feelings. The day Norton
visited Section 60 to announce his resignation in person, a carload of
recruiters tagged along. "Picture the scene," John Dos Passos wrote
his friend Arthur McComb:

> an automobile full of gentlemen with large jowls in U.S. Army
> uniforms — Richard Norton courtly in a monocle . . . in front
> a large crowd of ambulance drivers — behind them a much
> shrapnel-holed barnlike structure. An occasional shell
> screeches overhead, makes the fat-jowled gentlemen duck
> and blink and crashes on the riverbank opposite, making
> much dust fly but causing no apparent damage. Mr. Norton
> has just finished his very modest speech ending with the
> wonderful phrase "As gentlemen volunteers you enlisted in
> the service and as gentlemen volunteers I bid you farewell."
> What a wonderful phrase "gentlemen volunteers," partic-
> ularly if punctuated as it was by a shell bursting thirty feet
> away. Thereupon, to be truthful, the fat-jowled gentlemen lost
> their restraint and their expression of tense interest and bolted
> for the abris.

Dos Passos and the other men in the unit declared their unani-
mous decision: "We of the Norton Harjes ambulance refuse the
yoke."[35]

Some of the army's men were inept recruiters, to say the least.
One of the men Kean sent out, according to Norton's diary (October
3, 1917), "could not find his way about and so returned to Paris." A.
Piatt Andrew described another:

> Then a Captain was sent up to Soissons and Jouaignes to
> enlist our men, but on the day of his arrival he displayed
> another American proclivity and became dead drunk. . . .

> [Officially], he died of "heart failure," and . . . being the first
> American officer to die in service in France [received] special
> military honors.[36]

This was the same man who, Norton said, literally "died of
drink." Yet another recruiting officer, according to Norton, told the
volunteers " 'that he'd rather be a private in [the U.S. Army] than a
Captain in any damn foreign army.' The result of this talk," Norton
added, "was that not a single man in the section enlisted."[37] This was
probably the man Andrew described as "a blustering egotistical brag-
gart." He lasted two weeks.[38]

Perhaps accustomed to military machismo, some recruiters tried
to bully the drivers into accepting militarization, as Greayer Clover
noted in his portrayal of the man who visited the Bastard Section of
the Réserve Mallet. When they agreed to drive trucks for the French
Army, *camionneurs* such as Clover tacitly accepted an active part in the
fighting. Their trucks were free game for German artillery and, if
captured, they themselves would be treated like any prisoners of war.
Transferring over to the American Army, that is, was not a big change
for camion drivers. So, like Clover, most of them were receptive to, or
at least open-minded about, the army's takeover.

When Kean's recruiter showed up, the Bastard Section had just
returned from several days hauling munitions through fierce shelling
along the Chemin des Dames. Dirty and exhausted, the men were
suddenly startled by a loud, unfamiliar voice. "Come down here and
enlist in the United States army," the recruiter yelled from the barracks courtyard. "You are not in the French Army and you are not in
the United States army. You are nothing but a lot of Croix de Guerre
seekers — a bunch of outcasts."[39] Needless to say, the bedraggled
Bastards were in no mood to suffer insult from some big-mouth desk-
jockey. In the end, only two of the Bastard Section's sixty drivers
followed the recruiter's orders to transfer into the Transport Division
of the Quartermaster Corps. Over the long term, the Bastard Section's experience proved to be an exception for the AFS ambulance
and camion units. The response of Philip Orcutt's Section 31 was
more typical: "One evening," Orcutt wrote, "a large Pierce Arrow
pulls up beside our cars, parked in a walnut grove. Three American
medical officers step out with clanking spurs. . . ." The chief recruiter

then made a short speech, after which the drivers "form small circles, and discuss the situation." Most of the men, Orcutt reported, decided to accept militarization, recognizing that "the old volunteer Ambulance Service is dead. . . ."[40]

Colonel Kean came to believe that the source of Norton's personal rejection of militarization was an irrational, somewhat envious, suspicion of A. Piatt Andrew. "I understand," Kean wrote Wadsworth after Norton had resigned, "they [Norton and his aides] are unwilling to serve in the same office with Mr. Piatt Andrew, and seem, in spite of my assurances to the contrary, to fear that he will have some advantage over them."[41] Norton's regard for Andrew, or lack of it, can perhaps be discerned in one otherwise insignificant detail. In Norton's diary entries, in all his letters, cables, and other communiqués (notes, memos), and even in his correspondence with Andrew himself, from the first to the last, Norton invariably referred to Andrew as Andrew*s*. Norton's inability to get the name straight seems to reflect a stubborn refusal to acknowledge the man, if not a subconscious rejection of Andrew's individuality.

The first appearance of Andrew's name in Norton's diary — as Andrews — comes in the entry for January 15, 1917. An American organization called The Friends of Serbia had shipped some ambulances to France, intending them for service in Salonika, and Norton resented Andrew's attempt to take charge of these cars. No Norton-Harjes ambulances had ever operated out of Salonika, it should be noted, whereas the AFS had two sections attached to the French Army of the Orient, which was headquartered in the Macedonian city. In fact, six months earlier, when the French were talking about sending more ambulances and drivers to Salonika, Norton wanted nothing to do with the project.[42] Nevertheless, in January of 1917 Norton called Andrew's attempt to claim the Friends of Serbia ambulances "rather rank."

The first mention in Norton's diary of a meeting between these two men appears in the entry of April 24, 1917, when Norton "went with [Harjes] to . . . Major Logan's where Piatt Andrews [sic] joined us." The discussion that afternoon involved militarization, which was then still a rumor, and the possibility of taking on munitions-delivery work for the French. Neither Norton nor Harjes liked the idea of militarization, and Harjes in particular did not want to get involved in the camion service. Norton, however, was not as unreservedly opposed to munitions delivery as Harjes. On May 4, he had a "long talk with Harjes who is strongly against our undertaking the T.M. work [munitions transport], his feeling being the Red Cross should not try to do more than military & civil relief & the sanitary sections. I believe w : could organize the other also." In the end, Norton deferred to H rjes' judgment, and they let Andrew have the camion service all to himself. In so doing, Norton missed out on the medals, citations, and general acclaim that were heaped on Andrew and his truck drivers by the grateful French.

Throughout 1917, Norton grew increasingly resentful of Andrew and the AFS. Norton's diaries and letters suggest that during 1917 he grew gradually more distrustful of Andrew, and at times harbored feelings of jealousy. Although Norton's remarks from the early years of the war reveal that he believed his units superior to those in the AFS, there is little evidence to suggest that Norton initially regarded Andrew as a personal rival. Their relationship seems to have changed about the end of 1916. The two men exchanged a few letters in late 1916 and early 1917, and although these letters were generally professional in tone, they were abrupt and distant, with the chill at times of one-upsmanship. When Norton wrote Andrew, for example, to ask if a certain man had served the AFS ably, he pointed out that the prospective driver, who had left Andrew's ambulance corps, was applying to join his, Norton's, corps. *Touché*. Following the August 23 session in which Kean presented his militarization plan, Norton noted that Kean "offers me a major's commission — along with Piatt Andrews!!" The two exclamation points suggest sarcastic incredulity. Two weeks later, when the possibility arose of putting Norton in charge of the Red Cross ambulances to be sent to Italy, Norton declined, noting in his diary that he wanted "nothing to do with [the ARC's Italian campaign] if the Field Service had anything to do with it."[43] Norton, to put the matter simply, could not abide the notion that Andrew was his equal: "I would refuse under any circumstances," Norton wrote his brother, "to be put in this or any other service on a par with a man like Andrews."[44] Andrew was nothing more, Norton said derisively, than "a scamp."[45]

Actually, Colonel Kean had fed Norton's innate suspicion of Andrew. During the August 23 session, according to Norton's diary,

Kean "plainly stated that Andrews had neither the volunteers nor money sufficient to continue his service and did ask to have it taken over by the army." In the letter to his section leaders, Norton passed along Kean's information: "Mr. Piatt Andrews, who as Colonel Kean told us yesterday, has no longer the money nor the power to continue his Field Service and so wanted that Service taken in by the army."

However, Kean's account of Andrew's predicament was untrue. Henry Sleeper explicitly told Andrew in late April that a surplus of "splendid looking" volunteers had been applying at an average of seventy-five per week at his AFS recruiting office in Boston.[46] Driver C. Bryan counted a hundred new volunteers at the AFS Paris offices during each of the first two weeks of July.[47] Neither was there a shortage of capital, in that Andrew had sufficient funds in the spring of 1917 to order 500 Model Ts. According to Norton's diary of May 30, the head of the *Service Sanitaire*, Captain Aujay, confessed to blocking this order, so as to force Andrew to assign his new recruits to camion sections. Indeed, over $300,000 remained in the AFS budget when Andrew's service was formally disbanded in October of 1917.[48] The AFS, in short, was thriving, not failing. Norton's eyes could have told him as much, for when Kean arrived in August the AFS had thirty complete sections in the field. It is difficult to understand how Colonel Kean might have deduced that the AFS was in trouble, in that as commander of the army's militarization program he had all of the facts at his fingertips. It is equally difficult to understand why Kean would concoct such a story. Having known of Norton's distrust of Andrew, Kean surely realized that Norton would be inclined to resist any program Andrew supported. Perhaps Kean hoped that if Andrew's AFS was seen as benefiting from militarization, Norton would seek similar benefit for his ambulance corps and urge his drivers also to accept militarization. It is also possible, though unlikely, that when various options were first being considered, Kean misinterpreted Andrew's enthusiastic support of militarization as disguised pleas for help.

In any event, Norton eagerly believed Kean's erroneous account of Andrew's action, for it jibed squarely with his own assessment of Andrew. "Nobody who knows Andrew's character," Norton said, "will doubt for an instant that he used all possible influence to have the Red Cross taken over, so that it would not appear, what is fact, that his service had failed but that ours was a success."[49] To Norton's way of thinking, Andrew's involvement in the militarization program explained its inherent desperation and wrongheadedness.

Yet, Norton had been clearly told by his brother that it was their ambulance service, not Andrew's, that was losing volunteers. As early as March of 1917, Eliot Norton reported to the American Red Cross that the recruiting figures had severely fallen off and the future was no more promising. The causes of the difficulty, as Eliot laid them out, were threefold. For one thing, he said, the rigorous selectivity of the Norton-Harjes organization, as opposed to the low standards of the AFS, made for a small pool of acceptable volunteers. Yet the Nortons had always claimed that their outfit was more selective than Andrew's, and so its pool of prospects should have always been smaller. Eliot noted further that since the diplomatic break with Germany in early February, "practically no applications have come through the American Red Cross. . . ." The standard practice of local Red Cross chapters was to send the applications of candidates for ambulance work to Eliot's New York office. This source of applicants had apparently dried up, and, as Eliot conceded, "other applications have fallen off proportionately." He also explained that he detected a reluctance among likely prospects to make any commitment to the Red Cross ambulance service in March, now that war seemed imminent. Applicants patriotically eager to serve overseas presumably preferred to go over as fighting men, rather than as Red Cross volunteers.

Eliot also told the ARC that he had "advised Harjes and Richard that I thought it was going to be difficult to keep up their sections to their full numbers. . . ."[50] Despite this explicit information to the contrary, Norton chose to believe it was the AFS whose recruiting figures were down and that therefore Andrew was happy with the militarization program. Norton seemed willing to believe anything derogatory about Andrew and the AFS. In his diary for August 17, for instance, Norton wrote of hearing that the men in Andrew's Section 31 "lost their nerve & left their cars with wounded while they took shelter." The rumor seems to have pleased him. Also, when he was out explaining his resignation to his own sections, he was not disappointed to learn that "in all the sections are many who refuse to go into any service in which Andrews is an officer" (diary, August 29).

In fact, Andrew had mixed feelings about the matter. On the one hand, he was fiercely loyal to his AFS units, which he had once hoped would provide the ambulance service for the entire American Army. On the other hand, Andrew was resolutely devoted to France. If transferring his AFS men into the American Army would help defeat Germany, the demands of militarization must be accommodated, whatever the cost. Politics and power, two forces Andrew had always respected, were at play here: the preservation of French political and cultural integrity depended on the American Army's might. Consequently, his personal regard for the AFS or for his own well-being and reputation was of secondary importance. So, Andrew submitted to and, at least outwardly, supported militarization — at times even promoting it, as when he visited Alden Rogers' camion section and "painted golden pictures of life in the American army."[51]

But all was not golden for Andrew. Once the militarization process began, Andrew saw his entire organization, the AFS, dissolved and its ambulance service taken over by the U.S. Army Ambulance Service (USAAS). Positions of command were given to regular-army men, while Andrew was nudged out of the way — his experience discounted, his counsel largely ignored. "We have had our big days," Andrew wrote Sleeper, "and are now in the midst of many disappointments, but we have been doing everything possible to facilitate the militarization of the Field Service."[52] Although promoted from major to lieutenant colonel, Andrew took a backseat until the end of the war, frustrated and disappointed perhaps, but ever supportive of the cause of France.

Whereas Richard Norton was a casualty of his own stringent principles and unrestrained candor, A. Piatt Andrew was a different type of war victim. He ended up voluntarily suppressing his identity and experience as the organizer, administrator, and champion of a vastly successful ambulance service. He muted his private feelings about the instances of ignorance, ineptitude, and corruption around him, all the while gamely supporting the agencies of power and political expedience, however professionally clumsy or personally demeaning they might be, in the hope that ultimately France would have her victory.

Given the ubiquitous power and arrogance of the army, there was little Andrew could do to influence its conduct, other than make suggestions and offer advice. Unlike Norton, who could not abide foolishness, Andrew refrained from protesting the folly of the American Expeditionary Force once it had made its preposterous decisions. For example, contrary to his advice about ambulances, the AEF decided to use Ford light-truck chassis with compartments that could accommodate eight seated or four recumbent patients.[53] These vehicles proved, as Andrew had predicted, cumbersome and inefficient. Only after "several thousand Ford ambulances of an inconvenient and less practical model had been sent to France," Andrew observed, did the Americans join the French and others in adopting the original American Field Service model. The ambulance designers also failed to account for such details as the length of French stretchers. Wounded soldiers brought by French *brancardiers* to U.S. Army ambulances had to be painfully transferred to shorter American stretchers before they could be loaded. Some impatient USAAS drivers sawed off the handles of the French stretchers, which played havoc with the hospital orderlies' attempts to unload the *blessés* and carry them into the wards.[54]

Due in part no doubt to Andrew's ostensible support, the AFS men were generally receptive to militarization, and by the first of October, 1917, the transfer of those drivers who had agreed to be militarized was completed. Recruiting had gone so well in the AFS camion units, in fact, that in mid-September U.S. officials declared "the transport sections of the American Field Service will practically become the nucleus of the transport service of the American army in France."[55] In all, 304 *camionneurs*, or roughly 38 percent of the drivers (over 800) in the sixteen Réserve Mallet units, transferred into the AEF's Transport Division.[56] The ambulance sections had an even higher percentage. Henry Sleeper, who, like Andrew, regretted "having to yield all rights of administration" to the army, boasted nevertheless that a total of 600 of the 1,000 American Field Service ambulance drivers had joined the USAAS.[57] Colonel Kean and the army calculated that about 50 percent of the AFS ambulance drivers made the switch to the USAAS, which was "a great deal better" than the Norton-Harjes percentage.[58]

Although the exact figures are not available, the thirteen Norton-Harjes ambulance sections provided the USAAS with scarcely any drivers. As he noted in his journal on September 18, 1917,

AFS driver William Yorke Stevenson heard that "the Norton-Harjes crowd have quit 'en masse.' "[59] Stevenson's impression is supported by G. R. Gaeddert's official *History of the American Red Cross*: "Apparently only a small percentage of [Norton's] men enlisted with the Medical Corps of the United States Army when Colonel Kean came to take over."[60] Indicative of Kean's disdain for Norton, the Colonel didn't bother to keep count of the drivers from Norton's sections who were militarized.

The Norton-Harjes and AFS drivers who did transfer into the army's ambulance and transport corps discovered that making the psychological switch wasn't easy, because giving up the volunteer identity was difficult. Being a volunteer had been a source of honor and pride for these men; it gave them distinction. In a way, that is, Richard Norton was wrong: the club spirit, the sense of being part of a special and unique group, actually intensified and took on new significance when the volunteer sections were abolished. Ex-volunteers identified themselves in their letters to the AFS *Bulletin* by their old section numbers, including their new USAAS numbers parenthetically, if they bothered to give them at all. Former American Field Service drivers made jokes about the new USAAS sections. One driver said that if one looked closely at an ex-AFS man's uniform, "ten to one somewhere on [it] will shine forth the number of his old Field Service Section."[61] Ex-volunteers made sure their old AFS or Norton-Harjes section numbers on their cars could be made out, even faintly, beneath new army paint.

In another way, though, Richard Norton was correct: militarizing the body led to a militarization of the soul. Although the memories, like the old numbers beneath the paint, may have lingered, something vital, some energizing force, some *spirit* disappeared when the army took over. Drivers' memoirs from the transition period tend to close off with militarization, the newsy letters to hometown papers diminish in number, and the private journals or diaries become abrupt and terse.[62] The change is understandable, after all, in that the leisure hours, which had been spent jotting down impressions and transposing notes into letters, were now filled with daily routine: inspection, drill, KP duty, or jumping jacks and other P.T. busyness. Army life was a full-time occupation, and the Leisure-Hours Writer's Club was closed for the duration.

Before this transformation of spirit was finished, however, some drivers managed to capture in their private diaries or published memoirs certain moments from the transition, freezing in language, as it were, last-second views of volunteer life as the army began to take over. They wrote of early encounters, serene or fiery, with military personnel; told of lugubrious farewells to buddies who abhorred war and had scoffed at militarization; recounted anxiety-ridden internal debates with themselves about what to do; depicted hundreds of huge new army ambulances rolling, big-wheeled and unspoiled, into their miserable little encampment. Such incidents gave the world its last glimpse of the character and life of these gentlemen volunteers.

One day in late September of 1917, a chauffeur-driven sedan arrived unannounced at the camp of S.S.U. 18, bringing an army recruiter to sign up the section's drivers. The recruiter found the section gathering as if the drivers had expected him, and yet curiously indifferent, indeed oblivious, to his presence. The drivers were milling about in the graveled courtyard of their *cantonnement* wearing their spiffiest uniforms, nearly all with medals and some with medals on their medals. Their cars were lined up around the perimeter of the barracks square, meticulously scrubbed but withal rusty and dented and scraped, a few with frames noticeably sprung, others with fenders twisted or missing. The ambulance compartments had been scoured free of all smells and human detritus. Going about his business of recruiting the assembling drivers, the army man discovered that by coincidence the section was scheduled that afternoon to receive the Croix de Guerre, to be presented by a contingent of distinguished French officials and highly decorated *mutilés* in a full-dress ceremony complete with bugle and drums and many-colored flags.

During the previous month, Section 18 had been evacuating the casualties of the first mustard gas attack in the Verdun sector. The drivers, like the *poilus*, hardly knew what they were dealing with. The gas didn't immediately invade the respiratory system and kill a person directly; this new, highly lethal weapon (dichlor-ethyl-sulfide) delayed its effect, eventually producing (usually) large blisters and weeping lesions in the skin that grew and festered to become excruciatingly painful and sooner or later disabling, possibly fatal. Because mustard gas interacts chemically with moisture, it affects the lungs and the saliva in and around the mouth — and, unbearably, the damp, private places on one's body. As the *poilus* discovered, mustard gas is slow to vaporize, staying around for days on the ground and clinging to bandage wrappings, generally filtering into cracks and clothes everywhere, remaining inert until it is disturbed and finds a spot of moisture. Perhaps then it settles on the perspiring brow of an un-suspecting *ambulancier.* The section's Croix de Guerre, in other words, was indisputably deserved.

The drivers of Section 18 stood smartly, attentively, during the speeches and ceremonies that afternoon in the brilliant slant of an autumn sun, after which the section's slate-blue Tin Lizzies quietly pulled out in pairs, to pass beneath the still flags and join the closing processional, the *petites voitures* bouncing easily along, cartoonlike, high-axled and merry, behind the large, low touring cars of the illustrious French officials and the funereal sedan carrying the army's recruiter, and so, in the words of the section's diarist . . .

> . . . *the little American ambulances chugging slowly along in the rear of the procession slipped over the hill and back to their park and thus Section 18 of the American Ambulance Field Service, as a voluntary organization, passed out of existence.*[63]

Epilogue

After the war, A. Piatt Andrew and many of the 2,437 volunteers who served in his ambulance and camion sections, less the 127 who lost their lives, resurrected the American Field Service as a historical and charitable organization. In addition to starting a library and collecting historical documents, the revived AFS initiated a program to enable American students to study in France, and French students in the United States. The scholarship program was funded by the $300,000 left in the coffers after the AFS was disbanded, and by personal contributions, such as the earnings from Georges Clemenceau's 1922 American lecture tour. The former French Premier made this sizable donation out of gratitude for the work of Doc Andrew and the American Field Service.[1]

In 1921, Andrew renewed his political activity and won the congressional seat formerly held by the man who had defeated him in the Republican primary of 1914, Augustus Peabody Gardner. The people of the Sixth Congressional District of Massachusetts elected Andrew to the House of Representatives for seven consecutive terms. Andrew died at his home in Gloucester at the age of 63 on June 3, 1936.

Transferring into the American Expeditionary Force as a major in 1917, Henry Herman Harjes organized and ran the entire liaison service of General Pershing's army. Harjes was the perfect man for securing cordial, efficient cooperation between the French and the Americans. He had diplomatic skills, influential American and French contacts, and unique leadership experience as the former director of the American Relief Clearing House and as the head of his own ambulance corps. Harjes was wounded in August of 1918, promoted to lieutenant colonel two months later, and discharged in May 1919. Returning to his prewar position as Senior Partner of Morgan, Harjes & Co in Paris, Harjes was able to help stabilize the French franc and facilitate Belgian and French reconstruction through his financial savvy and his generous, but judicious, lending policy. Harjes, who had received the Croix de Guerre twice and the Order of the Crown of Belgium, was made a chevalier (1917) and an officer (1919) of the Legion of Honor. Harjes died from a fall while playing a polo match in Deauville, France, on August 21, 1926. He was 51.

Early in September of 1917, when Richard Norton was squabbling with Colonel Kean, he wrote his brother, "I am confident that I can find some work to do which will enable me to use my powers better than if I were to enter Col. Kean's service."[2] Apparently, Norton underestimated the number, vindictiveness, and clout of his enemies. Late in October of 1917, after the militarization process was over, Major Perkins reported to General Pershing that the French Service de Sanitaire had asked the Red Cross to set up a new, nonmilitary ambulance service for five or six of its base hospitals, with Norton in charge. The General fiercely insisted that Colonel Kean and the army should handle all of the ambulance units. Allowing Norton to manage such a unit, the General said, "would be a slap in the face to the army!"[3] To the befuddlement of the French, Pershing and the compliant ARC officials suspended the plan until Norton's part in it could be eliminated. When Major Perkins, who worked for the Red Cross, advised Norton that Pershing had blocked the new service because Norton was involved in it, Norton "asked Perkins whether this being the case he could give me [Norton] any work at all to do in the Red Cross & he said no, he couldn't. So I have received the order of the boot & must pack and go to England."[4]

As of this date, November 1, 1917, the day Norton "received the order of the boot," over three years had passed since Norton and his original American Volunteer Motor-Ambulance Corps first sailed from Folkestone to Boulogne. Pershing had been in France fewer than five months, and Norton's replacement, Colonel Kean, seventy-two days.

Before Norton was able to arrange his return to England, French officials, who still held him in high regard, requested one last favor of him. They needed someone they could trust to carry out a highly secret investigation for them. Over the previous months, several instances of what the French suspected to be sabotage had occurred along the French coast around St. Nazaire. The French were worried that an influx of new German agents or international provocateurs might be causing the trouble. The espionage and sabotage in the area didn't disturb General Pershing as much as the presence of legal prostitutes. (A copy of Pershing's memorandum of complaint to Commandant Sayles is inserted in Norton's diary between November 24 and 25.) Commandant Sayles, in charge of coastal security, asked Norton to seek out and identify any likely espionage agents and to make note of any suspicious activity in Nantes and St. Nazaire. Norton finished his counterintelligence assignment by mid-December and turned over to Sayles the names of a few suspects and the locations of several underpatrolled areas along the coast. His usefulness in France over, Norton left Paris on December 28, 1917, and arrived the following noon in London, where he happily reported that "everything [is] all right at my house." But everything was not all right with Norton himself. He died of meningitis on August 2, 1918, three months before the Armistice, at the age of 46.

Notes

INTRODUCTION

1. John S. Haller, Jr., *Farmcarts to Fords: A History of the Military Ambulance, 1790–1925*, p. 147.

2. Paul B. Williams, *The United States Tennis Association and the World War*, p. 255.

3. Stephen Thorn, "Notes, Experiences, and Suggestions . . . ," p. 415.

4. A good discussion of the types and functions of the various hospitals appears in Haller, pp. 154ff.

5. J. Halcott Glover, *Friends of France*, p. 162.

6. Naturally, there were other early volunteer groups that were not American, such as the Friends' Ambulance Unit, which Philip Baker had put together in London in August of 1914, and the group organized by Dr. Hector Munro, a celebrated British feminist, who included four women drivers (one an American) in his team. There was also the private Allies Field Ambulance Corps, whose English organizers bailed out when they were accused of espionage, surreptitiously abandoning three women drivers at the Belgium front. All three, incidentally, narrowly escaped the German advance and returned to England. One of the drivers, Olive King, was soon back in Europe as a volunteer driver for the Scottish Women's Hospitals (cf. King, *One Woman at War*, 1986).

CHAPTER ONE: THE HARJES FORMATION

1. Paul-Louis Hervier, *The American Volunteers with the Allies* (Paris: Edition de *La Nouvelle Revue*, 1918), p. 228. An article in the Paris edition of the New York *Herald*, which Hervier cites, sets the date of the requisition as August 12, 1914.

2. The conditions are mentioned in a speech by Myron T. Herrick, former U.S. Ambassador to France, quoted in *Literary Digest* (December 2, 1916), p. 168.

3. L. D. Geller, *The American Field Service Archives of World War I, 1914–1917* (New York: Greenwood Press, 1989), p. 1.

4. The Ambulance Committee was "in full control of the management" of the Military Hospital (cf. "General Order No. 1" in the papers of Samuel Newell Watson, in the Hoover Institution Archives, Stanford University). The Rev. Dr. Watson chaired the committee (W. S. Dalliba was the Honorary Chairman), which also included L. V. Benét, Charles Carroll, F. W. Monahan, and L. V. Twyeffort. One of the Hospital Board's attorneys (Charles B. Samuels) advised Dr. Watson that once the building construction was completed, the Committee's role had been legally reduced to "a very minor position," one of "a single, competent superintendent" (cf. letter from Samuels to Watson, October 24, 1914; Watson papers; Hoover Archives).

5. Cf. 2/22/15 letter to John J. Hoff; Watson papers; Hoover Archives.

6. Geller, pp. 2–3; Albright, *The Field Service*, pp. 30–31.

7. Brown, in *The History of the American Field Service*, George Rock, ed., p. 7.

8. Brown, quoted in Howe, ed., *The Harvard Volunteers in Europe*, pp. 77–78. In the Military Hospital's report filed with John J. Hoff in February of 1915, the date of the first load of *blessés* is given as September 6 (Report of Operations of the American Ambulance; Watson papers; Hoover Archives, p. 1).

9. See "The Backwash of Battle," pp. 300–302, 304; Hildebrand, pp. 624–625; and Howland, pp. 170–173.

10. The "Report of Operations of the American Ambulance," in a 2/22/15 letter to John J. Hoff (Watson papers; Hoover Institution Archives), puts the matter this way: "The utility of these special cars [ambulances] having been amply demonstrated in actual service . . . , and a sum of money having been offered for the particular purpose of purchasing and equipping several similar cars . . . , the Ambulance Committee decided, after careful consideration, to add this new department to the work already carried on (by the American Military Hospital)," p. 20.

11. The hospital was justifiably proud, for instance, of being the first to establish a department of dentistry, complete with modern dental operating rooms. Herrick [*Literary Digest* (12/2/16), p. 1468] mentions the dental department.

12. Cf. Geller, p. 2. There are numerous recorded anecdotes about the French soldiers' pleasure when they learned that they were being taken to the American Military Hospital. See, for instance, A. S. Hildebrand, "La Chapelle Station," *Outlook* (August 22, 1917), p. 625.

13. See H. Howland, "The American Flying Squadrons," *The Independent* (May 1, 1916), p. 172. The other major criticism, Howland noted, was that "the Americans spoil the French boys when they fall into their hands." Regardless, 95 percent of those treated were reported to have been saved, an unusually high ratio [Sheehan, *Munsey's Magazine* (November 1916), p. 198]. Cynics, however, claimed that the high success rate was the result of the hospital's policy of keeping patients long after the time they could have been safely released. In that beds were filled by men who didn't need to be there, the argument goes, the hospital lowered its risk by being unable to accept *blessés* who needed treatment (and who might reduce the success ratio, if the treatment failed).

14. *Outlook*, Dec. 6, 1916, p. 747.

15. Harvey W. Cushing, *From a Surgeon's Journal* (Boston: Little, Brown, 1936), p. 35. Cushing sets the opening of the hospital as August 7, a date much too early (the Germans were still stalled at Liège). Richard Norton's diary dates the opening as August 27, and in that he was directly involved in helping Mrs. Depew from time to time, he was in a position to know (see Chapter Two).

16. Personal diary of Richard Norton, entry of November 14, 1914. Norton had spent the 13th at Mrs. Depew's empty hospital.

17. Edward D. Toland, *The Aftermath of Battle* (New York: Macmillan, 1916), p. 3. Born in Philadelphia, Toland had a Litt.B. from Princeton. After helping organize the Harjes Formation, he left Europe to marry Esther Howell in the States in June of 1917. He spent the remainder of his life as headmaster of his alma mater, St. Paul's School, in Concord, N.H. In addition to *The Aftermath of Battle* (1916), which is an edited version of his 1914–1915 European diary, this unprepossessing, down-to-business man published only one other book, *Choosing the Right Career* (1925).

18. Toland, pp. 19, 23–24.

19. Toland, p. 20. Toland himself estimated a total of 900 empty beds throughout the city.

20. Ibid., p. 34.

21. Ibid., p. 28.

22. For a discussion of the machine gun and its use at the Battle of Somme, see John Keegan, *The Face of Battle* (New York: Viking, 1976), pp. 228 ff.

23. Haller, *Farmcarts to Fords*, p. 161.

24. For a commentary on the principle of *l'attaque à outrance*, see William R. Griffiths, *The Great War* (The West Point Military History Series; Wayne, New Jersey: Avery Publishing Group, 1986). Alistair Horne, in

The Price of Glory, notes the similarity between this principle and the celebrated slogan voiced by Danton during the 1792 defense of Verdun: *"il nous faut de l'audace, encore de l'audace, toujours de l'audace,"* p. 18.

25. Marc Ferro, *The Great War, 1914–1918* (New York: Military Heritage Press, 1989), p. 30.

26. Toland, p. 34.

27. Toland, p. 50. At the Claridge Hotel, meanwhile, the hospital service was organized by two British doctors, Garrett Anderson and Flora Murray, and was in full operation in September of 1914 (cf. McLaren, 1917).

28. Ibid., pp. 65–66.

29. Ibid., p. 48.

30. Ibid., pp. 62–63. The rationale for banning American drivers from the front was more complex than a simple desire to prohibit meddling, as A. Piatt Andrew would discover a few months later.

31. The British War Office was equally strict, as demonstrated by the experience of the Friends' Ambulance Unit, which was formed by Philip Baker in England in August of 1914. Baker and Geoffrey Young, a Quaker war correspondent who had seen the bloody consequences of the war in Belgium, persuaded Sir Arthur Stanley, head of the British Red Cross (BRC), to allow the Friends' Ambulance Unit to serve in Belgium under the auspices of the BRC and The Order of the Hospital of St. John of Jerusalem, popularly called the St. John Ambulance Association. In addition to several tons of medical supplies that were collected, eight ambulances were obtained and a staff of forty-three (including three doctors and six wound dressers) was hired. When the ambulance unit arrived in Dover on August 30, "they were told that the Belgians had been withdrawn from the line and that there was no need for them 'over there' " (van Shaick, *The Little Corner Never Conquered*, p. 166). The next morning the Quakers sailed away. "A terrible sight met their eyes" in Dunkirk. "In the half-darkness of these bare sheds lay hundreds upon hundreds of wounded men stretched on the straw-covered floor . . . , and here and there a few British and Germans. They had been there, many of them, for three full days and nights, practically unattended, mostly even unfed . . ." (Tatham and Miles, eds., *The Friends' Ambulance Unit*, p. 7). Despite the official military position that the Friends' Ambulance Unit wasn't needed, it clearly was, and the policy was changed in the spring of 1915. These indefatigable drivers proved to be in great demand throughout the remainder of the war.

32. Toland, pp. 79–80.

33. Ibid., pp. 82–83.

34. Ibid., p. 89.

35. Ibid., p. 89. Stephen Thorn, a leader of the Harjes Formation in the early years, lists no Ford ambulances until September of 1915 ("Notes, Experiences, and Suggestions . . . ," p. 426).

36. Ibid., p. 90.

37. Mitchell, *With a Military Ambulance in France 1914–15* (privately printed, 1915), p. 48; the letter is dated December 7, 1914. Mitchell's book was published anonymously, although at a couple of points in the text, the narrator is referred to as "Mitchell." Edwin Morse, *The Vanguard of American Volunteers,* 1919, explicitly identifies the author of *With a Military Ambulance* as Clarence V. S. Mitchell.

38. Toland, p. 131.

39. Ibid., pp. 133–139. Toland's book says the date of the transfer was November 2, which is probably a typographical error, for the preceding entry in the book (in his edited diary) is also dated November 2. There is another typo in this section: the village Warsy is spelled "Wassy." The entry just following this one in Toland's diary is dated November 6. Mitchell's account of the same events is set on November 5.

40. Toland, pp. 145–146; November 14.

41. Mitchell, p. 17. When Luther Nelson, another driver, decided to sign on with Harjes, he had entirely different motives. He chose Harjes' operations, rather than A. Piatt Andrew's American Field Service (AFS), Nelson said, partly because "the men there [in the AFS] are not as well taken care of as in the Harjes Corps." Another reason was that Nelson hoped if he "did good work with them [the Harjes Formation] now, there would be a good chance of getting a permanent job with [the Morgan-Harjes Bank] after the war" (6/9/16 letter to his sister; AFS Archives).

42. Ibid., p. 35. The comment about seeming to be part of the French army comes from Mitchell's letter dated November 9, 1914.

43. Ibid., p. 47. "F— C—" was Francis Colby, who had once driven for the American Military Hospital. When the Hospital de-emphasized its transportation service, Colby went to Belgium (in November of 1914) to form his own ambulance group.

44. Ibid., p. 79; Feb. 23, 1915.

45. Hervier, p. 230.

46. Mitchell, p. 68. He visited Mrs. Whitney's hospital on February 9, 1915.

47. Ibid., p. 74.

48. Thorn, "Notes, Experiences, Suggestions . . . ," pp. 422–423.

49. "The Genesis of the American Ambulance Service with the French Army, 1915–1917," *The Military Surgeon* (October 1925), p. 367.

CHAPTER TWO: RICHARD NORTON AND THE AMERICAN VOLUNTEER MOTOR-AMBULANCE CORPS

1. William Yorke Stevenson, *From Poilu to Yank* (Boston: Houghton Mifflin, 1918), p. 133. Stevenson drove for A. Piatt Andrew's American Field Service. Andrew once remarked of Richard Norton that he really didn't know him except for a brief previous meeting, "but [he] wears a monocle and that is enough" (letter to Henry D. Sleeper, 20 December 1916; in the archives of the American Field Service in New York).

2. John Dos Passos, "Introduction," *One Man's Initiation: 1917* (Ithaca, N.Y.: Cornell University Press, 1969), p. 25.

3. The diaries from September 1914 to December 1917 are held among the Richard Norton Papers in the Houghton Library, Harvard. When the text makes the date of a diary entry clear, the date is not repeated here in the notes.

4. Diary entry of September 23, 1914.

5. Diary entry of October 8, 1914.

6. Diary entry of November 28, 1914.

7. Diary entry of October 9, 1914.

8. This contradiction — a military man working for the Red Cross — was never fully explained. On April 23, 1915, Norton notes that he "saw Cuff at lunch time [Captain Cuff was with British Military Intelligence] . . . and he says the French authorities can not understand how a Lt. Col. like Barry can be doing Red Cross work. So far as that goes neither can I [Norton], but as I told him my job is not trying to run the war office."

9. Diary entry of October 2, 1914.

10. Diary entry of October 8, 1914.

11. Diary entries of October 14 and 16, 1914.

12. Diary entry of October 17, 1914.

13. James F. Muirhead's article in *Nation* (Dec. 16, 1915, p. 710) adds that

Norton "incorporated [his Corps] under the company acts of 1907 and 1913, with the certificate of the Board of Trade."

14. Diary entry of November 3, 1914.

15. Diary entry of November 20, 1914.

16. Reprinted in James, *Within the Rim, and Other Essays* (1968).

17. Diary entry of December 7, 1914.

18. Diary entry of December 7, 1914.

19. Diary entry of January 14, 1915.

20. Diary entry of January 18, 1915.

21. Diary entry of November 7, 1914.

22. Diary entry of November 9, 1914.

23. Norton's policy was that all cars going out should have two men assigned to them: a driver, whose job was simply to act as chauffeur, and a volunteer, who was in charge (see Chapter Six). Norton's Corps used drivers provided by the British Red Cross and later by the French Red Cross, who paid the drivers a small salary. Sometimes, just to be on the safe side, a well-to-do volunteer such as Arthur Kemp would retain his own personal chauffeur.

24. Diary entry of August 15, 1915.

25. Diary entry of August 19, 1915.

26. Diary entry of August 15, 1915.

27. Diary entry of September 13, 1915.

28. Diary entry of October 16, 1915.

29. Diary entry of December 30, 1915.

30. Diary entry of August 21, 1915.

31. From a letter printed in the Continental Edition of the *Daily Mail* (15 December 1915), quoted in Paul-Louis Hervier, *The American Volunteers with the Allies* (Paris: Editions de *La Nouvelle Revue*, 1918), pp. 275–276.

32. Diary entry of September 26, 1915.

33. Diary entry of July 5, 1915. Norton's response to this news was that "it would be better to give the Corps to the French who are ready to use them."

34. Diary entry of July 12, 1915.

35. Cf. diary entry for October 24, 1914.

36. Diary entry of January 13, 1915.

37. Diary entry of November 12, 1914.

38. Diary entry of December 7, 1914.

39. Diary entry of December 13, 1914.

40. First mentioned in the diary entries of December 26 and 27, 1914.

41. Diary entry of April 30, 1915.

42. Diary entry of May 3, 1915.

43. Diary entry of May 6, 1915.

44. According to the *New York Times* of August 8, 1915, Norton's section had twenty-five ambulances in Baizieux in June of 1915. The following November, after building up for the Battle of Champagne in October, Norton had sixty cars, and he was able to divide them into two sections (*Times*, November 16, 1915).

45. Diary entries of May 22 and 25, 1915.

CHAPTER THREE: A. PIATT ANDREW AND THE AMERICAN AMBULANCE FIELD SERVICE

1. Andrew Gray, "The American Field Service," *American Heritage*, vol. 26 (December 1974), pp. 60–62; hereafter "Gray." Gray, it might be noted, is Andrew's grandnephew. See also Geller, p. 8.

2. A. Piatt Andrew, *Letters Written Home from France in the First Half of 1915* (n.p.: privately printed, 1916), pp. 2–3; hereafter *LWHF*.

3. *LWHF*, p. 1.

4. *LWHF*, p. 14.

5. *LWHF*, pp. 18–19; letter of 1/7/15.

6. Francis Colby had written Richard Norton in October of 1914 that the American Military Hospital was considering just such an expansion into the field, causing Norton to conclude that the hospital in Neuilly had enough cars and drivers and wouldn't need the ambulance corps he was putting together in London.

7. L. D. Geller, *Friends of France: The American Field Service with the French Armies, 1914–1917, 1939–1945* (New York: AFS Archives, 1990), p. 1. However, this squad must have gone by December 7, when Richard

Norton stopped in Montrieux at the nearly finished hospital for Indian troops. The medical authorities there were in such desperate need of ambulances that Norton left the new Argyle he had been given that very day in Boulogne.

8. Richard Norton's diary entry of December 17, 1914.

9. L. D. Geller, *The American Field Service Archives of World War I, 1914–1917* (New York: Greenwood Press, 1989), p. 3; hereafter "Geller."

10. *LWHF,* p. 18.

11. Gray, 61.

12. Tardieu later became Premier of France, and Gaby had a distinguished career as a French diplomat.

13. *LWHF,* pp. 20–21.

14. According to *LWHF,* p. 23, the section planned to leave Monday morning, January 18; however, according to the Summary of the history of S.S.U. 1 in *History of the American Field Service in France,* Vol. I (Boston: Houghton Mifflin, 1920), p. 80, the unit did not leave until January 20.

15. *LWHF,* p. 31; his night-shift hours are mentioned on p. 39.

16. *LWHF,* p. 38.

17. Gray, p. 61.

18. Norton's diary entry of December 17, 1914.

19. *LWHF,* p. 52.

20. *LWHF,* pp. 53–58.

21. Gray, p. 61.

22. A. Piatt Andrew, "The Genesis of the American Ambulance Service with the French Army," *The Military Surgeon* (October 1925), pp. 364–365.

23. Gray, p. 62.

24. *LWHF,* p. 77.

25. McGrew's recollection is quoted in Gray, p. 62. His imagination probably has enriched his memory. It would be virtually impossible to start ten Model Ts simultaneously in such a manner, given the nature of the beasts (see Chapter Six). Yet, after reading of their exploits, one is uncomfortable suggesting that there was something these drivers couldn't do.

26. *LWHF,* p. 88.

27. *History of the American Field Service in France, 1914–1917,* Vol. I, p. 280.

28. *Friends of France* (Boston: Houghton Mifflin, 1916), p. 22.

29. *LWHF,* p. 90. In a letter of June 5, 1915, addressed to a critic of the operation, Andrew stressed "the request which has been made by the [French] General Staff that we provide additional sections of twenty cars each, as rapidly as we can" (*LWHF,* p. 129). In fact, some of the French officers seemed to believe they couldn't get along without Andrew's Model Ts. While an expanded Z Section (newly named Section 3) continued to work the Vosges in the winter of 1915, Herman Harjes sent a Ski Section of 50 volunteers, mostly Norwegians and Americans, to the Alpine sector. Harjes' men, led by Herman Webster of Chicago, used five ski-sleighs to help transport the wounded down from the mountain snows. Although the Alpine skiers had some advantages over the Model T drivers in the Vosges, the French seemed to prefer the AFS's light Fords. After Section 3 had been transferred to the Verdun front in the summer of 1916, General Villaret contacted Andrew within a week. Villaret's Army of the Vosges was desperate for "at least a detachment of [AFS Fords]," in that no other cars could do the work. Andrew called upon his reserve of Model Ts, and by the winter of 1916 he had put together a Vosges Detachment of six cars for Villaret's sector. [Cf. Claude Moore Fuess, *Phillips Academy, Andover, in the Great War* (New Haven: Yale University Press, 1919), pp. 16–17, and A. Piatt Andrew's opening essay ("The Service") in *History of the American Field Service in France,* Vol. I (Boston: Houghton Mifflin, 1920). Information about Harjes' Ski Section can be found in the *New York Times,* December 25, 1915, and in Harjes' January 19, 1916, letter to Mabel Boardman of the American Red Cross (National Archives).]

30. *LWHF,* pp. 88–89.

31. These are only four of the principal points. A translation of the complete document in slightly modified form appears in the Introduction to Volume I of *The History of the American Field Service in France,* pp. 21–23.

32. Andrew, "For Love of France," *The Outlook* (December 27, 1916), p. 924.

33. Andrew, "The Genesis of the American Ambulance Service with the French," *The Military Surgeon* (October 1925), p. 365.

34. Introduction, *History of the American Field Service in France,* p. 23.

35. *LWHF,* p. 165.

36. Diary entry of September 13, 1915.

37. In a letter to Mabel Boardman of the American Red Cross of January 21, 1916, Harjes noted that "some weeks ago" the French General Headquarters expressed their desire that all ambulance corps be united under the American Red Cross. In the same letter, Harjes noted that Richard Norton's corps had agreed to serve under the organizational sponsorship of the ARC (letter in the ARC files in the National Archives).

38. In a letter (August 7, 1916) to Robert Bacon, Harjes repeated what he had written to Boardman in January: "General Headquarters [suggested] that all American [ambulances] at work with the French Army in the field should come in and be centralized under one single organization, viz: the American Red Cross." Andrew, however, "took the stand," according to Harjes, "that the ARC was a neutral organization" and accordingly rejected the offer to join the ARC. The matter was thus dropped — by Harjes, Andrew, and General Headquarters.

39. When he asked Henry Sleeper to order the plates for the certificates, Andrew wrote, "I have arranged with Naudin, who is probably the best line draughtsman in France . . . , to include suggestions of Yorktown and the fraternity in arms of revolutionary days and the fraternity of American and French soldiers today" (letter dated April 7, 1916; AFS Archives).

40. Andrew, "For Love of France," *The Outlook* (December 27, 1916), p. 923.

41. S.S.U. 2 was first called Section Y; its designation was changed in July of 1915. After S.S.U. 4, the numbering system grows a bit confusing. The Harjes Formation was designated S.S.U. 5 and the Norton Section was S.S.U. 7. Therefore, Andrew's fifth section became S.S.U.8.

42. This letter is contained in the American Field Service Library and Archives in New York; hereafter "AFS Archives."

43. For example, see August 30, 1916, letter from Andrew to W. C. Heinkel. Through their correspondence, Andrew learned that Heinkel had contributed, on behalf of another party, $4,500 (intended for ambulances) to "the general account of the Ambulance." Andrew quickly advised Heinkel that he had never heard of that money — nor would he hear of it unless Heinkel requested the money back and deposited it in Andrew's Boston account at Lee Higginson and Company (AFS Archives).

44. Geller, p. 9.

45. In February of 1916, Section 2 was sent to Verdun, where the horrendous German offensive and monumental bombardment had just begun.

By June, when the massive destruction of the forts and villages throughout the Verdun sector had reached its peak, all five of Andrew's sections were working the region virtually around the clock. Norton and Harjes had units performing exemplary service at Verdun as well.

46. Or so Bacon told Henry Sleeper after the fact. See Sleeper's letter to Andrew (7/27/16); AFS Archives.

47. Letter to Sleeper of July 24, 1916; AFS Archives. Andrew is pretty harsh on Bacon in this hand-written letter. At one point, claiming that Bacon left the hospital "in the most miserable hands," Andrew charges that Bacon's lax supervision allowed the hospital administrators to keep patients longer than necessary, so that only a few new cases were admitted each day — a practice that kept the beds full, the expenses low, and the death rate down.

48. Letter of August 18, 1916; AFS Archives.

49. See Andrew's letter of August 30, 1916, to Charles Freeborn; AFS Archives.

50. Letter to Henry Sleeper, dated July 14, 1916; AFS Archives.

51. Letter of July 30, 1916; AFS Archives.

52. Mrs. Vanderbilt's account of the tour was published in *Harper's Magazine* (January 1917), pp. 175–186. Andrew gives a detailed summary of the tour in a letter to his parents, dated August 18, 1916 (AFS Archives). Several volunteers also mention Mrs. Vanderbilt's visit in their memoirs, letters, and diaries.

53. In a letter to Sleeper on July 14, 1916, Andrew wrote: "I will tell you confidentially, not for publication, they decided to turn us out." The letter to Bacon was written on August 4, 1916. Both letters are in the AFS Archives.

54. Geller, p. 9.

55. The deal was consummated on July 16, 1916, which is why Geller sets that date as the day of Andrew's independence; Geller, p. 30.

56. Letter of August 18, 1916, to his parents; AFS Archives.

57. Gray, p. 90. See also Hervier, *The American Volunteers with the Allies* (Paris, 1918), pp. 232–233.

58. The AFS loved the place, as is rapturously noted in the AFS *Bulletin* (no. 28, January 12, 1918).

59. Andrew quoted the note (from Paulding Brown of Harvard Law School) in a letter to Sleeper on July 27 and in a letter to Bacon on the

28th. He also quoted the comments of the two Yale men in the same two letters; AFS Archives.

60. The AFFW also had its own transportation corps to carry supplies from the *entrepôts des dons* (gift warehouses) in Paris to regional medical stations and hospitals. These cars and light trucks were driven by women — Miss Caspairs, Miss Arnold, Miss Amy Bradley, Miss T. Dunham, and Miss Hart — according to Hervier, p. 34. Bradley's fascinating letters were collected and published as *Back of the Front in France* (Boston, 1918).

61. See Andrew's letter of 20 August 1916 to Sleeper. Andrew mentioned the AFFW's 5,000 local committees, surely an unrealistic figure. He must have meant committee members, in that a subsequent letter to Bacon (8/31/16) mentions hundreds of committees; AFS Archives.

62. Henry D. Sleeper, "The Effort in America," *The History of the American Field Service in France*, pp. 44–46.

63. In the Preface to his 1916 *Harvard Volunteers in Europe*, Mark A. De Wolfe Howe claims that because Germany didn't ask for medical aid, those sympathetic to the German cause did not volunteer in large numbers (four out of four hundred, according to Howe, p. vii). Andrew got his leads to sympathetic campuses in ways other than through personal contacts in the Ivy League. For example, a volunteer from the University of Iowa gave Andrew the name of the "man who has two moving picture theatres in [Iowa City] and who is in touch with the students there." The recruit also suggested that Sleeper might communicate with Professor Bush of the Department of Romance Languages (Andrew's letter to Sleeper, August 20, 1916; AFS Archives).

64. Dunbar Maury Hinrichs, *We Met by the Way* (privately printed by author, 1975), p. 7.

65. Henry Sheahan, Dedication, *A Volunteer Poilu* (Boston: Houghton Mifflin, 1916).

66. Salter Storrs Clark and Caroline G. Clark, eds., *Soldier Letters* (Westfield, Conn.: Middleditch, 1919), p. 12.

67. Leslie Buswell, *Ambulance No. 10: Personal Letters from the Front* (Boston: Houghton Mifflin, 1915), p. 93.

68. Andrew, "For Love of France," *The Outlook* (December 27, 1916), p. 923.

69. Andrew, "The Genesis of the American Ambulance Service with the French Army, 1915–1917," *The Military Surgeon* (October 1925), p. 367. Geller says there were sixteen camion sections (p. 14).

70. Andrew, "The Genesis . . . ," p. 376.

CHAPTER FOUR: UNDER FIRE

1. This chapter consists of reconstructed anecdotes taken from various accounts of the drivers' experiences at the front. In some cases several incidents have been combined into one; in a few instances facts drawn from other sources have been added to enrich the incident; and still other anecdotes have been restructured to give them narrative coherence. In all cases, some selectivity has been employed. Some fictitious dialogue and descriptions have, at times, been spliced into the narrative. The exception to this disclaimer is the toast by Leslie Buswell that concludes this chapter.

2. Based on Lockwood, "The Section in Alsace Reconquise," *Friends of France: The Field Service of the American Ambulance Described by Its Members* (Boston: Houghton Mifflin, 1916), pp. 26–27. The stipulation that the ambulances carry only wounded men is what causes Ernest Hemingway's Frederic Henry to deny a ride in his ambulance to an Italian soldier with a severe hernia (Chapter VII, *A Farewell to Arms*). Suggesting that the man "get a bump on [his] head," Lt. Henry promises to pick him up on his return trip. The plan, incidentally, doesn't work.

3. Based on Sheahan, *A Volunteer Poilu* (Boston: Houghton Mifflin, 1916), pp. 216–218.

4. Based on William Yorke Stevenson, *From Poilu to Yank* (Boston: Houghton Mifflin, 1918), p. 117.

5. Based on Robert W. Imbrie, *Behind the Wheel of a War Ambulance* (New York: McBride, 1918), pp. 36–39.

6. Based on William Yorke Stevenson, *At the Front in a Flivver* (Boston: Houghton Mifflin, 1917), pp. 128–129, and on Robert W. Imbrie, *Behind the Wheel of a War Ambulance* (New York: McBride, 1918), pp. 114–115.

7. Based on William Yorke Stevenson, *At the Front in a Flivver* (Boston: Houghton Mifflin, 1917), pp. 115–116.

8. Based on H. Snyder Harrison, "At the Back of the Front: Dunkirk and Ypres," *Friends of France* (Boston: Houghton Mifflin, 1916), pp. 13–14. The quoted words are Harrison's.

9. Based on Nordhoff, "An Ambulance Driver in France," excerpted from the *Atlantic Monthly* (October 1917) by the National Board for Historical Service, *War Readings* (New York: Scribners, 1918), pp. 200–202. Nordhoff's *Atlantic Monthly* articles were edited and collected in *The Fledgling* (Boston: Houghton Mifflin, 1919). After the war, Nordhoff (with James Hall) gained fame as the author of *Mutiny on the Bounty* and other works.

10. Based on W. Kerr Rainsford, "An American Ambulancier at Verdun," *The World's Work* (December 1916), p. 185.

11. Based on Rice, *An American Crusader at Verdun* (Princeton: n.p. 1918), pp. 33, 68–71. Rice spells the name of the *poste de secours* "Houdremont." No such location has been found. His descriptions and mileage data suggest he most certainly meant Haudromont, near the famous quarries of the same name. Other memoirs, such as Edward Weeks, *My Green Age* (Boston: Little, Brown, 1973), mention the *poste* at Haudromont.

12. Based on *From Poilu to Yank* (Boston: Houghton Mifflin, 1918), p. 122.

13. Based on Philip D. Orcutt, *The White Road of Mystery: The Note-book of an American Ambulancier* (New York: John Lane, 1918), pp. 51–52.

14. Based on "An Ambulance-Driver's Fire-Baptism," *Literary Digest* (September 29, 1917), pp. 53–54.

15. Based on Philip D. Orcutt, *The White Road of Mystery: The Note-book of an American Ambulancier* (New York: John Lane, 1918), pp. 90–91.

16. Based on Salter Storrs and Caroline G. Clark, eds., *Soldier Letters: Coleman Tileston Clark and Salter Storrs Clark, Jr., Their Stories from Their Letters and Diaries* (privately published by L. Middleditch Co., Westfield, Conn., 1919), pp. 27–28.

17. Based on Read's letter, excerpted in *The Overseas War Record of the Winsor School, 1914–1919*, pp. 81–84.

18. Based on Richard Norton's letter to his sister, partially reprinted in the Boston *Post* (7 August 1916) and excerpted in Paul-Louis Hervier, *The American Volunteers with the Allies* (Paris, 1918), pp. 276–278; on Norton's diary entries for June 11–13, 1916; and on James F. Muirhead, "American Volunteer Ambulance Corps," *The Nation* (January 19, 1917), pp. 72–73. There are still other fragmented versions of this story, not all of which satisfactorily explain the reason for the order or agree on how the two drivers were rescued [e.g., Charles F. Horne, editor in chief, *Source Records of the Great War*, Vol. IV (National Alumni/American Legion, 1922), pp. 270–271]. In an article in the *New York Times* (August 5, 1916), Richard Norton calls it "an extremely stupid order given by some overexcited divisional doctor," which doesn't explain very much.

19. Based on Waldo Peirce, "Christmas Eve, 1915," *Friends of France* (Boston: Houghton Mifflin, 1916), pp. 139–147; and on Luke C. Doyle's letter of December 27, 1915, reprinted in "The Inspector's Letter Box," *Friends of France* (Boston: Houghton Mifflin, 1916), pp. 217–218. See also Perry Poore Sheehan, "In Memory of Lafayette," *Munsey's Magazine* (November 1916), pp. 183–194; and the *New York Times* (December 26, 1915).

20. Based on William Yorke Stevenson, *At the Front in a Flivver* (Boston: Houghton Mifflin, 1917), pp. 225–229. In Stevenson's tribute, he spells Kelley's name "Kelly."

21. From "The Inspector's Letter Box," *Friends of France* (Boston: Houghton Mifflin, 1916), p. 225.

CHAPTER FIVE: *EN REPOS*

1. *At the Front in a Flivver* (New York: Macmillan, 1918), p. 3.

2. [Anonymous], *Diary of S.S.U. 18* [Paris: n.p. (privately printed), 1917], p. 14.

3. Philip D. Orcutt, *The White Road of Mystery* (New York: John Lane, 1918), p. 88.

4. Julien Bryan, *Ambulance 464: Encore de Blessés* (New York: Macmillan, 1918), pp. 141, 143.

5. *The White Road of Mystery*, p. 88.

6. *Diary of S.S.U. 18*, p. 13.

7. Geller, *The American Field Service Archives of World War I, 1914–1917* (New York: Greenwood Press, 1989), p. 36.

8. William Yorke Stevenson, *At the Front in a Flivver* (Boston, 1917), p. 154. Stevenson spells the name of the village "Vaulecourt."

9. Richard S. Kennedy, *Dreams in the Mirror* (New York: Liveright, 1980), p. 145.

10. *The Enormous Room* (New York: Modern Library reprint, 1934), p. 3.

11. *Ambulance No. 10*, pp. 28, 67–68.

12. "Richard Norton's Ambulance," December 16, 1915, p. 710. Although Muirhead was speaking about the Norton section in particular, his description applies to all American volunteer ambulance corps.

13. Cf. Robert Imbrie, *Behind the Wheel of a War Ambulance*, pp. 45–46.

14. Preston Lockwood, "The Section in Alsace Reconquise," *Friends of France*, p. 32.

15. See, for example, A. Piatt Andrew's comment that the "French officers . . . were carefully selected, not merely for their competence and training, but for their tact and familiarity with American character and customs . . . ["The Genesis of the American Ambulance Service with the French Army, 1915–1917," *The Military Surgeon* (October 1925), p. 368]. However, the appointments were not always successful. For ex-

ample, when Harjes' Section 61, which was stationed next to Stevenson's AFS section, was to be transferred about the end of August of 1917, Stevenson wrote, "Fine as are the fellows [in Harjes' section], I shall not regret [losing] their very annoying Lieutenant, who is constantly butting into our affairs" (*From Poilu to Yank*, p. 150). Thorn is equally direct: "the French lieutenant ... rarely understands the American character, and ... sometimes does not even speak English ..." ("Notes, Experiences, ..." p. 422).

16. A thorough discussion of the comparable table of organization in a Harjes section can be found in Thorn, "Notes, Experiences, ..." pp. 420–421. The most common actual deployment of personnel, French and American, is summarized in Philip Orcutt, *The White Road of Mystery* (New York: John Lane, 1918), pp. 48–49.

17. The official (French) titles of the ARC staff: H. H. Harjes was *Chef des Sections Sanitaires*, Richard Norton was *Directeur du Service aux Armées*, A. T. Kemp was *Directeur du Service Intérieur*, and C. B. Brockway was *Adjoint-technique*.

18. The amount of pay varies in different accounts. The *Diary of Section VIII*, edited for the American Field Service by Sleeper, says that "each of us [volunteers] receives 5 sous per day, the regular pay of the *poilu*" (p. 29). Imbrie confirms the 5 sous figure (*Behind the Wheel of a War Ambulance*, p. 46). However, Lockwood says the pay was "one sou a day" (*Friends of France*, p. 30). This smaller figure is confirmed by a driver quoted by Gleason in *Our Part in the Great War* (p. 37). The apparent contradiction may be resolved, or perhaps intensified, by noting that Andrew claims in the *History of the American Field Service* that the AFS added 2 French francs a day to the volunteers' regular salary (Vol. I, pp. 25–26). Thorn says the drivers and the *poilus* got five cents a day ("Notes, Experiences, ..." p. 421).

19. James R. McConnell, "The Section in Lorraine," *Friends of France* (Boston: Houghton Mifflin, 1916), p. 64.

20. *Ambulance 464*, p. 18.

21. *We Met by the Way* (privately printed by the author, 1975), pp. 16–17.

22. Seabrook gave up a successful public relations business to volunteer for the ambulance service; Stevenson, a financial editor for a Philadelphia newspaper, had published a book called *The Joys of Sports*; and Pottle was an established poet.

23. For a fascinating account of censorship during the war and how it affected a journalist's habits of mind and reportorial tactics, see William G. Shepherd, *Confessions of a War Correspondent* (New York: Harper &

Brothers, 1917). Shepherd, a United Press correspondent, conceded (in his italics) *"it does not pay to try to beat the censor"* (p. 30), a lesson he learned the hard way. Growing irritated that he and his fellow reporters were not granted passes to visit the front, he took it upon himself to "get out and see things." However, "before midnight the French and British had arrested seventeen of us . . ." (p. 53). Things didn't get any better for the journalists as the war proceeded. They were restricted to the capitals (London and Paris): "We could not move from London. There were orders against us . . ." (p. 115). Later (in the early weeks of 1917), the journalists defined for themselves a new role — "the twentieth century war correspondent, who aligned himself with the military in return for an occasional pass to ['certain interesting places' at] the front, after which he returns to the capital [and] writes a story . . ." (p. 120). This twentieth-century war correspondent, according to Shepherd, spends most of his time making the rounds of military offices and filing stories given him by the officials and bureaucrats running the war.

24. *American Heritage History of World War I* (New York: American Heritage/ Bonanza Books, 1964), p. 48.

25. *The Real War, 1914–1918* (Boston: Little, Brown, 1930), p. 45.

26. *In Flanders Fields* (New York: Viking, 1958), pp. 340–342.

27. Cf. Clark, *Soldier Letters* (privately printed by L. Middleditch Co., Westfield, Conn., 1919), p. 77.

28. *With the American Ambulance in France* (Honolulu: Star-Bulletin Press, 1919), p. 140.

29. Ibid., p. 141.

30. Salter Storrs Clark and Caroline G. Clark, eds., *Soldier Letters* (privately printed by L. Middleditch Co., Westfield, Conn., 1919), p. 92. The letter also appeared in the New York *Tribune* of August 10, 1917.

31. Number 71, November 16, 1918.

32. *Trucking to the Trenches* (Boston: Houghton Mifflin, 1918), pp. 15–16.

33. *Behind the Wheel of a War Ambulance*, p. xi.

34. "The Day's Work," *The Harvard Volunteers in Europe*, M. A. DeWolfe Howe, ed. (Cambridge: Harvard University Press, 1916), p. 196.

35. Coudert, Foreword to C. de Florez, *No. 6: A Few Pages from the Diary of an Ambulance Driver* (New York: Dutton, 1918), p. viii.

36. Preface to Edward D. Toland, *The Aftermath of Battle* (New York: Macmillan, 1916), pp. viii–ix.

37. *No. 6*, p. 52.

38. From "The Inspector's Letter Box," *Friends of France*, pp. 154–155; the quotation can also be found in *History of the American Field Service in France*, Vol. III (Boston: Houghton Mifflin, 1920), pp. 136–137.

39. *At the Front in a Flivver*, pp. 37–38.

40. "My Trip to the Front," *Harper's Magazine* (January 1917), p. 178.

41. *History of the American Field Service in France, 1914–1918*, Vol. I, p. 86.

42. *Exile's Return* (New York: Penguin reprint, 1969), pp. 39–40. In "E. E. Cummings' Spectatorial View," *Lost Generation Journal* (Winter, 1977–1978), pp. 9, 19, Susan Gates applies Cowley's theory to the American poet.

43. C.R.M.F. Cruttwell, who was an infantry officer during the war, puts the matter this way: "The army and corps commanders became empty and unreal figures living ten or fifteen miles behind in luxurious and unmolested châteaux; even the divisional and brigade staffs lost much of their intimate significance, and were often regarded as fussy amateurs when they visited the trenches. The higher staffs studied the map, but seldom the ground itself" [*A History of the Great War, 1914–1918* (Chicago, 1991 rpt), pp. 107–108].

44. *The Face of Battle* (New York: Viking, 1976), p. 329.

45. *The White Road of Mystery*, p. 81.

46. W. Kerr Rainsford, "An American Ambulancier at Verdun," *The World's Work* (December 1916), p. 186.

47. Perhaps the most explicit statement about this duality of their daily lives was made by Carlyle H. Holt ["The Inspector's Letter Box," *Friends of France* (Boston: Houghton Mifflin, 1916), pp. 173–174]: "Our life here is one of highlights. The transition from the absolute quiet and tranquillity of peace to the rush and roar of war takes but an instant and all our impressions are kaleidoscopic in number and contrast. . . . Sometimes we sit in the little garden behind our *caserne* in the evening, comfortably drinking beer and smoking or talking and watching the flash of cannon. . . . Yet we may leave a spot like that and immediately be in the midst of the realities of war."

48. Eric J. Leed, *No Man's Land: Combat and Identity in World War I* (Cambridge University Press, 1979), provides an excellent analysis of the nature and impact of this aspect of the Great War.

49. "Many Soldiers Are an Answer to Three," *Harvard Crimson* (October 28, 1921).

50. *Ambulance No. 10* (Boston: Houghton Mifflin, 1916), p. 43.

51. *Diary of S.S.U. 18,* p. 14.

CHAPTER SIX: THE CARS

1. The entire poem appears in George J. Shively, *Record of S.S.U. 585* (New York: E. L. Hildreth, 1920), pp. 98–99.

2. Robert Lacey, *Ford: The Man and the Machine* (Boston: Little, Brown, 1986), p. 88.

3. Ibid., p. 107.

4. Prior to 1911, the Model T had a one-piece oil pan, which meant the engine had to be hoisted off the motor-mounts and, usually, completely out of the car, if the mechanic wanted to inspect or work on the crankshaft bearings or connecting rods. After 1911, the oil pan had a removable plate that allowed access to the bearings and rods.

5. Joshua G. B. Campbell, "The Section in Flanders," *Friends of France* (Boston: Houghton Mifflin, 1916), p. 125.

6. "An American Ambulance at Verdun," *Friends of France,* p. 99.

7. *Soldier Letters,* p. 37.

8. *Ambulance 464: Encore de Blessés* (New York: Macmillan, 1918), p. 173.

9. *Our Part in the Great War* (New York: Frederick A. Stokes, 1917), p. 41.

10. Ibid., pp. 38–39.

11. Andrew, "The Genesis of the American Ambulance Service with the French Army, 1915–1917," *The Military Surgeon* (October 1925), p. 371.

12. Ibid., p. 372.

13. "Some of the Early Problems," *The History of the American Field Service in France,* Vol. I (Boston: Houghton Mifflin, 1920), pp. 32–33.

14. "The Genesis . . . ," *The Military Surgeon,* p. 370.

15. Some volunteers claimed to find it difficult to drive cars with gear shifts. Lansing Warren and his brother, Skip, for instance, were not used to shifting the gears of the large Fiats they were assigned [cf. "Ambulancier," *Lost Generation Journal* (Winter, 1977–1978), p. 11]. On the other hand, the three foot pedals of the Model T, with its unique planetary transmission, no doubt frustrated more drivers than did the gear boxes of the Fiats.

16. Bowerman, *The Compensations of War: The Diary of an Ambulance Driver*

During the Great War, Mark C. Carnes, ed. (Austin: University of Texas Press, 1983), p. 31.

17. The particular makeup of an American ambulance section is set forth in the Introduction to the *History of the American Field Service,* Vol. I, p. 23. In his *Military Surgeon* article, Andrew recalls that "each section was endowed with . . . twenty small Ford ambulances actually in the field; two such ambulances in reserve; a Ford staff car; a light repair car (Ford) . . . ; a large repair car (2-ton truck) . . . ; a 2-ton truck arranged to carry from fifteen to twenty sitting cases and used especially for evacuating lightly wounded or gas cases . . . ; a kitchen trailer . . . ; and three tents . . . ," pp. 372–373. Clearly this disposition bespeaks Andrew's ideal, for it was seldom found in the actual sections.

18. From Andrew's letter to Henry D. Sleeper of April 7, 1916; held in the AFS Archives.

19. From J. Halcott Glover's biweekly "Historical Report" (11 to 30 June 1915) filed with the American Ambulance Hospital staff in Neuilly; held in the AFS Archives.

20. *With a Military Ambulance in France, 1914–1915* (privately printed, 1915), p. 31. An excellent description of the customizing of the ambulance compartments to hold stretchers, complete with diagrams, appears in Stephen Thorn, "Notes, Experiences, and Suggestions on the Automobile Ambulance Service of a Modern Army in the Field," *Military Surgeon* (1917), pp. 416–420, 424 ff.

21. Letter of 21 January 1916, from the files of the American Red Cross held in the National Archives.

22. "American Red Cross Ambulance Service in France," *Scientific American* (October 7, 1916), p. 325.

23. "Notes, Experiences, and Suggestions . . . ," *Military Surgeon,* p. 416.

24. Scribners paperback edition (1987), p. 30.

25. *Soldier Letters* (Westfield, Conn.: L. Middleditch Co., 1919), p. 47. L. D. Geller, *Friends of France: The American Field Service with the French Armies, 1914–1917, 1939–1945* (New York: American Field Service Archives, 1990), p. 31, notes that the Model Ts were not suitable for the Balkan topography.

26. Whether or not the Fiats, Berliets, and other makes burned more gas than the Fords is debatable. The Fords got better mileage than the larger cars, but the Model Ts held fewer passengers, so they had to make more trips. (In 1917, gasoline cost 3.60 FF — or 65 cents — for 5 liters, or about 50 cents per gallon.) Other factors involving wear on a

car's engine and tires should not be overlooked as hidden expenses when considering the increased number of trips the Model T had to make.

27. *No Hiding Place* (Philadelphia: Lippincott, 1942), p. 151

28. American Field Service *Bulletin*, No. 7 (August 15, 1917). The Vosges Detachment continued in operation until August 8, 1917. Other accounts vary only slightly, claiming that the appeal was made by General Villaret within a week after Section 3 had been sent to help out at Verdun in the summer of 1916. Villaret's Army of the Vosges, these accounts note, was desperate for "at least a detachment of [AFS Model Ts]," because "no other cars could do the work." So, Andrew put together a Vosges Detachment of six cars for Villaret's sector by the winter of 1916. Cf., Claude Moore Fuess, *Phillips Academy, Andover, in the Great War* (New Haven: Yale University Press, 1919), pp. 16–17, and A. Piatt Andrew's opening essay ("The Service") in *History of the American Field Service*, Vol. I (Boston: Houghton Mifflin, 1920).

29. William Yorke Stevenson, *From Poilu to Yank* (Boston: Houghton Mifflin, 1918), pp. 164–165.

30. Ibid., p. 158.

31. Joshua Campbell, "The Section in Flanders," *Friends of France* (Boston: Houghton Mifflin, 1920) p. 125.

32. Floyd Clymer, *Henry Ford's Wonderful Model T*, p. 107.

33. A. Piatt Andrew, "The Genesis . . . ," *Military Surgeon*, p. 373.

34. *At the Front in a Flivver* (Boston: Houghton Mifflin, 1915), p. 208.

35. The vivid simile is William Yorke Stevenson's; ibid., p. 2.

36. The poem appeared anonymously in the American Field Service *Bulletin*, No. 7 (August 15, 1917).

37. AFS *Bulletin*, No. 17 (October 27, 1917).

38. Cf. A. Piatt Andrew, "Some of the Early Problems," *The History . . .* , Vol. I, p. 32 (also in Andrew, "The Genesis . . . ," *Military Surgeon*, p. 372).

39. Ibid., pp. 36–37 (also ibid., p. 375).

40. George C. Brown, ed., "With the Ambulance Service in France: The Wartime Letters of William Gorham Rice, Jr.," *Wisconsin Magazine of History* (Autumn, 1981), p. 17.

41. "The Genesis . . . ," *Military Surgeon*, p. 375.

42. Richard Norton's section sometimes used drivers sent to him by the

British or French Red Cross, who covered their expenses. In these instances, the volunteer "outranked" the driver and assumed command of the ambulance, overseeing and taking responsibility for its employment.

43. "American Red Cross Ambulance Service in France," *Scientific American* (October 7, 1916), p. 325.

44. *Ambulancing on the French Front* (New York: Britton, 1918), pp. 34–35.

45. A. Piatt Andrew, "The Service," *History of American Field Service*, Vol. I, p. 24.

46. Ibid., p. 25.

47. *War Letters* (Paris: The Black Sun Press, 1932), p. 119.

48. See Steve Galatti's reminiscence in AFS *Bulletin* No. 46 (May 25, 1918).

49. See Norton's diary entry of January 14, 1917.

50. Imbrie, *Behind the Wheel of a War Ambulance* (New York: McBride, 1918), p. 72.

51. "The Inspector's Letter Box," *Friends of France*, p. 149.

52. "For Love of France," *The Outlook* (December 27, 1916), p. 929.

53. *Ambulance No. 10*, p. 26.

54. Gleason, p. 50.

55. *My Green Age* (Boston: Little, Brown, 1973), p. 48.

56. "An American Ambulancier at Verdun," *The World's Work* (December 1916), p. 185.

57. "The Inspector's Letter Box," *Friends of France*, p. 180.

58. White.

59. Or pot-hole.

60. "The Section in Alsace Reconquise," *Friends of France*, p. 39.

61. "The Inspector's Letter Box," *Friends of France*, p. 207.

62. Ibid., p. 183.

63. *Our Part in the Great War*, p. 42.

64. *Behind the Wheel of a War Ambulance* (New York: McBride, 1918), p. 14.

65. Ibid., pp. 14–15.

66. Ibid., p. 15.

67. Ibid., p. 15.

CHAPTER SEVEN: POLITICS, MOTIVES, AND IMPRESSIONS

1. C.R.M.F. Cruttwell, who mentions the figure of 90 percent in *A History of the Great War,* says that "this estimate may be accepted as approximately accurate as it is given independently by [Colonel] House, Spring Rice the British Ambassador, and by Bernstorff the German Ambassador at Washington" (pp. 199–200). Certainly the anti-involvement sentiment "He kept us out of war" proved to be a widely popular and perhaps decisive campaign slogan during President Wilson's bid for reelection in 1916.

2. George C. Brown, ed., "With the Ambulance Service in France: The Wartime Letters of William Gorham Rice, Jr., S.S.U. 1–66," p. 29. Rice spent a term in the AFS in 1916, and a second one in 1917. He made the comment about the ARC during his second tour. For a detailed picture of an American woman's experience running an ARC canteen, see Alice Lord O'Brian, *No Glory: Letters from France, 1917–1919* (Buffalo, N.Y.: Airport Publishers, Inc., 1936).

3. *A Stop at Suzanne's and Lower Flights,* pp. 251, 253.

4. Several references acknowledge this 1915 shipment: Edwin Morse, *Vanguard of American Volunteers,* p. 158; Charles A. Fenton, "Ambulance Drivers in France and Italy," p. 329; and *Lost Generation Journal* (Winter 1977–1978), p. 5. Neal English, Director of the ARC Office of Public Information, noted in a letter of November 3, 1944, that "Harjes was given charge of seventeen ambulances sent through the ARC — twelve purchased from contributions raised on the Yale campus and five at Harvard University." English was quoting (word for word) information in an ARC document (author anonymous; typescript; date unknown, but more recent than Charles Fenton's article) titled "Ambulance Service in Europe Before U.S. Entrance in World War I."

5. Stephen Thorn, a volunteer who served nearly all of his nineteen months as the head of Harjes' ambulance corps, noted that in June of 1915 "the French authorities suggested that the Harjes corps . . . act as a first line ambulance section" ["Notes, Experiences, and Suggestions on the Automobile Ambulance Service of a Modern Army in the Field," *Military Surgeon* (1917), pp. 425–426]. There is no reference in Thorn's article to the seventeen Yale-Harvard Fords. The only Model T ambulances Thorn mentions are six (not seventeen) added to Harjes' unit in September of 1915. Where Harjes placed the other eleven Fords is not recorded. As Parisian director of the ARC, Harjes had license to assign ARC ambulances to whichever hospital he chose.

6. Harjes' cable of May 21, 1915, and the ARC response of June 4, 1915, are contained in the American Red Cross files in the National Archives.

Thorn wrote about the matter somewhat ambiguously: "October [1915] found the section rechristened 'Section Sanitaire Américaine No. 5,' incorporated into the American Red Cross, and organized [according to French strictures]" ("Notes, Experiences, and Suggestions...," p. 426). Thorn's understanding of when the section was absorbed into the ARC (he implies October) is perhaps based on the date of the actual arrival of the identification cards, in that the ARC advised Harjes of its willingness (conditionally) to sponsor his section in a letter dated the previous June.

7. In a memorandum he prepared for the American Relief Clearing House, Herman Harjes appealed to various relief agencies to help him with the financial operation of the ambulance service. "I would personally be very glad," Harjes wrote, "if the Clearing House could see its way to making a great big appeal in America for money." Such an appeal, he said, was necessary because he had written "some months ago to the American Red Cross ... but their means did not permit him to do anything and ... so far they have not been able to accomplish very much." (Harjes attached a copy of this memo to his July 8, 1916, letter to Robert Bacon; the letter and the attached memo are in the ARC files in the National Archives.)

8. The letter (quoted in the previous paragraph) from Boardman to Harjes, dated August 14, 1915, and Harjes' January 30 letter to Wadsworth are located in the files of the American Red Cross held in the National Archives. Harjes did have plenty of volunteers. For instance, in the winter of 1915 he put together a ski section of fifty men, mostly Norwegians and Americans, to work in the Vosges. The ski section, led by Herman Webster of Chicago, used five ski-sleighs to help transport the wounded down the snowy mountain slopes [cf. *New York Times,* December 25, 1915, and Harjes' January 19, 1916, letter to the ARC's Mable Boardman (National Archives)].

9. The figures of growth pertain to the period between May 1 and November 1, 1917. *The Work of the American Red Cross. Report by War Council of Appropriations and Activities from Outbreak of War to November 1, 1917,* p. 27.

10. *Back of the Front in France,* p. 82.

11. The two quoted phrases (about "Red Cross issue" and "partial support") come from an anonymous, short, unpublished history of the "Ambulance Service in Europe Before U.S. Entrance in World War I" held in the national office of the American Red Cross.

12. See Thorn, p. 423, and letter from Eliot Norton to Robert Patterson, Director of the Bureau of the Medical Service of the ARC, November 19, 1916, in the ARC files held in the National Archives. Luther Nelson,

who joined the Harjes Formation (S.S.U. 5) in early September of 1916, told his sister that "the men in [the] Harjes section are furnished all equipment free" in a letter of 6 September 1916, held in the American Field Service Archives.

13. Richard Norton's volunteer unit became an official American Red Cross section in the winter of 1915–1916 (see Chapter Two: Richard Norton and the American Volunteer Motor-Ambulance Corps). By September of 1917, when the Red Cross units were militarized (assigned to the U.S. Army), at least 500 men had served six-month terms in the Red Cross (that is, Norton-Harjes) units according to the estimate of G. R. Gaeddert, *The American National Red Cross in World War I, 1917–1918*, vol. IV of *The History of the American Red Cross*, p. 363. Gaeddert based his numbers on a letter to the ARC (Joseph R. Hamlin) from Eliot Norton, July 18, 1917.

14. After the United States declared war in April of 1917, however, ARC policy changed drastically. When the U.S. Army began to militarize the volunteers and neutrality was no longer an issue, the ARC provided ample funds, cars, and personnel for ambulance service in both France and Italy. For instance, during the first six months after its inception on May 1, 1917, the ARC's War Council, charged by President Wilson to raise and oversee the distribution of Red Cross funds, allocated $103,800 to the Norton-Harjes ambulance service (*The Work of the American Red Cross. Report by the War Council from Outbreak of War to November 1, 1917*, p. 116). In total, the ARC formed forty-seven ambulance units to serve in the American Army medical corps. These ambulances primarily performed jitney duty, transferring wounded between hospitals or from train stations to urban medical centers (cf. H. P. Davison, *The American Red Cross in the Great War*, pp. 141–142). The front lines were still being worked by the militarized volunteers in the Norton-Harjes and AFS units, which remained under the command of the French Army. In Italy, the American Red Cross was particularly helpful and generous — sending drivers, funds, cars, parts, and ARC officials to the front as well as base hospitals (see the sections on Dos Passos and Hemingway in Chapter Eight). Even Henry Ford joined in the act and gave a $500,000 line of credit to the ARC for cars and parts (ARC *Bulletin*, Sept. 7, 1917).

15. Cited as a cautionary lesson in the letter granting conditional acceptance of Harjes' request for ARC sponsorship of his unit (from ARC to Harjes, June 4, 1915, in National Archives). The ARC was young and perhaps naive at the time of the Boer War. The 1863 Geneva Convention, which formally established various national Red Cross organizations, was signed by fourteen nations in 1864. The United States did not

sign until 1882, and the Act of Congress that officially designated the American Red Cross as the nation's official relief organization was not passed until 1905.

16. From Wilson's address to the Senate, August 19, 1914 (*The Public Papers of Woodrow Wilson...*, Baker and Dood, eds., vol. I, p. 158).

17. Claude Fuess, ed., *The Amherst Memorial Volume*, p. 3. One private school was manifestly candid, publicly declaring its position with regard to neutrality. According to *The Spence Newsletter* (Spring, 1992), at the outbreak of the war, Clara B. Spence, founder and director of the Spence School (for girls and young women) in New York, "announced that the United States might declare itself neutral but [her] school would not ... Miss Spence eliminated German from the curriculum and declared that parents who strongly believed in neutrality or sympathized with Germany should withdraw their daughters from the school."

18. Cf. Fuess, *Phillips Academy, Andover, in the Great War*, pp. 14 ff.

19. Wood is quoted in Philip Van Doren Stern, *Tin Lizzie*, pp. 81–82.

20. All Wilson quotations come from *The Public Papers of Woodrow Wilson*, pp. 152–155; my emphases.

21. *No Hiding Place*, pp. 144–145.

22. Brown, ed., *With the Ambulance Service in France: The Wartime Letters of William Gorham Rice, Jr.*, p. 293.

23. Howard's letters are in the Papers of Sidney Coe Howard held by the Bancroft Library at the University of California, Berkeley.

24. *From Poilu to Yank*, p. 112.

25. "The Service," *History of the American Field Service*, vol. I, p. 8.

26. *Out to Win*, p. 59.

27. "The Effort in America," *The History of the American Field Service*, vol. I, pp. 39–40.

28. *My Green Age*, p. 41.

29. *Behind the Wheel of a War Ambulance*, p. 10.

30. *American Volunteers with the Allies*, p. 281.

31. Fuess, *The Amherst Memorial Volume*, p. 9.

32. *We Met by the Way*, p. 17.

33. *History of the American Field Service*, vol. III, p. 310; L. D. Geller erro-

neously attributes this clever piece to Edward M. Ross (*The American Field Service Archives*, p. 64).

34. "An Ambulance-Driver's Fire-Baptism," *Literary Digest* (Sept. 29, 1917), p. 57.

35. "The Harvest of the Night," *Harper's Magazine* (May 1917), p. 801.

36. *Our Part in the Great War*, p. 44.

37. From a form letter (dated September 18, 1916) sent to all persons who inquired about serving in Richard Norton's corps; in the American Red Cross files housed in the National Archives.

38. *Soldier Letters*, p. 12.

39. "My Trip to the Front," *Harper's Magazine*, p. 185.

40. *A Stop at Suzanne's*, p. 14.

41. *Soldier Letters*, p. 11.

42. Geller, *The American Field Service Archives of World War I, 1914–1917*, p. 48.

43. "For France Today," p. 28.

44. *The American Field Service Archives of World War I*, pp. 10–11.

45. Ibid., p. 10.

46. Brown, ed., "With the Ambulance Service in France: The Wartime Letters of William Gorham Rice," *Wisconsin Magazine of History* (Summer, 1918), p. 292.

47. *Ambulancing on the French Front*, p. 20.

48. *At the Front in a Flivver*, p. 5.

49. *Ambulance 464*, p. viii.

50. McConnell is quoted in the editor's Introduction to McConnell's posthumous *Flying for France*.

51. *Vanguard of American Volunteers*, p. 241.

52. Morse, p. 241; McConnell's words also appear in *Source Records of the Great War*, vol. VII, pp. 266–267.

53. *No. 6: A Few Pages from the Diary of an Ambulance Driver*, p. 114.

54. "For Love of France," *The Outlook* (Dec. 27, 1916), p. 930.

55. *The Selected Correspondence of Kenneth Burke and Malcolm Cowley, 1915–1981*, p. 50.

56. Joshua G. B. Campbell, "The Section in Flanders," *Friends of France*, p. 122.

57. *Ambulance 464*, p. 51.

58. Sleeper, ed., *Diary of Section VIII*, p. 39.

59. *From Poilu to Yank*, pp. 182–183.

60. Karl Winwright, as interviewed by G. Frederic Lees in the Continental Edition of the *Daily Mail*, September 27, 1917; cited in Hervier, *The American Volunteers with the Allies*.

61. *At the Front in a Flivver*, p. 3.

62. *Letters Written Home from France*, p. 39.

63. *Somewhere in France: Personal Letters of Reginald Noël Sullivan, Sanitary Section Unit 65 of the American Ambulance Field Service*, p. 48.

64. *Ambulance 464*, p. 57.

65. *No Hiding Place*, pp. 151–152.

66. Letter of 21 September 1916 to Mrs. Duncan McDuffie, his sister.

67. *The Fledgling*, pp. 58–63.

68. Quoted in a photo caption in "Across Albania with an Ambulancier," *Travel* (April 1918), p. 12.

69. *Soldier Letters*, p. 45.

70. Ibid., p. 109; my emphasis.

71. *Camion Letters*, Martin W. Sampson, ed., p. 37.

72. Ibid., p. 74.

73. Byrd's letter is reproduced in *Camion Letters*, p. 38.

74. American Field Service *Bulletin* No. 85 (March 15, 1918).

75. "For Love of France," *The Outlook* (December 27, 1916), p. 930.

CHAPTER EIGHT: SOME FEMALE DRIVERS AND OTHER NOTE-WORTHY VOLUNTEERS

1. One recent treatment devotes several pages to female American ambulance drivers: Dorothy and Carl J. Schneider, *Into the Breach: American Women Overseas in World War I* (New York: Viking, 1991), pp. 98–101. Unfortunately, the material is rife with major errors of fact and inference, particularly with regard to some of the women who are said to have driven for the American Women's Hospital and the separate and

discrete paragraphs on Mrs. Guy Napier-Martin and Mary Dexter, who were in fact the same person.

2. *American Women's Activism in World War I*, p. 163.

3. "A Certain Restless Ambition: Women Physicians and World War I," *American Quarterly* (December 1989), p. 637.

4. "Miss Sinclair's Genius," London *Daily News* (August 24, 1915). Samuel Hynes's *A War Imagined* discusses Sinclair's book and West's review in some detail; pp. 93–96.

5. *A Journal of Impressions in Belgium*, p. 224.

6. Ibid., p. 4.

7. Ibid., p. 64.

8. Barbara McLaren, *Women of the War*, pp. 113–114.

9. *The Outlook* (October 3, 1917), pp. 170–172.

10. See Arthur Marwick, *Women at War, 1914–1918*, p. 21. Rather than being a VAD, Kauffman's driver was actually a "Fanny" — that is, a member of the First Aid Nursing Yeomanry (FANY), which was formed in 1914 by Miss Ashley-Smith. Shocked by the effrontery of Ashley-Smith and her group of women when they first proposed to drive their own cars as ambulances in the war zone, the British War Office responded with a terse "Women — nurses — no possible use for them in France." Unfazed, Ashley-Smith turned to the British Red Cross, who agreed to sponsor her First Aid Nursing Yeomanry. The Fannys (their own term for themselves) grew in number from an original dozen or so to over forty in 1918 (Cushing, *From a Surgeon's Journal*).

11. Mentioned more frequently, perhaps, than female English drivers were those from Scotland. For example, while serving in Macedonia, Cole-man Clark noticed "a lot of Scottish women driving ambulances down here. They are quite a famous organization." In a later letter he adopted a familiar line: "[A French doctor] who worked with the Scottish women . . . told me that nine out of ten were suffragettes, and that . . . it was their scheme to be as much like men as possible" (*Soldier Letters*, pp. 58, 67–68). Clark was undoubtedly referring to the women who drove for the Scottish Women's Hospital, a unit of doctors, nurses, and ambu-lance drivers organized by Dr. Elsie Inglis. One of the champions of female volunteers was Dr. Hector Munro, a Scotsman who organized an ambulance corps in early August of 1914. His group consisted of two English women (Lady Dorothy Fielding and Elsie Knocker), one American (Mrs. Helen Gleason), and an 18-year-old Scot (Mairi Chis-

holm, an avid motorcyclist). Dr. Munro's group began driving in September of 1914 for hospitals near Ghent and Furnes (Marwick, p. 105; see also McLaren, p. 47). Mrs. Knocker once drove her "ambulance car to and fro on the road between Dixmude and Funes under such heavy shell fire that men [on the same road] broke down and were unable to continue driving under the strain of the terrible ordeal" (McLaren, p. 47). In November of their first year, Knocker and Chisholm were stationed in the Belgian village of Pervyse just behind the trenches, where the papers called them "the heroines of Pervyse" (Marwick, p. 105). Both women were gassed in 1918 and their post was closed. Another remarkable ambulance driver — an Australian — was Olive King. First serving in Belgium with a "small private organization . . . , the Allies Field Ambulance Corps . . . ," King was abandoned there by the organization's (male) leaders. She and two other female drivers barely escaped a German advance and made their way to London (*One Woman at War: Letters of Olive King, 1915–1920*, p. 3). In May of 1915, King signed on as a driver for the Scottish Women's Hospitals, which at that time was beginning to set up a number of field hospitals near the battle lines in Belgium and France. In October of 1915, King and other members of Dr. Inglis's Scottish Women's Hospital Unit headed for Macedonia, where the working conditions were severe, the weather horrid, and the mountainous terrain impassable. King's letters, however, reveal her to be inimitably courageous, resolute, and resourceful. Eventually, she left the Scottish Women's Hospital Unit and took the challenging position of driver for the Serbian Army.

12. *The House of the Good Neighbor*, pp. 206–207.

13. In 1921 a consortium of these groups was formed as the "Women's Overseas Service League." In addition to the text statistics, the official history of the WOSL catalogues a total of ninety-one World War I "major service organizations," including military units and selected British and Canadian groups (Sillia, pp. 1–2, 300–301).

14. Bradley, *In Back of the Front in France*, pp. xi–xii.

15. Paul-Louis Hervier, *American Volunteers with the Allies*, p. 33.

16. Ibid., p. 34.

17. Bradley, p. 10.

18. Bradley had to remove religious tracts and chewing gum from the comfort kits. "The French Government," she said, "disapproves of the first article, and the all-confiding stomach of the poilu of the second" (*In Back of the Front*, p. 36).

19. Ibid., p. 89.

20. *The Overseas War Record of the Winsor School, 1914–1919,* pp. 2 ff.

21. Ibid., p. 55.

22. Ibid., pp. 20–21.

23. The Winsor School material varies in content and vividness, and not all of the fifty-eight Winsor alumnae who served overseas drove ambulances or light camions. Nora (Eleanor) Saltonstall was not officially an *ambulancier,* but did do some unusual driving. Saltonstall worked in a French *autochir* (a vehicular hospital accompanying troops) and sometimes ended up driving the clumsy thing herself. One squally evening, for example, she was driving a doctor over a barely visible road and got the motorized contraption stuck in the mud. After several similar experiences, she felt like "a regular camion driver, dirty, but so accustomed to the job that it is no longer tiring" (*The Overseas War Record . . . ,* p. 86).

24. Hervier, pp. 43–44.

25. Mary Beth Rogers, *We Can Fly: Stories of Katherine Stinson and Other Gutsy Texas Women,* pp. 11–23. Having been turned down as a reconnaissance pilot, in 1918 Stinson volunteered as an ambulance driver, a duty she carried out in London and France during the autumn and winter of 1918 until she was incapacitated by the flu after the war. Also, see Claudia M. Oakes, *U.S. Women in Aviation Through World War I* (Washington, D.C.: Smithsonian Institution Press, 1978), p. 37.

26. Jane Darlington Irwin, Thomson's daughter, is quoted in a photo caption in the (often unreliable) section on female ambulance drivers in Schneider, *Into the Breach,* p. 99.

27. *Lest We Forget: A History of the Women's Overseas Service League,* p. 217.

28. *From Pinafores to Politics,* p. 226.

29. Ibid., pp. 286, 290. Harriman was less interested in her work directing a unit of female drivers for the ARC during the autumn of 1918 than in dropping dozens of names and reciting the political gossip about the post-Armistice Peace Conference, of which she liked to think she was a part (pp. 292–325).

30. The first American Women's Hospital was established at Luzancy (near Château-Thierry), before moving to Blérancourt at the end of March of 1919. According to Esther Lovejoy, it had a corps of six women drivers, who "were lithe, strong, and . . . fair to look upon. The appearance of our chauffeuses was a valuable asset for the reason that men are men the world around, and all the gasoline in France was controlled by poor, easy man. Surely it was wise to have chauffeuses who found favor in his eyes" (*Certain Samaritans,* p. 28). Lovejoy, it will be remembered, was

the one who spoke so patronizingly of the "little chauffeuress" who drove her around the embattled roads of the Pont-à-Mousson sector.

31. Lorraine Nelson Spritzer, *The Belle of Ashby Street: Helen Douglas Mankin and Georgia Politics*, pp. 12–13; see also Sillia, *Lest We Forget . . .*, p. 219. Supported by such a compelling background, Douglas went on to become perhaps the most influential and respected Georgia politician during the 1930s and 1940s.

32. Despite de Milhau's achievements as an artist, *ambulancier*, police-woman, civic leader, and honorary Shinnecock Indian, no biography of this fascinating woman has yet been written.

33. Schneider, *Into the Breach*, p. 100.

34. Dexter, *In the Soldier's Service*, pp. 137 and 202 n; see also *The Overseas War Record of the Winsor School*, p. 81.

35. Ibid., p. 144.

36. Ibid., p. 151. Dexter's GMC had a governor on it that restricted its speed to 25 mph, which made it difficult for her to keep up with Lowther's Wolseley when the group finally caravaned to their forward base.

37. Ibid., p. 153.

38. Dexter's moving account of this period, which appears in her letter of March 23, 1918, is filled with selfless praise for the work and courage of others (*In Back of the Front*, pp. 183–185).

39. Ibid., p. 191.

40. Another American woman, Charlotte Read, had joined the Hackett-Lowther Unit just prior to this time. Read's lifesaving body slide into the farmhouse cellar is described in Chapter Four: Under Fire. Read was one of the "very few women" who preceded Dexter to a front-line *poste*.

41. Ibid., pp. 205–206.

42. *The Overseas War Record of the Winsor School* mentions these awards (p. 81). In addition to Dexter's letters in *In a Soldier's Service*, another letter from Dexter appears in the Winsor School collection (pp. 71 ff) under her married name, Mrs. Guy Napier-Martin.

43. *New York Times* (April 13, 1992), A 13:4–5.

44. San Francisco *Chronicle* (April 13, 1992), A 12:2–3.

45. Schickel, *The Disney Version: The Life, Times, Art, and Commerce of Walt Disney*, pp. 63–65.

46. Diane Johnson, *Dashiell Hammett: A Life*, pp. 22–23, 307 n.

47. "The Spirit of Henry Tanner," reprinted in "Henry Ossawa Tanner: The Life and Work of an African American Artist," supplement to the San Francisco *Sunday Examiner & Chronicle* (February 16, 1992), p. 3.

48. Ibid., p. 5.

49. Marcia Mathews, *Henry Ossawa Tanner: American Artist*, pp. 160–162, 173.

50. Anderson, *Louis Bromfield*, p. 24. The *Cambridge Biographical Dictionary* (1990 edition) claims that Bromfield joined the French Army in 1914, whereas in fact he was in college until 1917.

51. However much it might be inspired by idealism and conscience, enlisting for service in a military organization, at base, is an act of irrevocable contract tacitly sanctioned and endorsed by political, legal, and cultural (patriotic) consensus. As such, *enlisting* in the army differs significantly from *volunteering* to serve in a charitable organization consisting of fellow volunteers, who are presumably mainly motivated by their personal conscience or by selfless, humanitarian considerations.

52. Excerpts from Peirce's richly descriptive letter to Professor C. T. Copeland discussing the region and explaining the formation of the Club can be found in Howe, *The Harvard Volunteers in Europe*, pp. 118 ff. An equally vivid discussion of the Thur (valley) is included in Peirce's account of Richard Hall's death in "Christmas Eve, 1915," *Friends of France*, pp. 139–147. Clips from his November journals, alternatingly hilarious and somber, also appear in *Friends of France*, pp. 182–186.

53. Prior to World War I, Peirce studied painting at the Julien Academy in Paris. During World War II (1944), Peirce won the national "Artists for Victory" contest. His *Haircut by the Sea* is in the Metropolitan Museum of Modern Art, New York, and other paintings by him hang in the Whitney (New York), the Brooklyn Museum, the Pennsylvania Academy of Fine Arts, and the AFS Museum in Blérancourt.

54. Quotations come from Geller, *The American Field Service Archives*, p. 31. One of Peirce's parodies was a poem, "Captain Kipling and Doctor Gros," which Geller also mentions, p. 8.

55. See Gleason, *Our Part in the Great War*, pp. 58–59.

56. On July 7, 1916, Lovering Hill, the American head of Section 3, wrote A. Piatt Andrew, asking that two of his men be given an early and permanent leave — one for "his stupidity" and Peirce for his "Quartier Latin existence [which] without doubt had caused a lot of the harm for which the Section is notorious." In the same letter, Hill protested that

"they are both good fellows . . . so you can see how I hate doing this and why I should so much prefer to have them spirited away [by Andrew's putting them on permanent leave] than to have a public firing. . . ." Andrew apparently agreed to go along with Hill's request, for on July 21 Hill reported that the two men are "leaving [for Paris] today," having been "notified . . . that I [Hill] don't want them back" (letters in the AFS Library and Archives).

57. Weeks, *My Green Age,* p. 43.

58. Crosby's mood swings began to alternate between the extremes of what Weeks called "his pious mood" (Weeks, p. 49) and that of resigned fatalism. Indicative of the former is a letter to his sister (Nov. 23, 1917) in which he describes surviving a near miss. "I was reading the Bible yesterday morning," he wrote, "and I noticed a passage (Romans X, 15): 'Whosoever shall call upon the name of the Lord shall be saved.' And a few hours later I was praying as I've never prayed before" (*War Letters,* p. 165). As for the other extreme, on October 2, 1917, he wrote his mother that the war makes a person feel "so small and useless that one gets to feel what difference does it make whether you get killed or not? After all, you've got to die sooner or later," he wrote, "so what's the difference?" (Ibid., p. 89). His periodic fluctuations of mood are also evident in Crosby's journals (edited by Geoffrey Wolff). In December of 1929, Crosby fulfilled a suicide pact with another woman in a dingy New York hotel room.

59. The date comes from Philip Sidney Rice, who met Hillyer on the passage over, according to Rice's *An American Crusader at Verdun.* Although he could claim some standing as a poet in the 1920s and 1930s, Hillyer was perhaps even more influential as a teacher of poetry at Harvard and Delaware, as evinced by the testimonials in a special issue of *Venture* (1962), a University of Delaware publication.

60. Townsend Ludington, *John Dos Passos: A Twentieth-Century Odyssey,* p. 131. Dos Passos converted part of this novel into his "Seven Times Round the Walls of Jericho," which went unpublished for several decades.

61. Nordhoff, *The Fledgling,* pp. 66–69.

62. Lawson, "No Man's Land" (an excerpt from his unpublished autobiography), *Lost Generation Journal* (Winter, 1977–1978), p. 12.

63. A complete roster of the forty-five men in Section 60 appeared in the Paris *Herald.* Richard Norton pasted the news item in his diary on the page reserved for June 2, 1917 — although that was probably not

the date of the story, in that June 2 does not match up with Ludington's information or with the dates of Dos Passos' letters.

64. Ibid., p. 20.

65. Cf. Seabrook's autobiography, *No Hiding Place*.

66. Howard's papers and letters are held in the Bancroft Library, University of California, Berkeley.

67. French truck (camion) sections were called Transport Materiale Units. Using five-ton Pierce-Arrows, the TMU drivers hauled ammunition, 75- and 37-mm cannons, trench mortars, baby tanks, machine guns, baggage, barbwire, engineering supplies, food, and even troops. American TMUs were grouped into the Réserve Mallet, named in honor of the head of the corps, Captain Richard Mallet. They constituted a reserve because, as one camion driver explained, the trucks are "attached to no Army Corps, but rather [are] held in reserve for emergency duty whenever a crisis [occurs] . . ." (Introductory Note, *Camion Cartoons* by Kenneth Day, p. vii).

68. Cowley, *Exile's Return*, p. 37.

69. The Cornell Unit, which was the first to accept camion duty, maintained that the matter was initiated by French governmental authorities when they approached Andrew and asked him "to take over as much as was feasible of the transport work" (*Camion Letters*, p. vi). In the *History of the American Field Service*, vol. III, p. 7, however, A. Piatt Andrew says the reverse: in early April, *he* approached *the French* and asked if the AFS could help transport munitions. In view of a letter (April 17, 1917) in the AFS archives from Henry Sleeper to Andrew, the latter seems likely. Sleeper told Andrew that he had recently talked to "quantities of splendid looking fellows" who showed up at his Boston office to volunteer for the AFS, "determined to do something." Sleeper realized that although the AFS could use some of these men, it could not use all "75 a week," which had been the average rate the previous month. Sleeper was particularly reluctant to turn any of them away, he said, lest "the man who is refused spreads the rumor that we do not need and can not use any more men." He pleaded with Andrew, therefore, to "*use all your wits to find a temporary way of placing the men I send over* . . ." [my emphasis]. To find places for the surplus of volunteers, Andrew may well have initiated the idea of using his new drivers in the French camion service. Whatever the case, a detailed history of the Réserve Mallet's duties and movements can be found in AFS *Bulletin* 84 (March 8, 1919).

70. A more curious explanation is logged in Richard Norton's private diary.

On May 30, 1917, Norton met with Captain Aujay, the French officer in charge of the *Service Sanitaire,* and according to Norton, "Aujay said he had recently stopped Andrews [sic] from cabling for 500 Ford cars & that he, Aujay, was going to keep Andrews [sic] to the Transport work & give all the Sanitary section work to the Red Cross [that is, the Norton-Harjes sections]." Curiously, nowhere does Andrew mention Aujay's canceling his 500-car order. Meanwhile, the number of AFS volunteers was increasing dramatically (see note 57). In *Ambulance 464,* Bryan noted that 110 volunteers arrived during the week of July 19, 1917, and 100 had arrived the previous week — as compared with 15 in January, before the United States declared war (p. 121).

71. *Camion Letters,* p. 7.

72. "Here was a new request for help, and only one reply was possible," Andrew wrote, attributing his positive response to all volunteers (*History of the AFS,* vol. I, p. 50). Yet, some volunteers refused to accept truck driving duty. For instance, when Lansing and Skip Warren "were told that we had been registered to drive munitions trucks instead of ambulances . . . , we notified Headquarters that we would only keep to our enlistments if we were given ambulances as originally proposed." They got their ambulances ["Ambulancier," *Lost Generation Journal* (Winter, 1977–1978), p. 11]. William G. Rice, an ambulance driver, saw several new volunteers mutiny when confronted with the news that they were to drive French Army trucks instead of AFS ambulances. "Twenty-four joined the ambulance service of the American [Military] Hospital in Neuilly," Rice noted on July 13, 1917, "and thirty-six went into the [Norton-Harjes sections] run by the American Red Cross" [Brown, ed., "With the Ambulance Service in France . . . ," *Wisconsin Magazine of History* (Autumn, 1981), p. 13].

73. *Camion Letters,* p. 33.

74. Ibid., p. 38. Similar pleas for suspension of judgment are found in many of the camion drivers' letters home.

75. At least five men in the Andover Unit, for instance, were killed in the service (cf. Fuess, *Phillips Academy: Andover in the Great War,* p. 187). Greayer Clover, a casualty of the war, wrote a striking piece for *Collier's Weekly,* called "A Night with the Camion Convoi," describing the nature — and dangers — of camion driving. This article and another narrative essay about his experience in the camion service, "When Our Luck Deserted Us," have been collected in Clover, *A Stop at Suzanne's and Lower Flights* (pp. 55–64, 70–78).

76. *Camion Letters,* p. xi.

77. *Somewhere in France,* p. 39.

78. Ibid., p. 23.

79. Ibid., p. 39.

80. Brown, ed., *With the Ambulance Service in France,* p. 15.

81. Hinrichs, *We Met by the Way,* p. 43.

82. Much of the Cummings material comes from Kennedy, *Dreams in the Mirror,* pp. 134 ff.

83. From a letter to Cummings' father, quoted in *Dreams in the Mirror,* p. 137.

84. Quoted in George Wickes, *Americans in Paris, 1903–1939* (New York: Doubleday, 1969), p. 72.

85. Kennedy dates the arrest as occurring on September 23. However, Richard Norton's daily diary indicates that he heard about their arrest from Herman Harjes on September 18.

86. From a letter to his parents, quoted in *Dreams in the Mirror,* p. 150; Cummings' emphasis.

87. Townsend Ludington, *John Dos Passos: A Twentieth-Century Odyssey,* provides much of this material.

88. From his July 12 letter to Rumsey Martin, *Letters and Diaries of John Dos Passos,* p. 88.

89. *Letters and Diaries,* p. 93.

90. Quoted in Ludington, p. 138.

91. Even though the United States did not declare war on Italy's principal enemy, Austria, until December, the American Red Cross began to consider sending ambulances to Italy as early as September 4, 1917, according to a rumor passed along by Herman Harjes to Richard Norton (as noted in Norton's diary entry of that day). After the Caporetto offensive in late October of 1917, however, the ARC firmed up and accelerated its plans for Italy. In that Caporetto was mostly a German offensive, and because the United States *was* at war with Germany, the ARC felt its plans were justifiable. The first units to go (Sections 1, 2, and 3) were "picked and seasoned men," recruited and selected for the ARC by the Transportation Committee of the American Military Hospital in Neuilly from the available volunteers (such as Dos Passos, Jack Lawson, and Julian Green) who had refused militarization. Dos Passos' Section 1 arrived in Milan on December 6, 1917, and on the 18th left for the front. The other two sections

followed shortly thereafter. In June of 1918, a new section of stateside volunteers (Hemingway's Section 4) was operating in the field, with Section 5 on its way.

92. See the letters and notes in *Letters and Diaries*, pp. 150 ff.

93. Dunbar Maury Hinrichs, *We Met by the Way*, p. 55. In *The Hard White Road*, p. 5, Alden Rogers expressed a similar opinion: "The American Military Police . . . took half the joy of life for everyone on leave [in Paris]."

94. *Letters and Diaries*, p. 142.

95. Ludington, p. 164.

96. Carlos Baker, *Ernest Hemingway: A Biography*, p. 42. Baker's study provides much of this information. Another rich source of information is Michael Reynolds, *Hemingway's First War* (Princeton, N.J.: Princeton University Press, 1976).

97. See Hemingway's letter to Ruth Morrison, in which he wrote, "I left the Croce Rosa Americana Ambulance service a while back . . ." (*Selected Letters*, Carlos Baker, ed., p. 11). Although the date is somewhat open to question, Professor Baker's best estimate sets it at June 22, 1918.

98. *Letters*, pp. 13–15.

99. In fact, the odds are that Hemingway may have *never* driven an ambulance. The figures work out this way: Assuming the accuracy of Professor Baker's date of June 22 for the letter in which Hemingway says he left the ambulance service "a while back," Hemingway's career as an ambulance driver could not have exceeded the seventeen days from June 4 to June 21. That is assuming "a while back" meant no more than one day before the letter was written (on the 22nd). However, if "a while back" meant more than one day, Hemingway would have left the corps sooner, having actually served no more than fifteen or sixteen days. In that three cars were sent out daily during this seventeen-day period, there was a total of 51 trips made (3 x 17). Hemingway, as we know from his remarks in *A Moveable Feast*, drove a Fiat. If Fiats were used for all 51 trips, each Fiat would make three trips (51 trips divided by 17 cars), because a strict rotation of the cars was normal. (If, however, any of the six Fords were sent out, the Fiats would have averaged fewer than three trips per day.) Moreover, each Fiat normally had two drivers who traded off driving. So, each Fiat driver averaged one-and-a-half days driving (and one-and-a-half days riding shotgun).

Thus, Hemingway, like all the other Fiat drivers in the ARC's Italian Section 4, drove an ambulance either one or, at most, two days between June 4 and 21.

CHAPTER NINE: MILITARIZING THE GENTLEMEN VOLUN-TEERS

1. Cable of April 16, 1917. All letters and cables involving the American Red Cross are herein noted as "ARC letter" or "ARC cable" and can be found in the American Red Cross materials held in the National Archives. Technically, former U.S. President William Howard Taft had been named Chairman of the ARC by President Woodrow Wilson (who was *ex officio* President of the ARC). Frequently addressed as Chairman, Eliot Wadsworth was actually Vice-Chairman, but it was he who functioned as the ARC's chief of operations. Mabel T. Boardman served at times as the ARC's Acting Director. Henry P. Davison was an elected member of the ARC's equivalent of a Board of Directors. Along with Wadsworth and Boardman, Davison sat on the nine-person Executive Board. Most significantly, Davison was Chairman of the War Council, created by President Wilson to expand the ARC's membership, enlarge its revenues, and focus its efforts on war relief. Major Grayson Murphy, who worked with Herman Harjes and Richard Norton in Paris, was the army's representative on the War Council.

2. Cf. Andrew, "The Genesis of the American Ambulance Service," p. 376.

3. As DeWitt Millen explained in *Memoirs of 591*: "They [the French people] took better care of the ambulance boys with the French army (with what they had to work with) than the American army did" (p. 15). Moreover, such an arrangement, Lansing Warren noted, "made it easy for us to show the French papers to American MP's and to use our American identifications with the French" ("Ambulancier," p. 138; papers, Hoover Institution Archives).

4. Gaeddert, *History of the American Red Cross*, vol. iv, p. 362 n.

5. Quoted in Andrew Gray, "The American Field Service," *American Heritage* (December 1974), p. 91.

6. The quoted phrase is from Andrew's cable to Henry Sleeper, received on April 26, 1917; in the AFS Archives. Ambulance driver Charles Nordhoff's patriotic fever was also excited by the prospect of the U.S. Army's takeover. "I hope we shall be transferred [militarized]," Nordhoff wrote, "because the pay will make us self-supporting, and any American would rather be in United States uniform nowadays, in spite of the bully way the French treat us . . ." (*The Fledgling*, pp. 134–135). The editor of the AFS *Bulletin* for September 8, 1917, was nearly as supportive as Nord-

hoff and Andrew. (John H. McFadden, the editor of the *Bulletin*, was absent because of illness when this number [10] was put together.) When militarized, he wrote, the AFS "shall, of course, lose some of our independence, but on the other hand, we shall gain in efficiency and stability." The editor also pointed out that by being "detailed back to the French army there will be little disruption of the character of the work done." A few volunteers especially liked the idea of receiving a soldier's wages, although none was as exuberant as Reginald Nöel Sullivan, who exclaimed, "I am really quite excited at the prospect of earning something!" Sullivan was elated because, being independently wealthy and accustomed to a life of leisure, he had never before held down a salaried job (*Somewhere in France*, p. 10).

7. From the cable Sleeper received from Andrew, April 26; in the AFS Archives.

8. From Norton's diary, June 22, 1917. Norton repeated this point in his diary two days later (June 24): "Beatty [from one of Norton's sections] came to talk over various matters. Find he has the same idea about not putting our ambulances under the army as Harjes and I." It is apparent from these comments that Norton did not know that, as of May 26, the issue of militarization had already been officially decided.

9. ARC letter; Kean to Wadsworth, September 7, 1917. American Red Cross officials had expected Harjes to endorse the militarization policy, in that prior to the U.S. declaration of war on April 6 he had pledged his support of such a policy. "Should the situation so develop [as] to involve our becoming absorbed in the army," Harjes wrote Wadsworth in early February, "we shall only be too willing to cooperate and serve to the utmost of our capacity" (ARC letter; February 9, 1917). Having ventured his own support, Harjes believed others would do likewise. "Fully believe," he cabled Eliot Norton the day the United States declared war, "that all our men including their chiefs, that is, the heads of sections as well as your brother [Richard], Kemp [Richard's aide] and myself, would be willing to sign any necessary engagements with the army" (ARC cable; Harjes to Eliot Norton, April 6, 1917). Harjes obviously had a change of heart between the 6th and the 26th of April, when he and Norton told Andrew that they didn't want their ambulance corps militarized.

10. ARC letter; emphasis provided.

11. ARC letter; Eliot Norton to Henry P. Davison, July 27, 1917, emphasis provided.

12. Norton's diary (July 30, 1917).

13. ARC letter; from the Acting Director of the ARC to Eliot Norton, July 13, 1917; written in the presence and presumably under the direction of Colonel Kean.

14. Norton's diary for 22 August 1917; Norton left Paris to visit his men on August 12.

15. ARC letter; Richard Norton, August 25, 1917. According to another ARC letter (Kean to Wadsworth, October 6), when Kean offered Norton a commission as major, he also offered Arthur Kemp one as captain.

16. If a volunteer did not accept militarization, he would be allowed to finish out his term. Then he would be sent back to America "unless [he found] some other occupation," according to Norton's understanding of Kean's plan (ARC letters; Richard to Eliot Norton, August 25, 1917, and Richard Norton to his section leaders, August 25, 1917).

17. ARC letter; Richard to Eliot Norton, August 25, 1917.

18. Norton described this meeting in his August 25 letter to Eliot. An outline of this meeting appears in Norton's diary (August 24, 1917): "[Went] to see Col. Kean in a.m. & give him my resignation & that of [Arthur] Kemp, [Frederick] Havemeyer, [Duncan] Ellsworth, [Herbert] Warden, [Morton] Stelle." Stelle later changed his tune. By September 10, according to Norton's diary, the man was doing "propaganda work for Col. Kean." On the 12th Norton added, "Stelle getting himself disliked by all of us because of the violent propaganda he is preaching for Col. Kean." On the 15th Norton wrote that Stelle was saying "I had misrepresented things to them [the volunteers]." Stelle later helped confiscate (for Kean) a copy of Norton's August 25 letter to his section chiefs.

19. Cf. Andrew, "The Genesis . . . ," p. 369.

20. *Wisconsin Magazine of History,* p. 25

21. ARC letter; Richard to Eliot Norton, August 25.

22. "Ambulancier," p. 142; papers, Hoover Institution Archives.

23. On Sunday, August 26, Norton set off to inform his volunteers of his decision to resign. C. de Florez's account shows the emotional impact of Norton's visit to Section 59: "He [Norton] said a few words, words that come straight from a man's heart and go to others, and then he was gone, this fellow we all love, who will no longer be our chief" (*No. 6,* p. 90). De Florez himself later refused militarization.

24. Norton himself used the "club" analogy when he told William Yorke

Stevenson that because the army was in charge, "the old club volunteer spirit must now be eliminated" (*From Poilu to Yank*, p. 185). The other information and quotations in this paragraph come from ARC letter; Richard to Eliot Norton, August 25, 1917.

25. ARC letter; Norton to Anderson (one of the section chiefs), August 25, 1917.

26. ARC letter; Kean to Wadsworth, October 6, 1917.

27. ARC letter; Kean to Boardman, November 23, 1917.

28. ARC letter; Kean to Davison, November 27, 1917.

29. ARC letter; Richard to Eliot Norton, September 18, 1917.

30. Kean at the time was making an issue of the releases because, much to his unending irritation, Norton had given a story to the Paris *Herald* that ran September 13, 1917. Under the headline "Harjes-Norton Ambulance Is Taken Over by Army," the story's lead began, "The Harjes-Norton Ambulance has been disbanded. . . ." Kean called planting the story "one of the most mischievous of [Norton's] activities," because it caused "all the men . . . [to demand] their releases at once and [to come] pouring into Paris" (ARC letter; Kean to Wadsworth, October 6, 1917).

31. Norton's diary, September 24, 1917.

32. Norton first cited Kean's pledge of lieutenancies for the section leaders in his diary of August 23, 1917. Norton also mentions Kean's promise in an ARC letter, Richard to Eliot Norton, September 4, 1917. Kean's retraction of the promise is mentioned in an ARC letter, Richard to Norton, September 18, 1917.

33. There were several inconsistencies in Kean's implementation of the plan. One involved sections in which only a few drivers accepted militarization. When most of the men in a particular ambulance section transferred into the U.S. Army Ambulance Service, fine. That section was given a USAAS number and allowed to continue its work uninterrupted. However, when nearly all of the drivers in a section rejected militarization, as was common in the Norton-Harjes units, the section was retained only until an army ambulance unit could be brought in to replace it. Then, the men who had rejected militarization were released and sent home, whereas the few drivers who had accepted militarization were sent to Sandricourt (the training camp taken over by the USAAC) as "casuals."

They were held there until enough casuals from other disbanded sections had gathered to constitute a new unit, which would then be immediately returned to ambulance duty. That, supposedly, was the plan. However, Robert Bodfish of Section 647 tells a different story. Bodfish was himself a casual at Sandricourt in October of 1917. By November, enough men had come in for a new ambulance unit, Section 647, to be formed, and on November 9 Harry Anderson, who had been the chief of the disbanded Norton-Harjes Section 21, was assigned to head the new section. However, the section was not returned to the field as its men had been led to expect. Instead, Section 647 found itself relegated to menial maintenance and janitorial duties while inexperienced, raw, and cocky units from the army's stateside camp at Allentown arrived, trained for a few days, and were dispatched to the front lines. Bodfish's section did not leave Sandricourt until February 8, 1918, after which the unit was shuffled around behind the lines. Although officially formed in early November of 1917 and consisting of experienced volunteer drivers from a variety of units, Section 647 was given no significant ambulance duty until mid-April of 1918 (*A History of Section 647*, pp. 11–23).

34. *The Hard White Road*, p. 30.

35. This letter of September 12, 1917, is quoted in the Introduction to the 1968 edition of Dos Passos' autobiographical *One Man's Initiation*, p. 25. Major Murphy is the only military officer known for sure to have accompanied Norton on his first visit to his sections after his resignation.

36. Gray, "The American Field Service," p. 91.

37. Diary entry for October 3, 1917.

38. Gray, p. 91.

39. Clover, *A Stop at Suzanne's*, p. 92. The man's language made such an impression on Clover that he virtually repeated it word for word in his letter home on September 29. " 'Join the United States army,' " Clover quoted the man as saying (in Clover's letter). " 'I want you men to come down here tomorrow morning and become soldiers, you are nothing now — you are nothing but a bunch of outcasts' " (*A Stop at Suzanne's*, p. 232; see also p. 108). Of the drivers who rejected militarization into the Transport Division, some went home and others joined aviation, infantry, or artillery units.

40. *White Road of Mystery*, pp. 153–154.

41. ARC letter; Kean to Wadsworth, September 7, 1917.

42. Norton's diary, September 10, 1916.

43. Norton's diary, September 6, 1917. Whether or not Norton wanted anything to do with the ARC ambulances going to Italy, the issue was soon moot. When the diplomatic details were being worked out in

Rome, Norton's name came up, and the Italian officials eliminated him at once, saying "that owing to the old trouble over Cyrene, it would be better to send someone else" (Norton's diary, October 5, 1917). John Dos Passos suggests what the "old trouble" was in his identification of Norton as "the man who smuggled half the Ludovici throne out of Italy" (*One Man's Initiation*, p. 25). Norton was director of the excavation of the Cyrene ruins in 1910–1911 for the Archaeological Institute of America (of which his father had been the first President) and for the Boston Museum of Fine Arts. Whatever the reason, Norton was *persona non grata* in Italy.

44. ARC letter; Richard to Norton, September 4, 1917.

45. Ibid.

46. The letter from Sleeper to Andrew of April 27, 1917, is in the AFS Archives. See also note 57 of Chapter Eight.

47. *Ambulance 464*, p. 121.

48. Gray, p. 92.

49. ARC letter; Richard to Norton, September 6, 1917 (attached by R. N. as an addendum to the letter of September 4).

50. ARC letter; Eliot Norton to Wadsworth, March 12, 1917.

51. *The Hard White Road*, p. 25.

52. Gray, p. 91.

53. Cf. *Scientific American* (Feb. 17, 1917), p. 179.

54. Norton's diary, October 22, 1917.

55. AFS *Bulletin* (No. 12), September 22, 1917.

56. AFS *Bulletin* (No. 84), March 8, 1919.

57. *History of AFS*, vol. I, pp. 54–55. Sleeper's figure is corroborated by the numbers in American Field Service *Bulletin* No. 84 (March 8, 1919).

58. ARC letter; Kean to Wadsworth, 6 October 1917. Kean may have been thinking of the entire AFS, not just its ambulance drivers. If so, his 50 percent is correct: 300 (of 800) truck drivers plus 600 (of 1,000) ambulance drivers equals 900 (of 1,800), or 50 percent of the total drivers.

59. *From Poilu to Yank*, p. 184.

60. *The American National Red Cross in World War I, 1917–1918*, vol. iv, p. 363. Like Kean, Gaeddert laid the blame for the low percentage at the feet of

Richard Norton, who "discouraged his men" from accepting militarization (ibid., fn 302).

61. AFS *Bulletin* (No. 52), July 6, 1918.

62. Diaries and journals from the USAAS days were rarely edited into books for publication, though there are numerous works of this sort from the volunteer period before the American Army took over the ambulance and camion service. Guy Bowerman's *Compensations of the War* (edited by Carnes) is the diary of a USAAC man, and its daily entries typically run a couple of lines in length. In contrast, for example, the entries (though not accounting for every day) in William Yorke Stevenson's *At the Front in a Flivver,* an edition of the journal he kept during his first term as a volunteer, seldom run under two or three pages each.

63. *Diary of S.S.U. 18,* p. 27.

EPILOGUE

1. Gray, pp. 91–92. The AFS also participated in World War II, after which it expanded its scholarship program into a worldwide student exchange.

2. ARC letter; Richard to Eliot Norton, September 4, 1917.

3. Norton's diary, October 23 and November 1, 1917.

4. Norton's diary, November 1, 1917. Norton had been warned of this eventuality on October 15, according to his diary: "Saw [Ralph] Preston at the Red Cross who gave me little hope of getting any work. He says the trouble is Genl. Pershing is still angry about my speaking in a letter I wrote the sections of 'mere privates.' "

Bibliography

Albrecht-Carrie, Rene. *The Meaning of the First World War* (Englewood Cliffs, N.J.: Prentice Hall, 1965).

Albright, Alan. *The Field Service: From Assistance to the War Wounded to Educating World Citizens* (n.p.: privately printed, 1993).

Aldridge, John W. *After the Lost Generation* (New York: McGraw-Hill, 1951).

"Ambulance-Driver's Fire-Baptism," *Literary Digest*, 55 (Sept. 29, 1917).

"American Ambulance," *Literary Digest*, 55 (Aug. 18, 1917).

"American Ambulance," *Outlook*, 114 (Dec. 6, 1916).

"American Ambulance Hospital at Neuilly: Pictures by Georges Pavis," *Scribner's Magazine*, 61 (May 1917).

"American Ambulance Hospital in Paris," *Science*, 41, n.s. (Jan. 8, 1915).

American Field Service. *Diary of Section VIII: American Ambulance Field Service*, Henry D. Sleeper, ed. (Boston: privately printed [T. Todd], 1917).

The American Field Service Archives of World War I, compiled by L. D. Geller (New York: Greenwood Press, 1989).

American Field Service Bulletin, nos. 1–87, original series (July 4, 1917–April 26, 1919).

American Red Cross, *The Work of the American Red Cross: Report by the War Council of Appropriations and Activities from Outbreak of War to November 1, 1917* (Washington, D.C.: American Red Cross, 1917).

"Americans Behind the Lines in France," *Literary Digest*, 51 (Aug. 21, 1915).

"America's Men," *Bookman*, 44 (Oct. 1916).

Anderson, David D. *Louis Bromfield* (New York: Twayne Publishers, 1964).

Andrew, A. Piatt. "For the Love of France," *Outlook*, 114 (Dec. 27, 1916).

―――. "The Genesis of the American Ambulance Service with the French Army, 1915–1917," *Military Surgeon*, 57 (Oct. 1925). This article is a slightly revised version of Andrew's essay, "Some of the Early Problems," contained in the Introduction to *History of the American Field Service in France: "Friends of France," 1914–1917*, 3 vols. (Boston: Houghton Mifflin, 1920).

―――. *Letters Written Home from France in the First Half of 1915*, Boston: n.p., privately printed, 1916).

Anonymous. "The Ambulance Corps: A Collegiate Crusade," *Lost Generation Journal*, V:2 (Winter, 1977–1978). Compiled, according to the editor, from articles in the files of the American Red Cross by H. B. Atkinson ("Ambulance Service, 1914–1918," 1939) and by Clyde E. Buckingham ("Ambulance Service in Europe Before U.S. Entrance in World War I," 1964).

"The Backwash of the Battle," *Outlook*, 117 (Oct. 24, 1917).

Baker, Carlos. *Ernest Hemingway: A Life Story* (New York: Charles Scribner's Sons, 1969).

Bakewell, Charles. *The Story of the American Red Cross in Italy* (New York: Macmillan, 1920).

Baldridge, C. LeRoy, and Hilmar R. Baukage. *I Was There* (New York: G.P. Putnam's Sons, 1919).

The Battle of Verdun (1914–1918), Michelin Illustrated Guides to the Battlefields (1914–1918) Series (Clermont-Ferrand, France: Michelin & Cie., 1920).

Beveridge, Albert. *What Is Back of the War* (Indianapolis: Bobbs-Merrill, 1915).

Bicknell, Ernest Percy. *With the Red Cross in Europe 1911–1922* (Washington, D.C.: American National Red Cross, 1938).

Blond, Georges. *Verdun*, tr. by Frances Frenaye (New York: Macmillan, 1964).

Bodfish, Robert W. *A History of Section 647: United States Army Ambulance Service with the French Army* (Worcester, Mass: Stobbs Press, 1919).

Bowerman, Guy E. *The Compensations of War: The Diary of an Ambulance Driver During the Great War,* Mark C. Carnes, ed. (Austin: University of Texas Press, 1983).

Bradley, Amy O. *Back of the Front in France: Letters from Amy Owen Bradley, Motor Driver of the American Fund for French Wounded* (Boston: Butterfield, 1918).

Brittain, Vera. *War Diary 1913–1917: Chronicle of Youth,* Alan Bishop, ed. (London: Victor Gollancz, 1981).

Brown, George C., ed. "With the Ambulance Service in France: The Wartime Letters of William Gorham Rice, Jr., S.S.U. 1–66," *Wisconsin Magazine of History;* Summer, 1981; Autumn, 1981; Winter 1981–82.

Brown, J. Paulding. "Letter," *Harvard Alumni Bulletin* (June 23, 1915).

Bryan, Julien H. *"Ambulance 464": Encore de Blessés* (New York: Macmillan, 1918).

Buckingham, Clyde E. "Ambulance Service in Europe Before U.S. Entrance in World War I"; typescript ms held in the files the American Red Cross.

Buswell, Leslie, ed. *Ambulance No. 10: Personal Letters from the Front* (Boston: Houghton Mifflin, 1916).

Camion Letters from American College Men: Volunteer Drivers of the American Field Service in France 1917, Martin W. Sampson, ed. (New York: Henry Holt, 1918).

Canfield [Fisher], Dorothea. *The Day of Glory* (New York: Henry Holt, 1919).

Carmichael, Jane. *First World War Photographers* (London and New York: Routledge, 1989).

Cartwright, Reginald. "Motor-Ambulance Driver's Notes from the Front," *Scientific American* Supplement 83 (June 16, 1917), 84 (Nov. 17, 1917).

Chapman, Guy. *Vain Glory* (London: Cassell, 1968).

Chomel, Vital. "Les Archives des Benefices de Guerre, 1914–1919," *La Gazette des Archives*, 1968, no. 62.

Church, J. R. *The Doctor's Part* (New York: Appleton, 1918).

Clark, Glen W., ed. *"Lest We Forget": A History of Section 503 of the U.S. Army Ambulance Service with the French Army* (Philadelphia: Westminster Press, 1920).

Clark, Salter Storrs, and Caroline G. Clark, eds. *Soldier Letters: Coleman Tileston Clark and Salter Storrs Clark. Jr., Their Stories in Extracts from Their Letters and Diaries* (privately printed by L. Middleditch Co., Westfield, Conn., 1919).

Clarke, Ida Clyde Gallagher. *American Women and the World War* (New York: Appleton, 1918).

Clover, Greayer. *A Stop at Suzanne's and Lower Flights* (New York: George N. Doran, 1919).

Clymer, Floyd. *Henry's Wonderful Model T: 1908–1927* (New York: McGraw-Hill, 1955).

Cowley, Malcolm. *Exile's Return* (New York: Viking Press, 1951).

Coyle, Edward R. *Ambulancing on the French Front* (New York: Britton, 1918).

Crosby, Harry. *War Letters* (Paris: Black Sun Press, 1932).

Cruttwell, C.R.M.F. *A History of the Great War 1914–1918* (Chicago: Academy of Chicago Publishers, 1991).

Cummings, E. E. *The Enormous Room* (New York: Boni and Liveright, 1922).

Cushing, Harvey W. *From a Surgeon's Journal: 1915–18* (Boston: Little, Brown, 1936).

Davison, Henry Pomeroy. *The American Red Cross in the Great War* (New York: Macmillan, 1919).

Dawson, Coningsby. *Out to Win: The Story of America in France* (New York: John Lane Co., 1918).

Day, Kirkland H. *Camion Cartoons* (Boston: Marshall Jones Co., 1919).

Dexter, Mary. *In the Soldier's Service: War Experiences of Mary Dexter, England, Belgium, France, 1914–1918* (Boston: Houghton Mifflin, 1918).

Diary of S.S.U. 18 (Paris: n.p., privately printed, 1917).

Diary of S.S.U. 19, in three parts (Paris: n.p., privately printed, 1917, 1918).

"Directory of Former Fellows of the American Field Service Fellowships, 1919–1942," *Institute of International Education*, XXIII (May 1, 1942).

Donaldson, Robert A. *Turmoil: Verses Written in France* (Boston: Houghton Mifflin, 1919).

Dos Passos, John. *The Fourteenth Chronicle: Letters and Diaries of John Dos Passos*, Townsend Ludington, ed. (Boston: Gambit, 1973).

———. *One Man's Initiation: 1917* (Ithaca, N.Y.: Cornell University Press, 1969; orig. pub. 1920 by Allen & Unwin Ltd.).

Eksteins, Modris. *Rites of Spring: The Great War and the Birth of the Modern Age* (Boston: Houghton Mifflin, 1989).

Fenton, Charles A. "Ambulance Drivers in France and Italy: 1914–1918," *American Quarterly* , III (Winter, 1951).

Ferro, Marc. *The Great War, 1914–1918* (London: Routledge & Kegan Paul, 1973).

Florez, Carlos de. *"No. 6": A Few Pages from the Diary of an Ambulance Driver* (New York: Dutton, 1918).

"Ford Company Gives $500,000 Worth of Ambulances and Equipment," *American Red Cross Bulletin*, September 7, 1917 (from the files of the American Red Cross).

Forsythe, D. P. *Humanitarian Politics: The International Committee of the Red Cross* (Baltimore: Johns Hopkins University Press, 1977).

"Friends of France," Supplement, *New York Herald* (Paris Edition), December 17, 1916.

Friends of France: The Field Service of the American Ambulance Described by Its Members (Boston: Houghton Mifflin, 1916). Includes Stephen Galatti, "The Organization of the Service"; Henry Sydnor Harrison, "At the Back of the Front: Dunkirk and Ypres"; Preston Lockwood, "The Section in Alsace Reconquise"; Everett Jackson, "Last Days in Alsace"; James R. McConnell, "The Section in Lorraine" (orig. appeared in *Outlook* III, Sept. 15, 1915); Frank Hoyt Gailor, "An American Ambulance in the Verdun Attack" (also appeared in 1916, *Living Age* 290, Aug. 12, 1916); Harry Sheahan, "The Section at Verdun"; Joshua G. B. Campbell, "The Section in Flanders"; George Rockwell, "The Beginnings of a New Section"; Emery Pottle, "Un Blesse a Montauville"; Waldo Pierce, "Christmas Eve, 1915." A French edition of this book, translated by Firmin Roz, with a preface by Jules J. Jusserand (French Ambassador to the United States), appeared as *Amis de la France* (Paris: Plon-Nourrit, 1917).

Fuess, Claude Moore, ed. *The Amherst Memorial Volume: A Record of the Contribution Made by Amherst College and Amherst Men in the World War, 1914* (Amherst, Mass.: Amherst College, 1926).

———. *Phillips Academy, Andover, in the Great War* (New Haven: Yale University Press, 1919).

Fussell, Paul. *The Great War and Modern Memory* (New York: Oxford University Press, 1975).

Gaeddert, G. R. "Ambulance Service," *The American National Red Cross in World War I, 1917–1918,* Vol. IV of *The History of the American National Red Cross* (Washington, D.C.: The American National Red Cross, 1950).

Gaines, Ruth Louise. *Helping France: The Red Cross in the Devastated Area* (New York: E. P. Dutton & Co., 1919).

Geller, L. D. *Friends of France: The American Field Service with the French Armies, 1914–1917, 1939–1945* (New York: American Field Service Archives, 1990).

The George C. Marshall Research Foundation. *Posters of World War One and World War Two* (Charlottesville: University of Virginia Press, 1979).

Georges-Renard, Louis. "Ambulanciers Americains," *Revue Politique et Literaire,* XIX (September 29, 1917).

Gibson, Preston. *Battering the Boche* (New York: Century, 1918).

Gilbert, Martin. *Atlas of World War I* (London: Weidenfeld and Nicolson, 1970).

Gilmour, John. "Transportation of Wounded," *Military Surgeon* (Jan. 1918).

Gleason, Arthur H. *Our Part in the Great War* (New York: Frederick A. Stokes, 1917).

Gray, Andrew. "The American Field Service," *American Heritage,* XXVI (Dec. 1974).

Griffiths, William R. *The Great War* (The West Point Military History Series; Wayne, New Jersey: Avery Publishing Group, 1986).

Grissinger, Jay W. "Field Service," *Military Surgeon* (Sept. 1927).

Haller, John S., Jr. *Farmcarts to Fords: A History of the Military Ambulance, 1790– 1925* (Carbondale, Ill.: Southern Illinois University Press, 1992).

Harriman, Florence Jaffray (Hurst). *From Pinafores to Politics* (New York: Henry Holt and Co., 1923).

Harrison, Carter Henry. *With the American Red Cross in France, 1918–1919* (Chicago: R. F. Seymour, 1947).

Hemingway, Ernest. *Green Hills of Africa* (New York: Scribner's, 1935).

———. *Selected Letters 1917–1961,* Carlos Baker, ed. (New York: Charles Scribner's Sons, 1981).

Henniker, Alan. *Transportation on the Western Front: 1914–1918* (London: His Majesty's Stationery Office, 1937).

"Henry Ossawa Tanner: The Life and Work of a Pioneering African American Artist," supplement to the *San Francisco Sunday Examiner & Chronicle* (February 16, 1992).

Hervier, Paul-Louis. *The American Volunteers with the Allies* (Paris: *Edition de La Nouvelle Revue,* 1918). Orig. published in French as *Les Volontaires Americains dans les Rangs Alliés* (1917).

Hildebrand, A. S. "La Chapelle Station," *Outlook,* 116 (Aug. 22, 1917).

Hillyer, Robert S. *The Collected Verse of Robert Hillyer* (New York: Alfred A. Knopf, 1934).

Hinrichs, Dunbar Maury. *We Met by the Way: An Account of a Life* (privately printed by author, 1975). Two volumes. Part 1, Volume I, treats the years up to April 1919; Part 2, Volume I, covers April 1919 to April 1937; Part 3, which makes up the whole of Volume II, treats the years through World War II. Unpublished, Volume II is in type-script.

"His Christmas Letter to His Mother," *Ladies Home Journal*, 34:12 (Dec. 1917).

History of the American Field Service in France: "Friends of France," 1914–1917, 3 vols. (Boston: Houghton Mifflin, 1920).

Horne, Alistair. *The Price of Glory: Verdun 1916* (London: Macmillan, 1962).

"How an American Won the Croix de Guerre," *Literary Digest*, 55 (Sept. 15, 1917).

Howe, Mark A. De Wolfe, ed. *The Harvard Volunteers in Europe: Personal Records of Experience in Military, Ambulance, and Hospital Service* (Cambridge: Harvard University Press, 1916).

Howland, Harold. "American Flying Squadrons," *Independent*, 86 (May 1, 1916).

Hungerford, Edward. *With the Doughboy in France: A Few Chapters of an American Effort* (New York: Macmillan, 1920).

Hynes, Samuel. *A War Imagined: The First World War and English Culture* (New York: Atheneum, 1991).

Imbrie, Robert W. "Across Albania with an Ambulancier," *Travel*, XXX (April 1918).

———. *Behind the Wheel of a War Ambulance* (New York: McBride, 1918).

Irwin, Will. *The Latin at War* (London: Constable & Co., 1917).

James, Henry. "The American Volunteer Motor-Ambulance Corps in France: A Letter to the Editor of an American Journal" (first issued as a pamphlet, 1914), as *Within the Rim* (reissued as *The American Motor Ambulance Corps in France: A Letter to the Editor of an American Journal*, London: W. Collins Sons & Co. Ltd., 1918).

Jay, Paul, ed. *The Selected Correspondence of Kenneth Burke and Malcolm Cowley, 1915–1981* (New York: Viking, 1988).

Johnson, Diane. *Dashiell Hammett: A Life* (New York: Random House, 1983).

Judd, James Robert. *With the American Ambulance in France* (Honolulu: Star-Bulletin Press, 1919).

Kahn, Sy M. "No Armistice for Harry Crosby," *Lost Generation Journal* (Winter, 1977–78).

Kauffman, Ruth Wright. "Woman Ambulance-Driver in France," *Outlook*, 117 (Oct. 3, 1917).

Kautz, John Iden. *Trucking to the Trenches: Letters from France June–November 1917* (Boston: Houghton Mifflin, 1918).

Keegan, John. *The Face of Battle* (New York: Viking, 1976).

Kellogg, Paul. *What the American Red Cross Did to Help Save Italy* (Washington, D.C.: The American Red Cross, 1918).

Kempf, James Michael. *The Early Career of Malcolm Cowley: A Humanist Among the Moderns* (Baton Rouge: Louisiana State University Press, 1985).

Kennedy, Richard S. *Dreams in the Mirror: A Biography of E. E. Cummings* (New York: Liveright, 1980).

Kimber, Arthur Clifford. *The Story of the First Flab: An Account of the Mission of Arthur Clifford Kimber;* comp. by Clara E. Kimber from his letters and other documents (*Friends of France*: San Francisco, 1920).

King, Olive. *One Woman at War: Letters of Olive King, 1915–1920,* ed. with intro by Hazel King (Carlton, Victoria: Melbourne University Press, 1986).

La Motte, E. M. "American Nurse in Paris," *Survey,* 34 (July 10, 1915).

Lacey, Robert. *Ford: The Men and the Machine* (Boston: Little, Brown & Co., 1986).

Lawson, John Howard. "No Man's Land" (an excerpt from his autobiography), *Lost Generation Journal* (Winter, 1977–78).

Leed, Eric. *No Man's Land: Combat and Identity in World War I* (Cambridge: Cambridge University Press, 1979).

"Letters from the Front," *Literary Digest,* 55 (Nov. 3, 1917).

Letters of William Cooper Procter (Cincinnati: privately printed, McDonald Printing Co., 1957).

Liddell Hart, Basil H. *The Real War 1914–1918* (Boston: Little, Brown & Co., 1930).

Lovejoy, Esther Pohl. *Certain Samaritans* (New York: Macmillan, 1933; revised/reset ed.).

———. *The House of the Good Neighbor* (New York: Macmillan, 1919).

Ludington, Townsend. *John Dos Passos: A Twentieth-Century Odyssey* (New York: Dutton, 1980).

Maloney, John. *Let There Be Mercy: The Odyssey of a Red Cross Man* (Garden City, N.Y.: Doubleday, Doran & Company, 1941).

Marshall, S.L.A. *The American Heritage History of World War I* (New York: American Heritage/Bonanza Books, 1964).

Marwick, Arthur. *Women at War, 1914–1918* (Glasgow: William Collins Sons, Fontana Paperbacks/Imperial War Museum, 1977).

Masefield, John. "The Harvest of the Night," *Harper's Magazine,* CXXXIV (May 1917).

Massie, Robert K. *Dreadnought: Britain, Germany, and the Coming of the Great War* (New York: Random House, 1991).

Mathews, Marcia M. *Henry Ossawa Tanner: American Artist* (Chicago: University of Chicago Press, 1969).

McLaren, Barbara. *Women of the War* (New York: Hodder and Stoughton, 1917).

Metz, Donald L. *Running Hot: Structure and Stress in Ambulance Work* (Cambridge, Mass.: Abt Books, 1982).

Millen, DeWitt C. *Memoirs of 591 in the World War* (Ann Arbor: DeWitt C. Millen, 1932).

Mitchell, Clarence V. S. *With a Military Ambulance in France, 1914–1915* (privately printed, 1915).

More, Ellen S. " 'A Certain Restless Ambition': Women Physicians and World War I," *American Quarterly*, 41:4 (December 1989).

Morse, Edwin W. *The Vanguard of American Volunteers: In the Fighting Lines and in Humanitarian Service, August 1914–April 1917* (New York: Scribners, 1919).

Muirhead, James F. "The American Volunteer Ambulance Corps," *Nation*, 104 (Jan. 18, 1917).

————. "Richard Norton's Ambulance," *Nation*, 101 (Dec. 16, 1915).

Murdock, Kenneth B. "Many Soldiers Are an Answer to Three," *Harvard Crimson*, LXXX (Oct. 28, 1921).

National Board for Historical Service. *War Readings* (New York: Charles Scribner's Sons, 1918).

Nordhoff, Charles B. *The Fledgling* (Boston: Houghton Mifflin, 1919).

O'Brian, Alice Lord. *No Glory: Letters from France 1917–1919* (Buffalo, N.Y.: Airport Publishers, c. 1936).

"Odd Ways of Transporting Wounded Soldiers," *Scientific American*, 119 (Aug. 31, 1918).

Orcutt, Philip D. *The White Road of Mystery: The Note-book of an American Ambulancier* (New York: John Lane, 1918).

"Poetry and Art to Repay Their Debt to Italy," *Literary Digest*, 55 (Sept. 29, 1917).

Pottle, Emery. "How the Amherst Spirit Works 'Somewhere in France,' " *Amherst Graduates' Quarterly*, 19 (May 1916).

Rainsford, W. K. "American Ambulance at Verdun," *World's Work*, 33 (Dec. 1916).

Reynolds, Michael. *Hemingway: The Paris Years* (Oxford: Basil Blackwell, 1989).

————. *Hemingway's First War* (Princeton: Princeton University Press, 1976).

————. *The Young Hemingway* (Oxford: Basil Blackwell, 1986).

Rice, Philip Sidney. *An American Crusader at Verdun* (Princeton: by author, 1918). Published earlier in Wilkes Barre, Pa., as *An Ambulance Driver in France*.

Rice, William. See Brown, George C., ed. "With the Ambulance Service in France: The Wartime Letters of William Gorham Rice, Jr., S.S.U. 1–66."

Rickards, Maurice. *Posters of the First World War* (New York: Walker and Company, 1968).

Rock, George, ed. *The History of the American Field Service* (New York: Platen Press, 1956).

Rodgers, Alden. *The Hard White Road: A Chronicle of the Reserve Mallet* (Buffalo, N.Y.: privately printed, 1923).

Rogers, Mary Beth, Sherry A. Smith, and Janelle D. Scott. *We Can Fly: Stories of Katherine Stinson and Other Gutsy Texas Women* (Austin: E. C. Temple; Texas Foundation for Women's Resources, 1983).

Sager, Xavier. "Letters from the Firing Line: The Care of the Wounded," *Scientific American*, 111 (Dec. 19, 1914).

Sanders, Michael, and P. M. Taylor. *British Propaganda During the First World War, 1914–1918* (London: Macmillan, 1982).

Sanger, William Cary, Jr., *Verse* (Utica, N.Y.: Widtman Press, 1954; orig. printed by William Cary Sanger, Sr., 1920).

Schaffer, Ronald. *America in the Great War: The Rise of the War Welfare State* (New York: Oxford University Press, 1991).

——. *The United States in World War I: A Selected Bibliography* (Santa Barbara: Clio Books, 1978).

Schmitt, Bernadotte E., and Harold C. Vedeler. *The World in a Crucible, 1914–1919*, Vol. 18 of *The Rise of Modern Europe* (New York: Harper & Row, 1984).

Schneider, Dorothy, and Carl J. *Into the Breach: American Women Overseas in World War I* (New York: Viking, 1991).

Seabrook, William. *No Hiding Place: An Autobiography* (Philadelphia: Lippincott, 1942).

Service, Robert W. *Rhymes of a Red Cross Man* (New York: Barse & Hopkins, 1916).

Seymour, James William Davenport, ed. *Memorial Volume of the American Field Service in France, "Friends of France," 1914–1917* (Boston: American Field Service, 1921).

Sheahan, Henry. *A Volunteer Poilu* (Boston: Houghton Mifflin, 1916).

Sheehan, Perley P. "In Memory of Lafayette: How Americans Are Paying Their Debt of Gratitude to France," *Munsey's Magazine*, 59:2 (November 1916).

Shepherd, William G. *Confessions of a War Correspondent* (New York: Harper & Brothers, 1917).

Shivery, George J., ed. *Records of S.S.U. 585 : Yale Ambulance Unit with the French Army, 1917–1919* (New York: E. L. Hildreth, 1920).

Silver, Kenneth E. *Esprit de Corps: The Art of the Parisian Avant-Garde and the First World War, 1914–1925* (Princeton: Princeton University Press, 1989).

Sinclair, May. *A Journal of Impressions in Belgium* (New York: Macmillan, 1915).

Source Records of the Great War, 7 vols., Charles F. Horne, editor-in-chief (National Alumni, American Legion, 1923).

Spritzer, Lorraine Nelson. *The Bell of Ashby Street: Helen Douglas Mankin and Georgia Politics* (Athens: University of Georgia Press, 1982).

"Standard U.S. Army Ambulance," *Scientific American*, 116 (Feb. 17, 1917).

Steinson, Barbara J. *American Women's Activism in World War I* (New York: Garland, 1982).

Stern, Philip Van Doren. *Tin Lizzie* (New York: Simon & Schuster, 1955).

Stevenson, William Yorke. *At the Front in a Flivver* (Boston: Houghton Mifflin, 1917).

──────. *From Poilu to Yank* (Boston: Houghton Mifflin, 1918).

Stokesbury, James L. *A Short History of World War I* (New York: William Morrow, 1981).

"Stories from the Front," *Literary Digest*, 55 (Aug. 18, 1917).

Sullivan, Reginald Nöel. *Somewhere in France: Personal Letters of Reginald N. Sullivan, Sanitary Section Unit 65 of the American Ambulance Field Service* (San Francisco: n.p., privately printed, 1917).

Tatham, Meaburn, and James Edward Miles, eds. *The Friends' Ambulance Unit, 1914–1919* (London: Swarthmore Press Ltd., [1920]).

Thorn, Stephen. "Notes, Experiences, and Suggestions on the Automobile Ambulance Service of a Modern Army in the Field," *Modern Surgeon* (1917).

"To Systematize Our War Charities," *Literary Digest*, 53 (Dec. 2, 1916).

Toland, Edward Dale. *The Aftermath of Battle: With the Red Cross in France*, with a preface by Owen Wister (New York: Macmillan, 1916).

Truslow, Neal. "American Red Cross Ambulance Service in France — Personal Experiences of a Volunteer at Verdun," *Scientific American*, 115 (Oct. 7, 1916).

Tuchman, Barbara. *The Guns of August* (New York: Macmillan, 1962).

van Schaick, John, Jr. *The Little Corner Never Conquered: The Story of the American Red Cross War Work for Belgium* (New York: Macmillan, 1922).

Vanderbilt, Mrs. W. K. "My Trip to the Front," *Harper's Magazine*, CXXXIV (January 1917).

Venture: Special Memorial Issue for Robert Hillyer (University of Delaware, 1962).

Verdun: An Illustrated Historical Guide (Verdun: Frémont, Editions Lorraines, n.d.).

Warren, Lansing. "Ambulancier," *Lost Generation Journal*, V:2 (Winter, 1977–78).

Warren, Lansing, and Robert A. Donaldson. *En Repos and Elsewhere Over There: Verses Written in France, 1917–1918*, with a preface by Lt. Colonel A. Piatt Andrew (Boston & New York: Houghton Mifflin, 1918).

Wedborn, Helena. *Women in First and Second World Wars: A Checklist of the Holdings of the Hoover Institution on War, Revolution, and Peace* (Stanford: Hoover Institution, 1988).

Weeks, Edward. *My Green Age* (Boston: Little, Brown, 1973).

White, J. W. "American Ambulance," *Survey*, 34 (Sept. 18, 1915).

Wickes, George. *Americans in Paris* (Garden City, N.Y.: Doubleday, 1969).

Williams, Paul B. *United States Lawn Tennis Association and the World War*, n.p., n.d. (603d Section Sanitaire).

Wilson, Francesca. *In the Margins of Chaos: Recollections of Relief Work in and Between Three Wars* (New York: Macmillan, 1945).

Wilson, Woodrow. *The Public Papers of Woodrow Wilson: The New Democracy —*

Presidential Messages, Addresses, and Other Papers (1913–1917), Ray Stannard Baker and William E. Dodd, eds., vol. I (New York: Harper & Brothers, 1926).

Winsor School. *The Overseas War Record of the Winsor School, 1914–1919* (Boston: Winsor School Graduate Club, n.d.).

Winter, Francis A. "The American Red Cross with the A.E.F.," *Military Surgeon* (December 1919).

Wolff, Leon. *In Flanders Fields: The 1917 Campaign* (New York: Viking, 1958).

Women's Overseas Service League, Helene M. Sillia, ed. *Lest We Forget: A History of Women's Overseas Service League* (privately printed, n.p., 1978).

Worthington, Marjorie. *The Strange World of Willie Seabrook* (New York: Harcourt, Brace & World, 1966).

Index